IMAGES
of America

SHAMONG

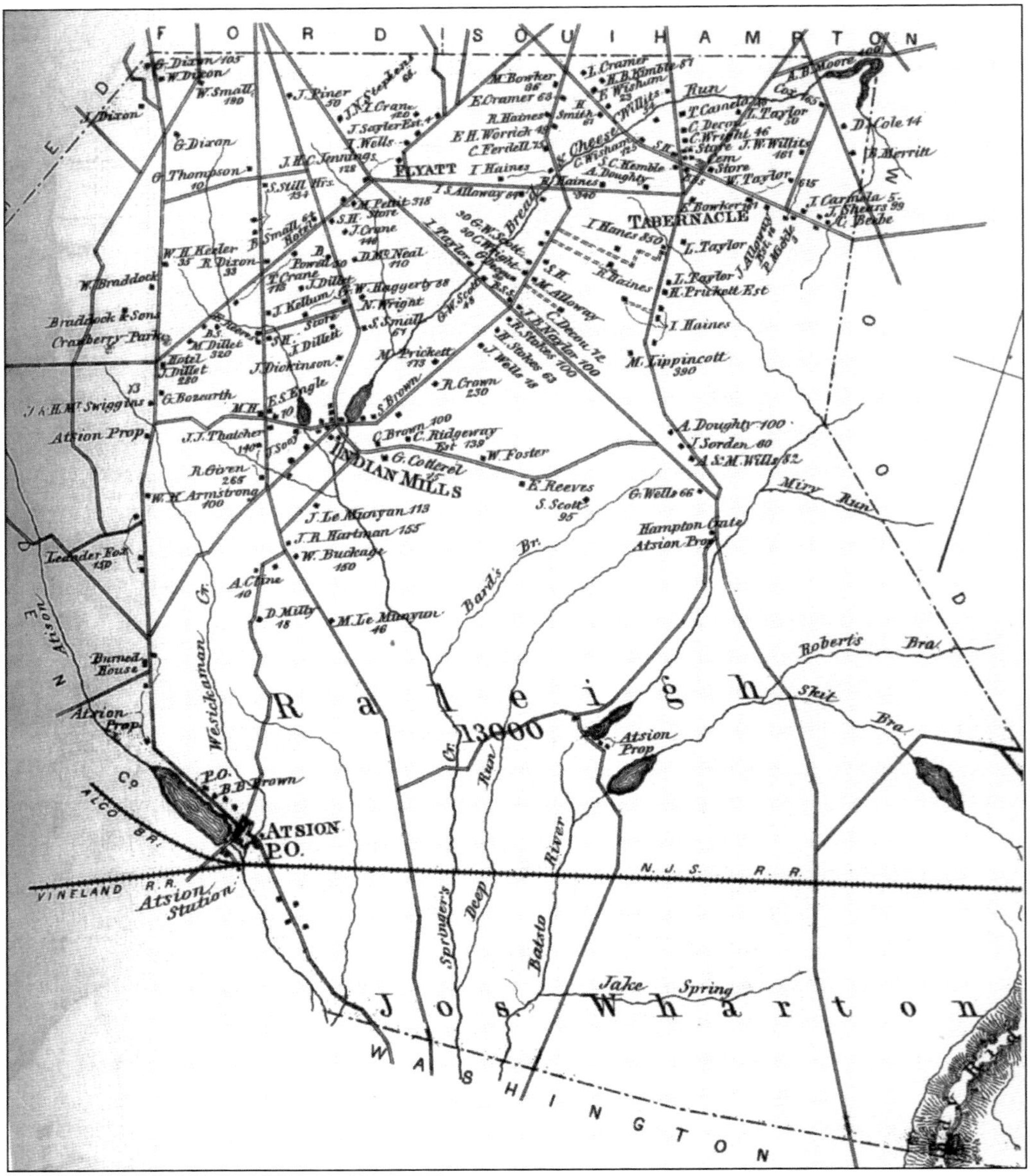

This image is taken from Scott's atlas of Burlington County and was published in 1876. It depicts Shamong Township in its entirety at that time. The villages of Atsion, Indian Mills, and Tabernacle are prominent. All the roads were then unpaved and most remained so well into the 20th century.

On the cover: This photograph was taken in the 1920s. Harold Bozearth stands next to the eight-point buck that he killed. John "Bull" Miller is kneeling at the far left. Further details are given in chapter 8, on pages 104 and 105. (Courtesy of the Indian Mills Historical Society.)

IMAGES
of America

SHAMONG

George D. Flemming

ARCADIA
PUBLISHING

ISBN 978-0-7385-6497-5

Published by Arcadia Publishing
Charleston, South Carolina

Printed in the United States of America

Library of Congress Control Number: 2008938749

For all general information, please contact Arcadia Publishing:
Telephone 843-853-2070
Fax 843-853-0044
E-mail sales@arcadiapublishing.com
For customer service and orders:
Toll-Free 1-888-313-2665

Visit us on the Internet at www.arcadiapublishing.com

To Robert (Bob) Erisman, former mayor of Shamong, who died at a young age. He was also a prominent ballplayer in Indian Mills and a friend to all he came in contact with.

CONTENTS

ACKNOWLEDGMENTS

The Indian Mills Historical Society was founded by a small group of concerned citizens in 1973. It is dedicated to the preservation of Shamong Township heritage and has adopted these words as its trademark. For many years, friends and members of the society have donated photographs that would have otherwise been forgotten in time. The images that appear are from the collections of the Indian Mills Historical Society.

INTRODUCTION

Shamong Township is one of many communities presently contained in the Pinelands National Reserve. This reserve was designated as this country's first national reserve in 1978. It is the largest open space on the eastern seaboard between Boston and Richmond, Virginia. It covers all or part of 56 municipalities over 7 counties in New Jersey. The region is home to more than 850 plant and 500 animal species and contains an aquifer of an estimated 17 trillion gallons of pure water. The Native Americans anciently referred to the area of Shamong as Edgepillock or "place of pure clear water." Shamong lies in the heart of the Wharton State Forest, which itself lies in the heart of the Pinelands National Reserve.

Shamong Township was incorporated on February 19, 1852, from parts of Medford, Southampton, and Washington Townships, although originally it was part of Evesham Township. It covers a land area of 46 square miles with 59 percent of the land included in the Wharton State Forest.

The name Shamong was derived from the correlation of the Lenape words *chummo* and *ong*, signifying "place of the horn" or "place of many deer." There are still many hunting clubs in Shamong, attesting to the deer population that is so prevalent. The Native Americans had lived in the area of Shamong for many thousands of years. They called themselves Lenape, which simply meant "men" in the Algonquian tongue. To other tribes, they were often considered to have the wisdom of grandfathers or peacemakers. Their stone tools are still being found in the plowed fields of area farms. It is no small wonder that Shamong is part of the Lenape Regional School District, which has its headquarters in Shamong. The high schools in the area also pay tribute to Native Americans by their names, Lenape, Cherokee, Shawnee, and Seneca.

Shamong Township was once the site of the first and only Native American reservation in New Jersey. It has often been cited that it was the first in the country, but this is incorrect. Earlier ones were established in Pennsylvania and Massachusetts. The reservation in Shamong was founded by the colonial government in 1758 and named Brotherton by Royal Gov. Francis Bernard. A Presbyterian missionary named Rev. John Brainerd was appointed by the governor to provide guidance to some 200 Native Americans who settled here. It was difficult for these native people to adjust to farming pursuits and to the "white man's" way of doing things. Drinking of alcohol, although forbidden by law, was also a continuing problem. The reservation comprised some 3,284 acres, but sadly much of it was left untilled and eventually leased out to area farmers. Disenchanted with their circumstances and the loss of Reverend Brainerd in 1781, the Native Americans accepted an invitation to join their cousins in New York State in 1802. The Brotherton lands were then sold by auction to area farmers and divided into 100-acre lots. Many of these same 100-acre parcels exist today as area farms.

After the demise of the Brotherton Reservation, the land area of old Shamong was gradually developed. Some farmers had previously worked this land but now could actually live on the land with the natives gone. Farmhouses, barns, and outbuildings began to spread across the township. Sawyers and millers took over the long-neglected sawmill at Indian Mills, and the gristmill there was rebuilt. A village gradually emerged known as Hartford, then Shamong, and finally called Indian Mills. Tabernacle also followed the same path. It was originally called Tabernacle in the Wilderness, and then finally just plain Tabernacle. The village of Atsion was another story. It was coexistent with the Brotherton Reservation but outside the reservation boundaries. Charles Read, a prominent statesman and entrepreneur, established the Atsion Iron Works in 1765. It changed ownership many times and expanded into an industrial complex with a bog-iron furnace, two forges, sawmills, and a gristmill and employed over 100 people. When the iron industry gave out in the 1840s, a paper mill and then cotton mill were established and flourished well into the 19th century. Atsion has become one of the lost and forgotten towns of the Pinelands. Some buildings still survive of the original Atsion Village such as the community church and two graveyards, a one-room school, mansion house, and village store. Workers homes have all disappeared. The once-large cotton mill is in ruins, as are the forges and furnace, which have disappeared. The lake, known as Atsion Lake, that once provided the waterpower for the iron and cotton industries, is now providing recreation as a state park. It remains one of the most serene and beautiful lakes in the Pinelands National Reserve.

Many of the streams and waterways of Shamong were converted into bogs used for growing cranberries, as this is a permitted crop in the Pinelands. It has flourished from the mid-1800s to the present. Likewise, the production of blueberries began. The wild plants known as huckleberries were also cultivated and still abound in the area. They are a major crop to area farmers. The sandy soil in areas of the township is very conducive to this crop and goes side by side with the cranberry bogs.

The present population of Shamong Township hovers around 7,000 people. A survey of new home construction reveals that from 1940 to 1969, only 98 homes were constructed. The real surge in new home construction occurred between 1970 and 1982, when 864 homes were built. Since then, there has been a steady decline in building, due to a scarcity of buildable land. This has been caused in part by certain restrictions that have been imposed by the Pinelands Commission and local authorities in compliance with township master plans.

The Shamong of today remains a vibrant rural and residential area. Numerous large farms remain and blend in among the small residential developments. The ravages of time have claimed many historical properties in the township, but thankfully the older residents and their families have donated photographs to the Indian Mills Historical Society, which appear on the following pages. These photographs provide an excellent visual reminder of the past, especially of buildings, places, and people that are no longer here. The society has also placed descriptive historical markers at all important sites within the township, helping to recall the days of yesteryear. Likewise, the Tabernacle Historical Society has also placed historical markers within the borders of Tabernacle Township, incorporated in 1901 and formed from a part of Shamong Township.

One

IN THE BEGINNING

Shamong Township is located in Burlington County and lies within the Pinelands National Reserve. A substantial portion of Shamong Township remains in a virtual wilderness state.

The prehistoric natives of this land comprised small family groups who had a nomadic lifestyle. They frequently moved from one campsite to another in search of large game animals. The campsites were nearly always close to a source of water. They fished the area streams and hunted wild turkey, elk, bear, and deer. They also gathered wild berries such as huckleberry and cranberry that still abound in the area. The bear and elk are gone, but the turkey and deer are still plentiful. The natives referred to themselves as Lenape, which meant "men." The early colonists referred to them as the Delaware as their principal villages were along the Delaware River and major tributaries. Other historians have also referred to the Lenape simply as the Jerseys, meaning natives who lived in east and west New Jersey.

The Native Americans were essentially living in the Stone Age until the coming of the Europeans in the early 17th century. They had no exposure to things made of metal and had functioned this way for thousands of years before the colonists came. The Lenape were fascinated by all implements introduced by the colonists, particularly tools, cooking pots, and utensils of all kinds. The age-old custom of making and using stone tools and clay cooking pots was rapidly coming to an end.

As the colonists traded and interacted with the Lenape, it became apparent that tools and utensils of brass, iron, and copper were greatly preferred by the aboriginal population. The colonists began buying large tracts of land from the Native Americans and in exchange provided them with various household goods. The use of stone tools quickly disappeared. Examples of stone tools utilized by the Lenape are shown on the following pages.

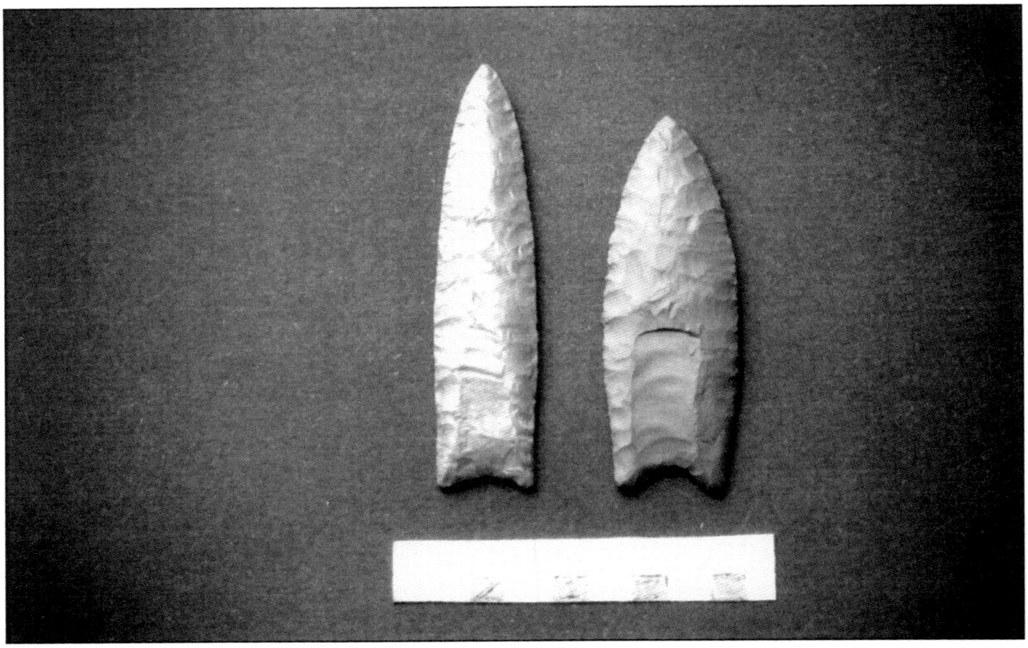

Early man used this type of projectile point at the end of a spear in his quest for large game such as elk, moose, and even mastodon. The spear was usually propelled with the use of an atlatl or throwing stick to cause the spear point to penetrate even deeper into the flesh of the animal. Points of this type, known as Clovis, date from 10,000 to 12,000 years ago.

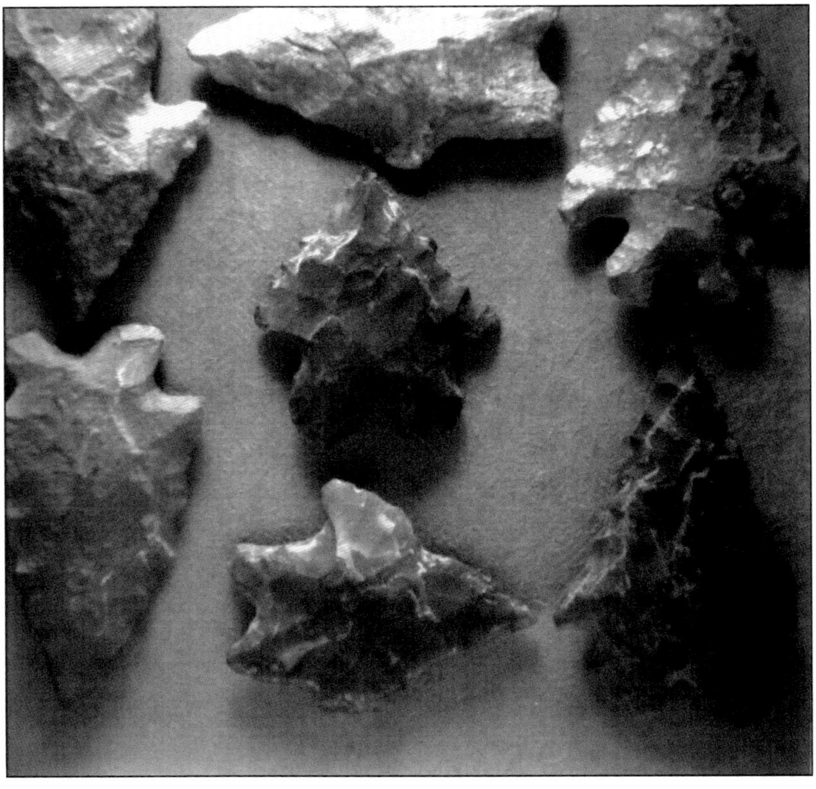

Small points such as these often had serrated edges to facilitate their use as possibly a cutting tool or knife. They also had a bifurcated base and date from 6,000 to 8,000 years ago. It has been theorized that they may have been hafted into a wooden handle.

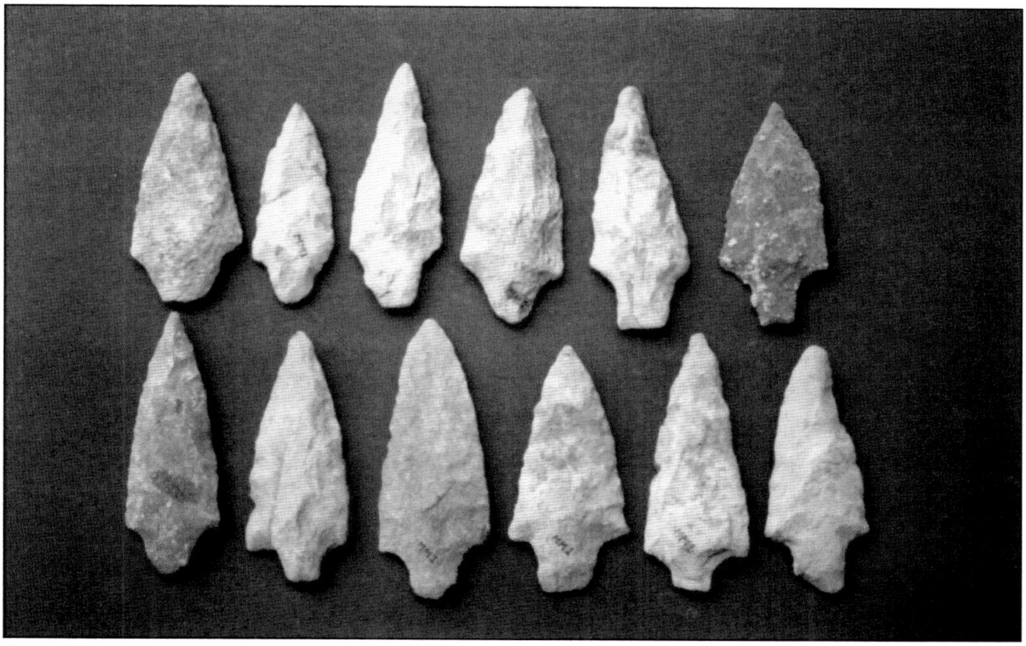

Seen here are projectile points from the Terminal Archaic Period that date to over 4,000 years ago. They were fastened onto the end of a spear and utilized in the hunting of large game animals of the area such as bear, deer, elk, and moose. They have survived as relics of the past on several sites in Shamong Township.

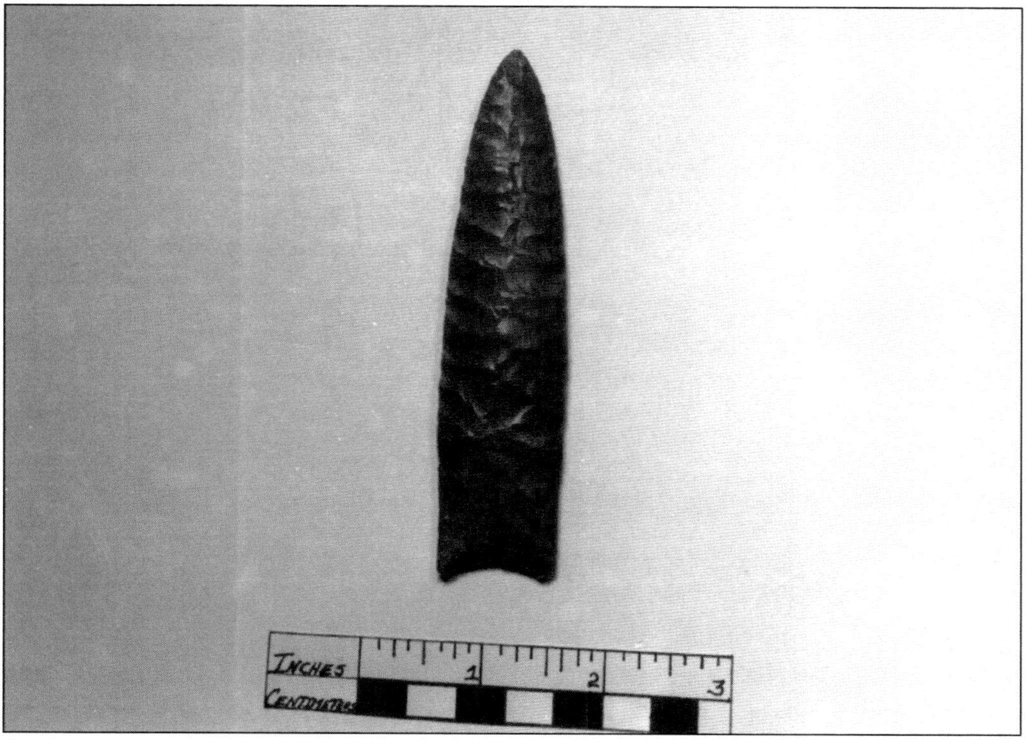

Finely made projectile points were crafted by the prehistoric flint knapper many thousands of years ago and fastened onto the end of a spear for hunting.

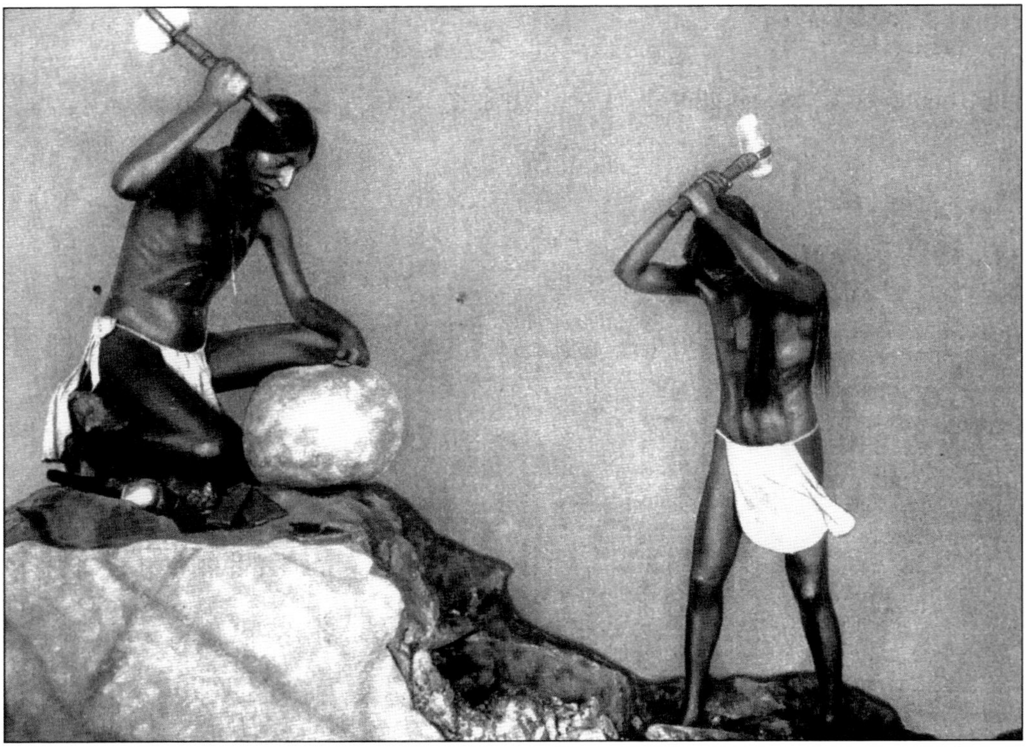

Native Americans followed the ways of their forefathers in working at extracting pieces of stone to later be crafted into projectile points. Most stone quarries for this stone were great distances away as southern New Jersey has no ready supply of stone such as jasper and argillite.

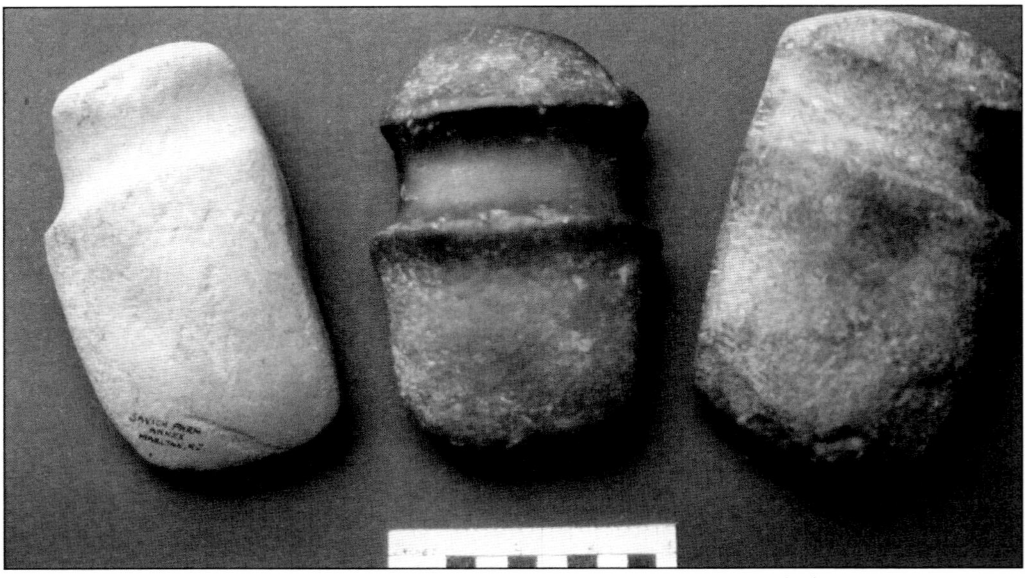

Stones such as these were gathered from the shores of the Delaware River and adjacent outcroppings of stone in Pennsylvania. They were made into axe heads and fastened onto a wooden handle with sinew. These are the full grooved variety and were used in various hammering chores. Their sharpened blades were remarkably capable of cutting down a tree, usually after the tree had been girdled by fire.

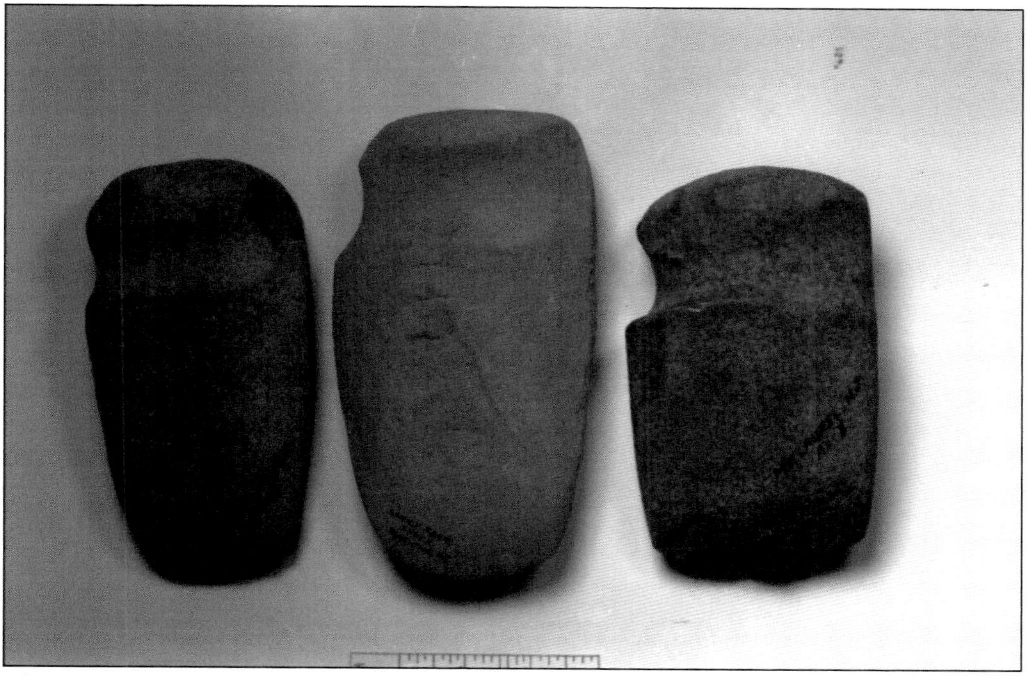

These stone axe heads, also fastened to a wooden handle, were three-quarter grooved by the natives. In so doing, they were able to tighten the thongs of sinew around the stone and handle by forcing wedges of wood down the straight side of the stone.

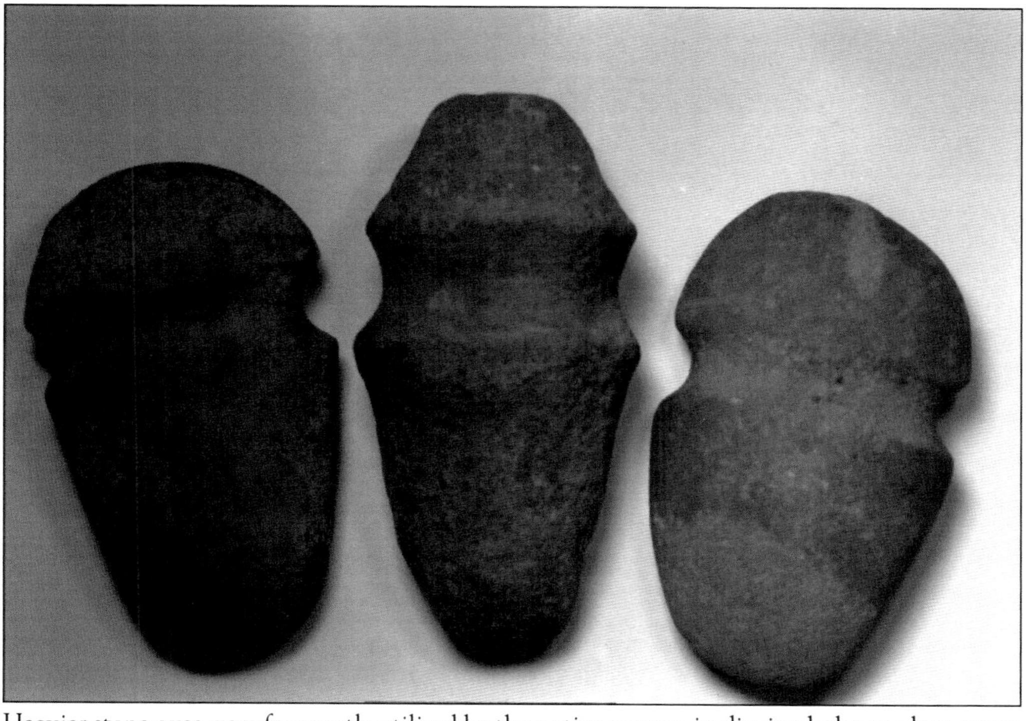

Heavier stone axes were frequently utilized by the native women in digging holes to plant crops. The women did most of the work of this type, while the men engaged in hunting and fishing. Household work was also mainly carried out by the women.

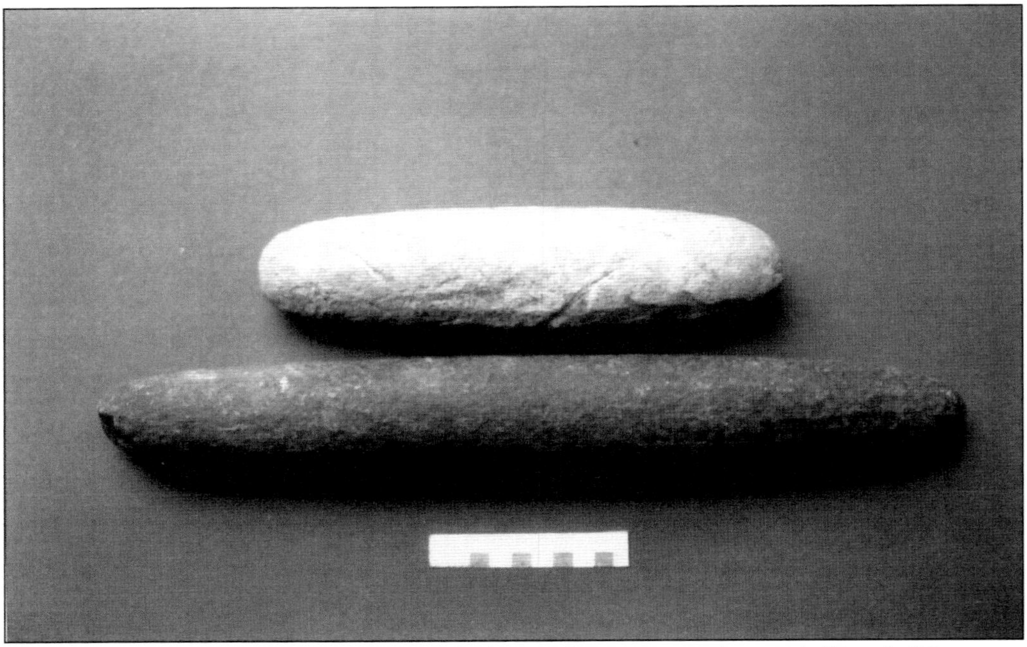

Roller-type stone pestles were used primarily for grinding grains and nuts of all kinds. They were used by the native women in stone and wooden mortars in preparing meals for the family.

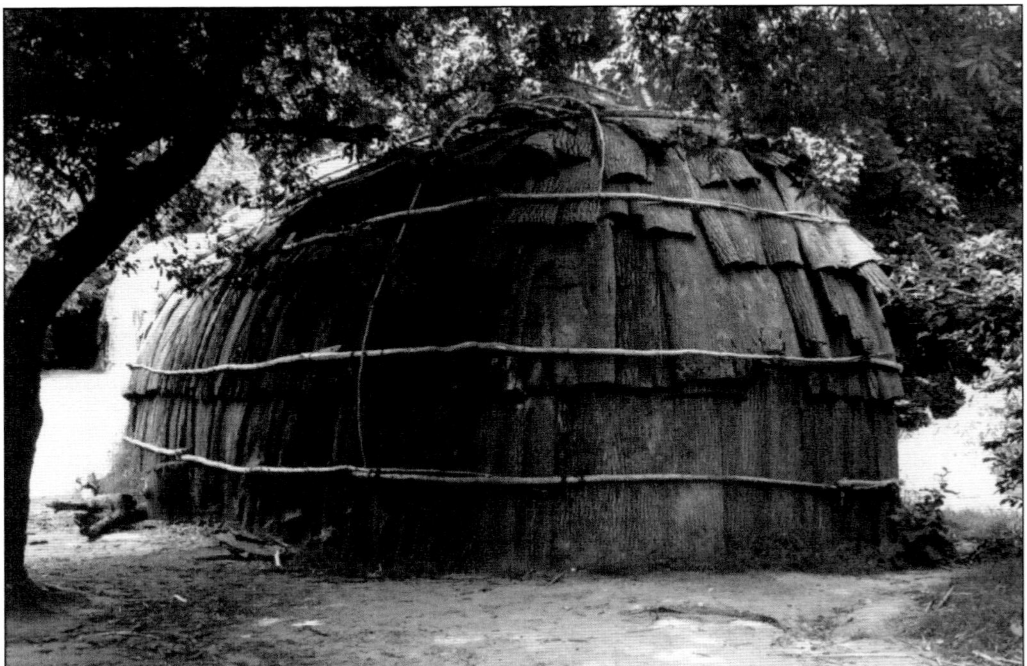

Saplings were cut down and shaped either in a circle or elongated. They were then bent over and lashed together. The wigwam was covered with tree bark. Several families could live in a structure of this size.

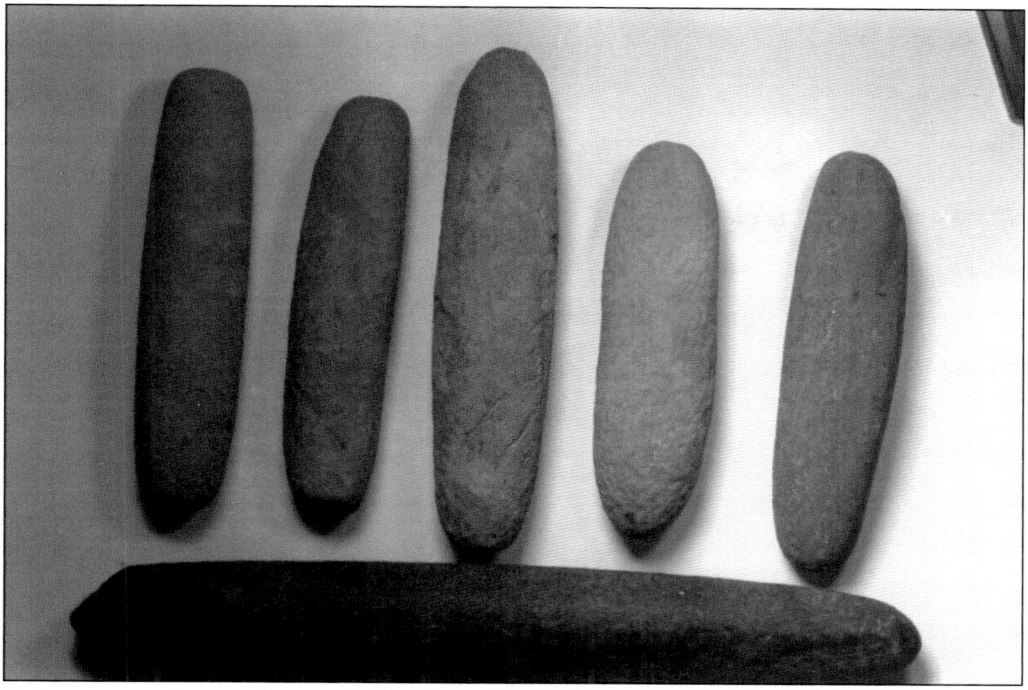

Roller-type pestles are frequently found on Native American habitation sites. They were an important household tool in use primarily by the women.

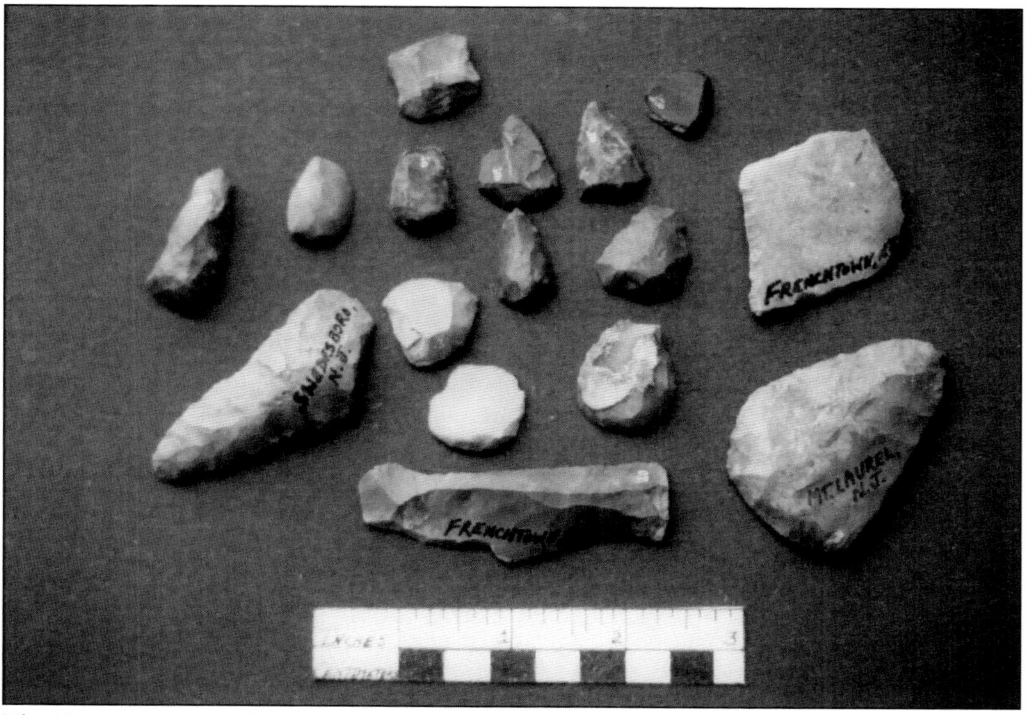

The Native American lifestyle involved considerable hunting and trapping. An important tool was the scraper. It was fashioned out of waste flakes and pieces of jasper or flint. Scrapers came in all sizes and shapes. Some were as small as a man's thumb and have been called "thumb scrapers."

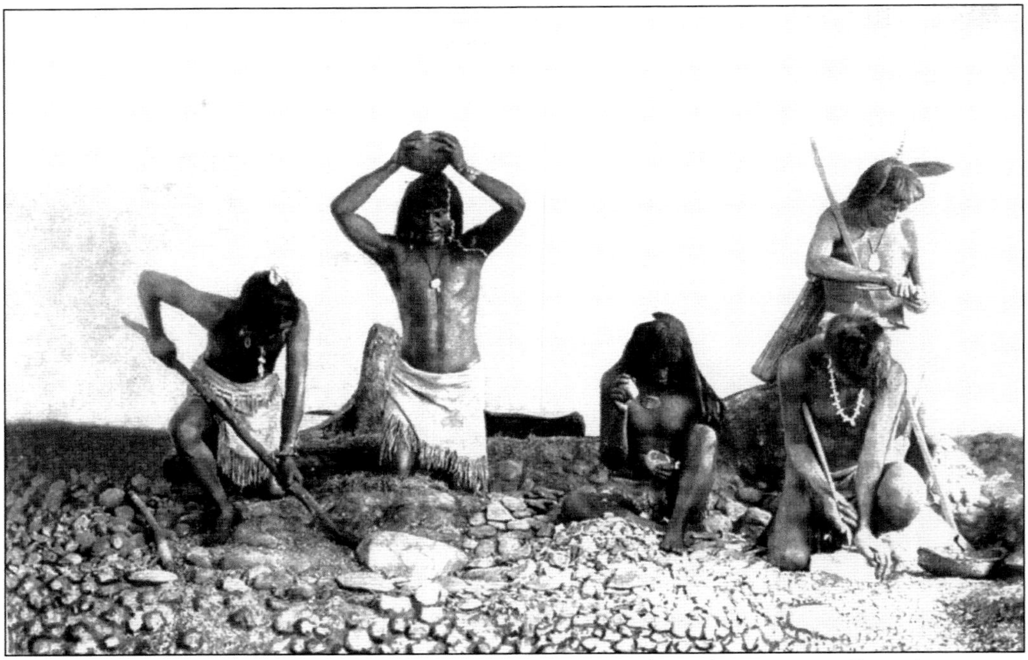

Native American men are engaged in a quarry-type setting where they are actually making stone implements or taking large blanks back to their village for completion. Anvils of stone and also hammerstones are used in work at a quarry.

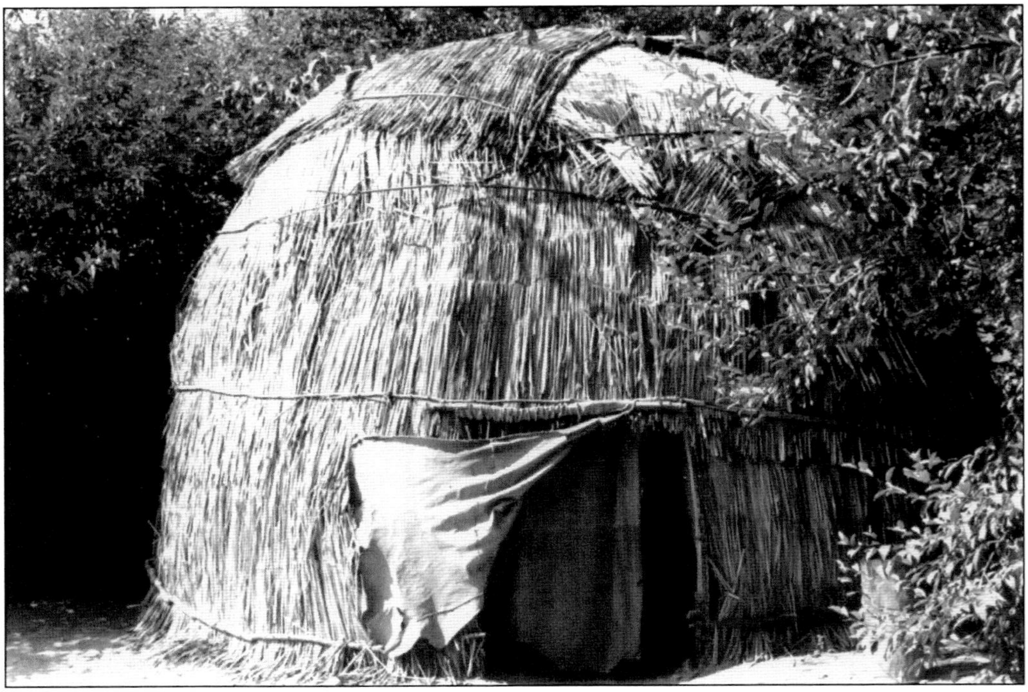

Here is a typical Native American dwelling made of bent saplings and covered with grasses or reeds. A deerskin hide is in place for a door. Possibly two small families could live in a dwelling this size.

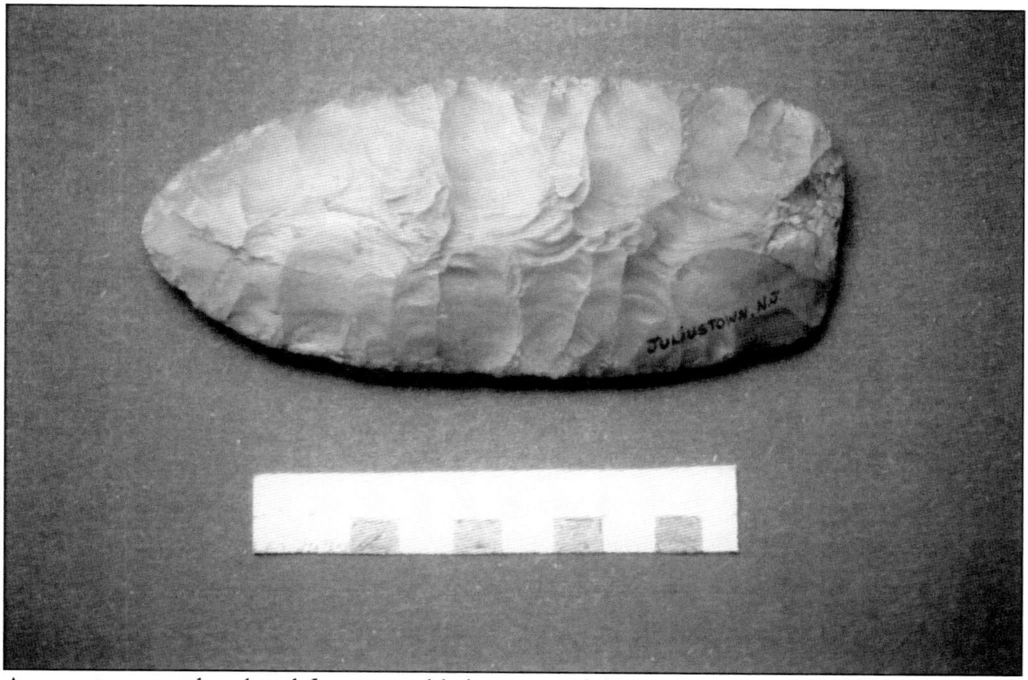

An exotic greenish-colored flint, most likely imported from afar, was used to make this knife. It fits comfortable in the hand and was most likely utilized like this. There is no indication of hafting into a wooden handle. It was used for a variety of cutting chores.

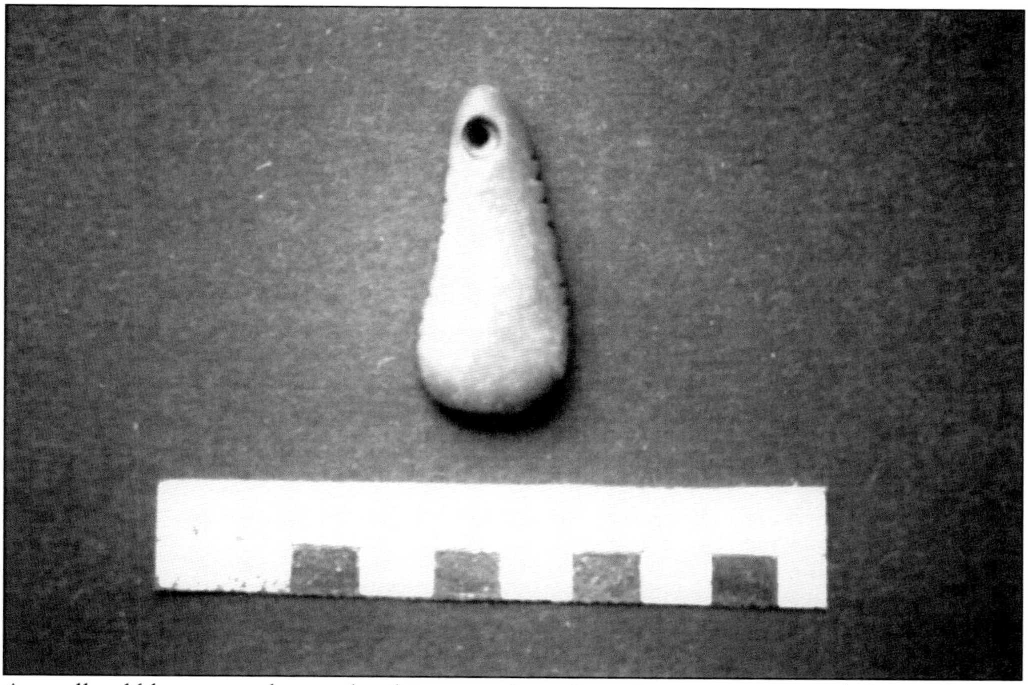

A small pebble was used to make this unusual pendant. It was worn around the neck as an adornment. It is drilled through from both sides of the stone. There are also 12 tally marks on each edge of the stone. These possibly indicate the number of days it took to make or are just there for decoration.

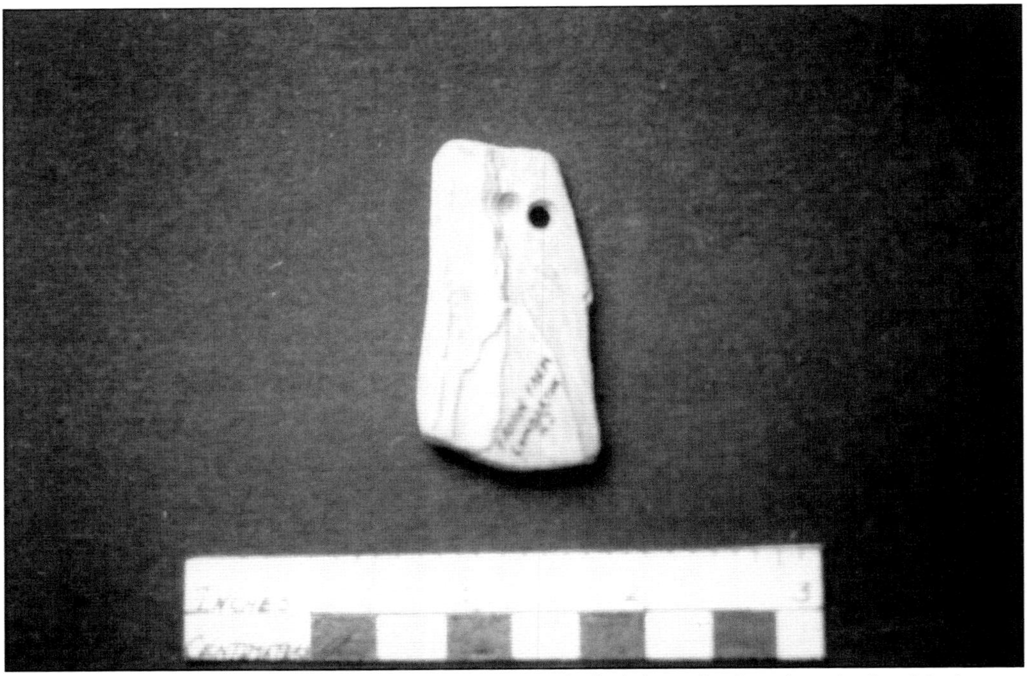

This pendant was also used for decoration. It is drilled from both sides. A third hole was attempted on one side but never completed. This pendant is unusual because it was made from petrified cypress wood.

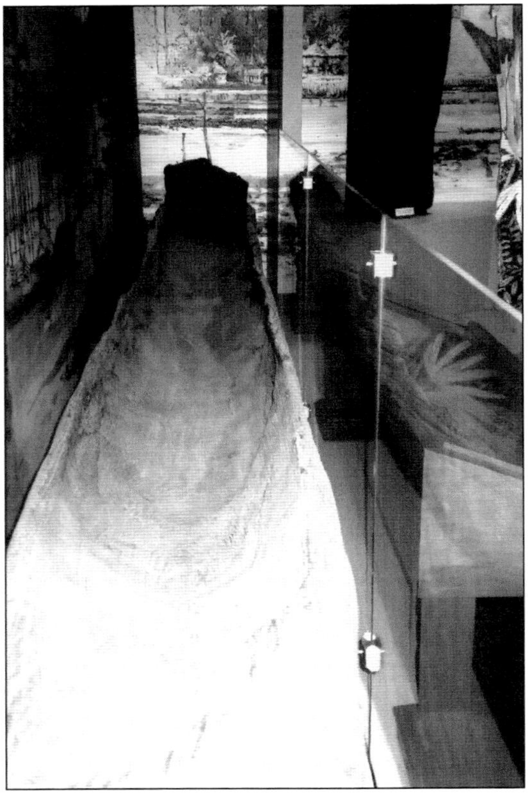

An ancient dugout canoe that had been preserved for centuries in the mud is now in a museum on display. It was remarkably preserved for hundreds of years. It was clearly gouged out with the use of stone tools.

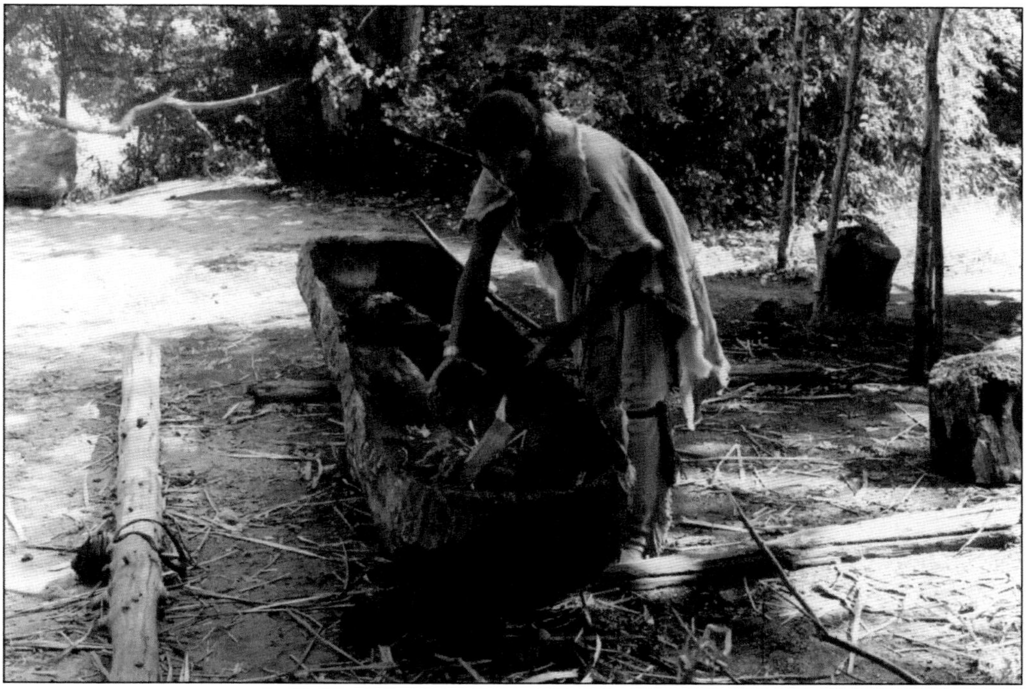

Here is a Native American engaged in burning the inside of a tree log into a canoe. The charred remains are then chopped out using stone tools called celts or adzes.

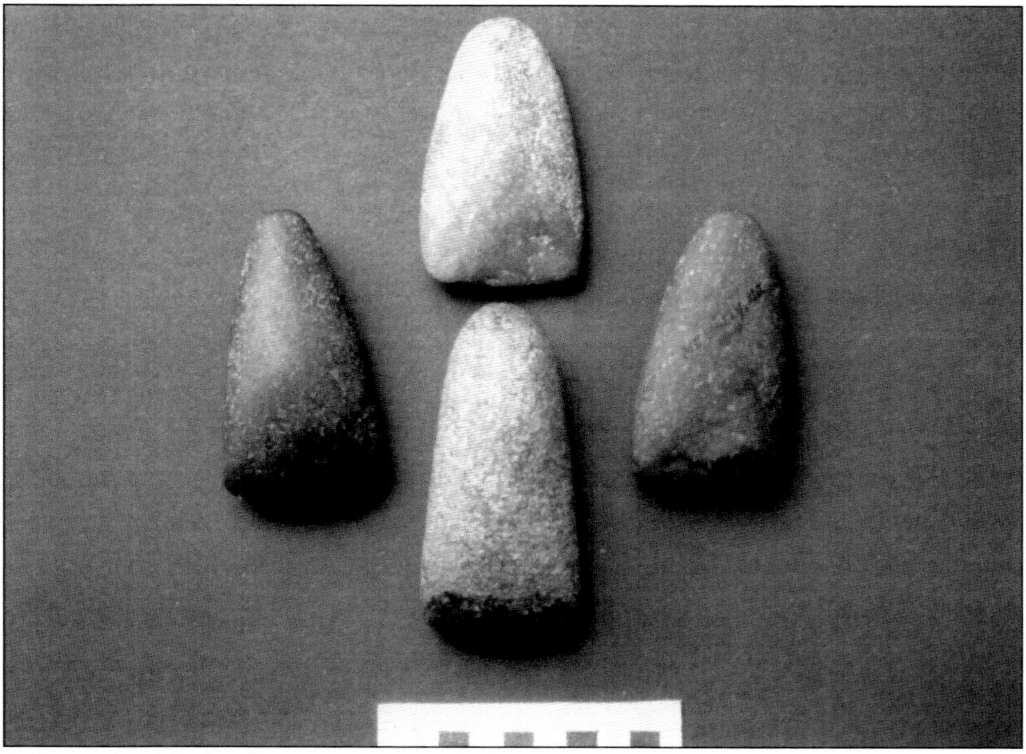

Celts, made of the hardest stone, were wedged or lashed into a wooden handle. They were ideal stone tools in the making of a dugout canoe.

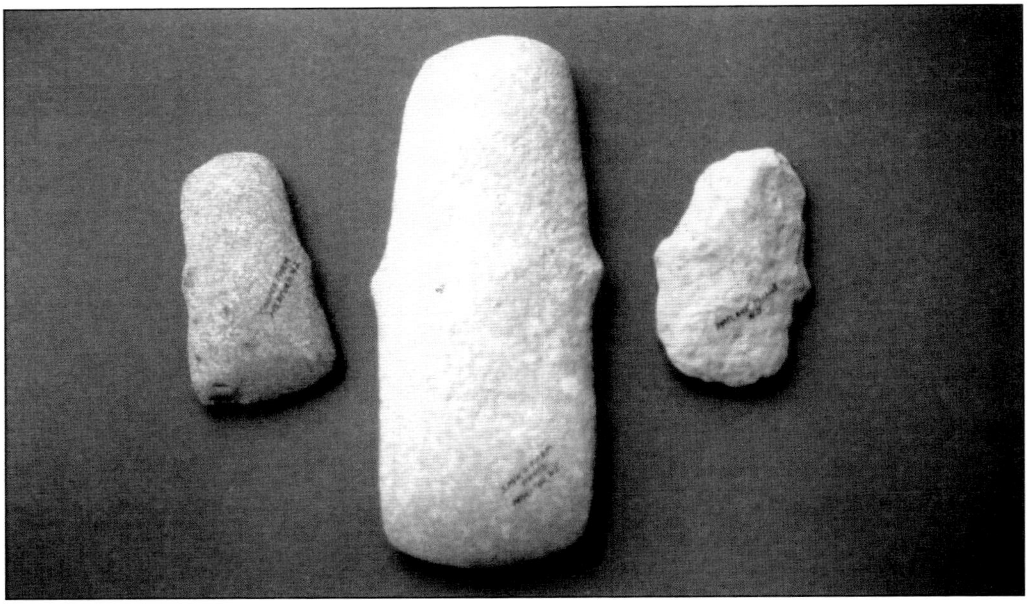

Knobbed adzes were flat on one side and curved into a blade on the other. They were hafted into wooded handles and used in various woodworking projects one of which was in the making of the dugout canoe. Many of these adzes have been found on Late Archaic sites over 4,000 years old.

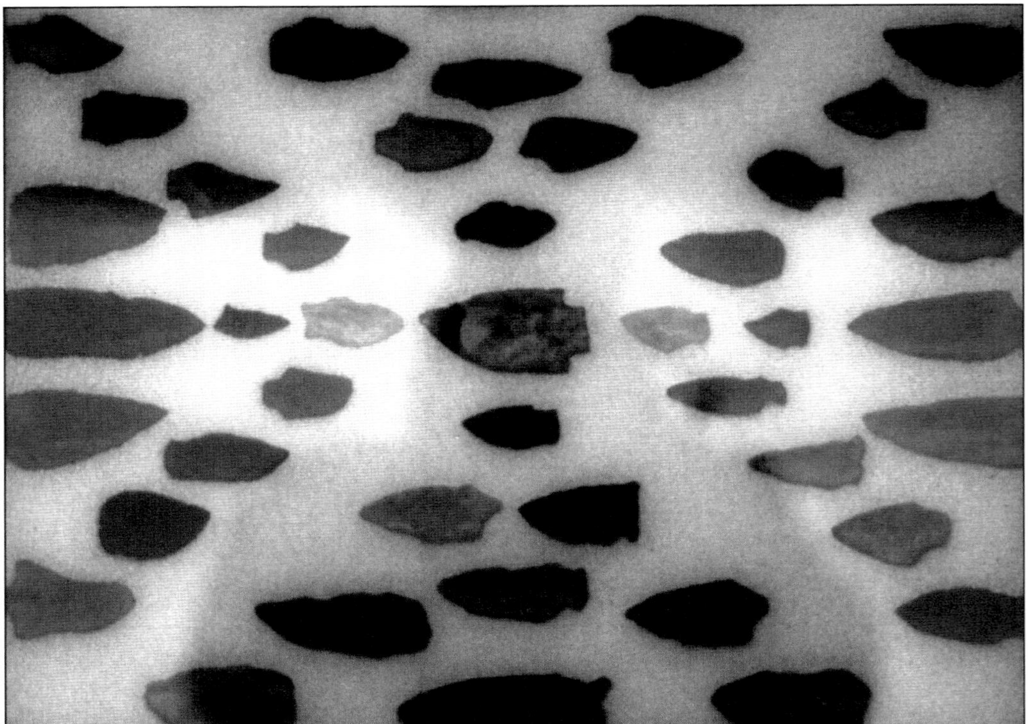

Seen here is a display of stone knives that were an important tool to the Native American in all cutting types of endeavors. They are easily distinguished by having an off-center point with a curving blade on one side. They were hafted into a wooden handle and lashed with sinew.

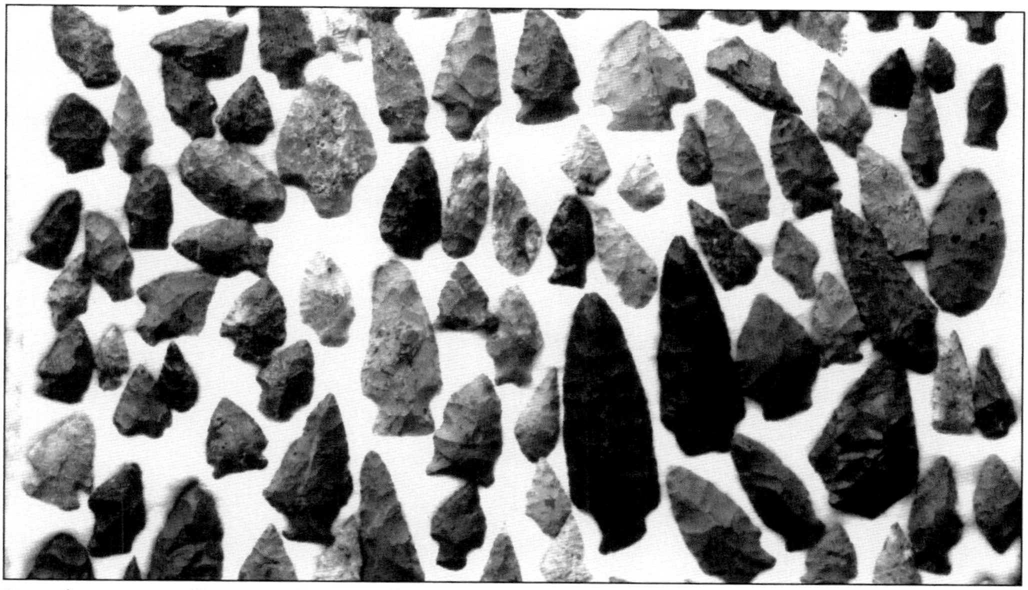

Seen here is a collection of projectile points spanning thousands of years and cultures in the Lenape history. Most were utilized on the tips of spears or on a thrusting-type javelin. A few could have been used on the tips of arrows. The bow and arrow had only been in use for about 1,500 years prior to the coming of the Europeans.

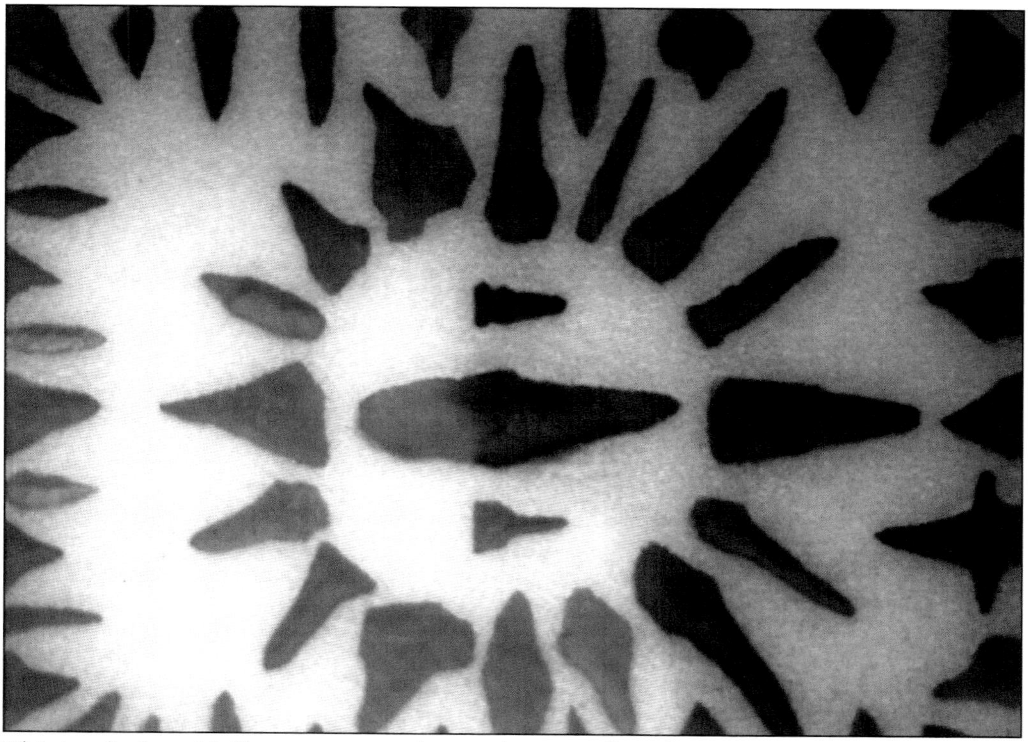

This is a display of drills, reamers, punches, and gravers all made of stone. The drills were mostly hafted into wooden handles. A few were held in the hand. The reamers and gravers were used in working hides and skins. Gravers were utilized in making incised lines on pottery bowls and other decorative items.

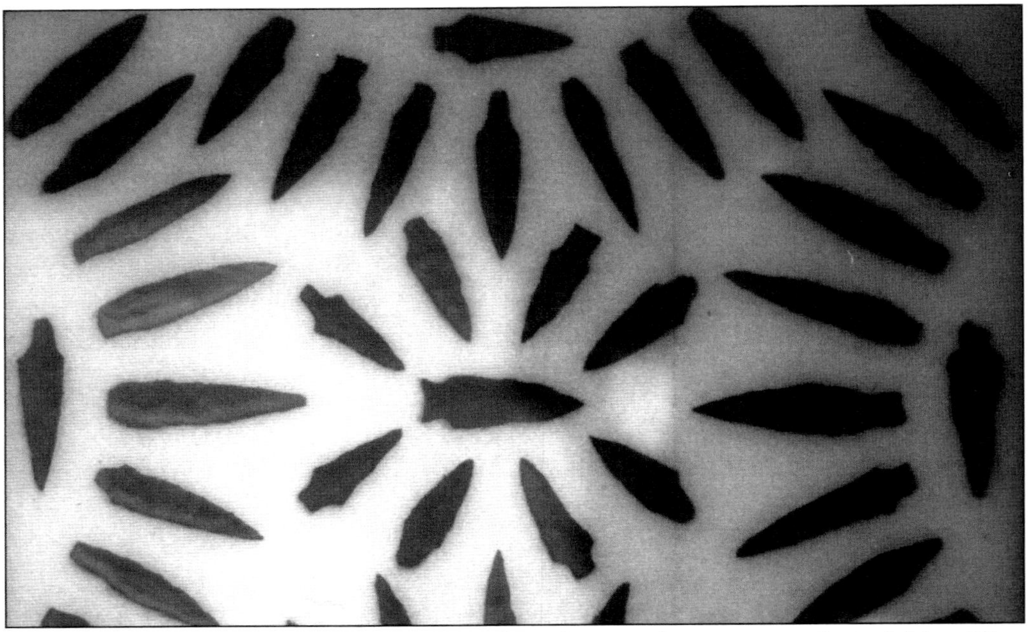

These long slender projectile points were used on the tips of spears primarily in fishing. They are commonly referred to as fish spears, however the scientific term for most of these points is lackawaxen.

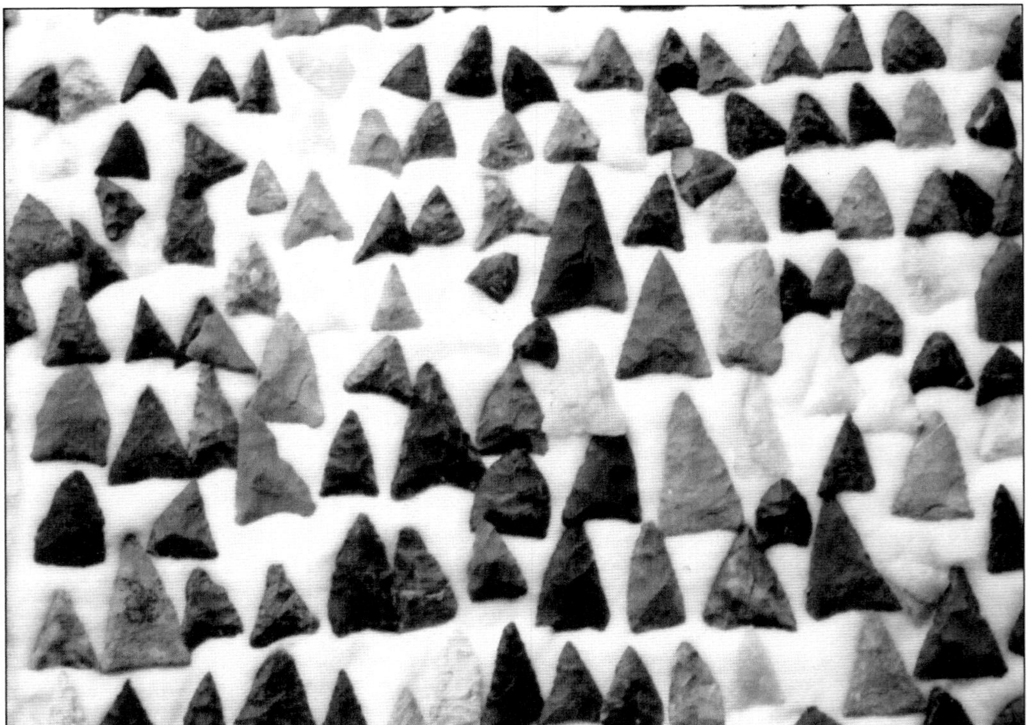

The most common example of a true arrowhead is the small triangular point, which was propelled with use of a bow and arrow. The larger triangular points had been in use for thousands of years but on the tips of spears.

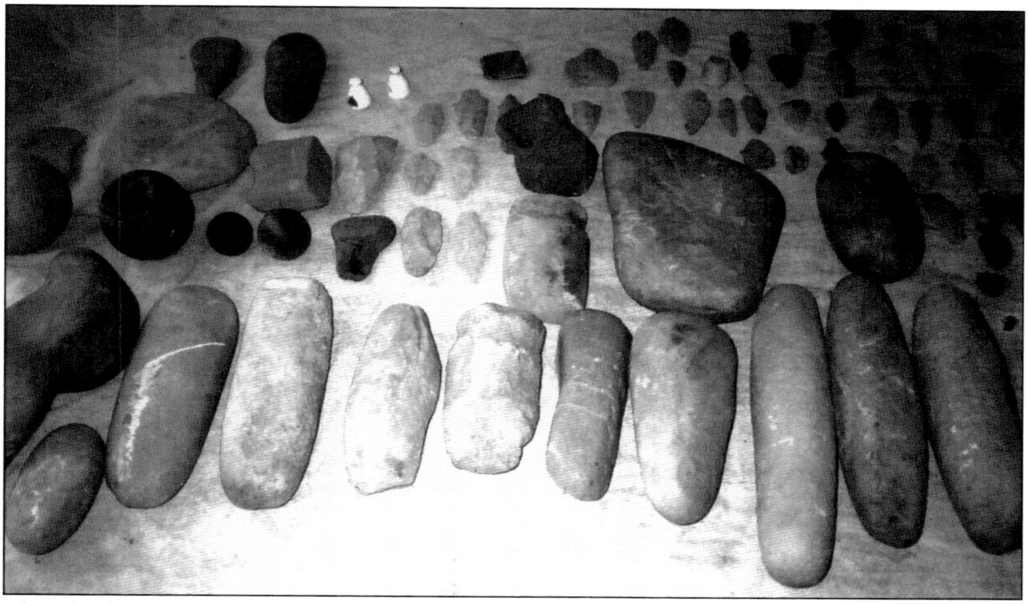

This display is part of the collection of Leon "Dinkey" King. He is a lifelong resident of Shamong Township. The projectile points, which include some arrow points, span a period of many thousands of years. All were found as surface finds in the plowed fields of Shamong. A number of roller-type pestles are shown. Also on display are three cannonballs that were found along Atsion Road near the King Farm. This road was an ancient one and used to transport munitions made at the nearby Batsto Furnace during the Revolutionary War. It is a possibility that these cannonballs fell from one of the wagons during transport to the landing wharves in Lumberton. Supposedly no munitions were made during this war at Atsion Iron Works, as the owners were pacifists.

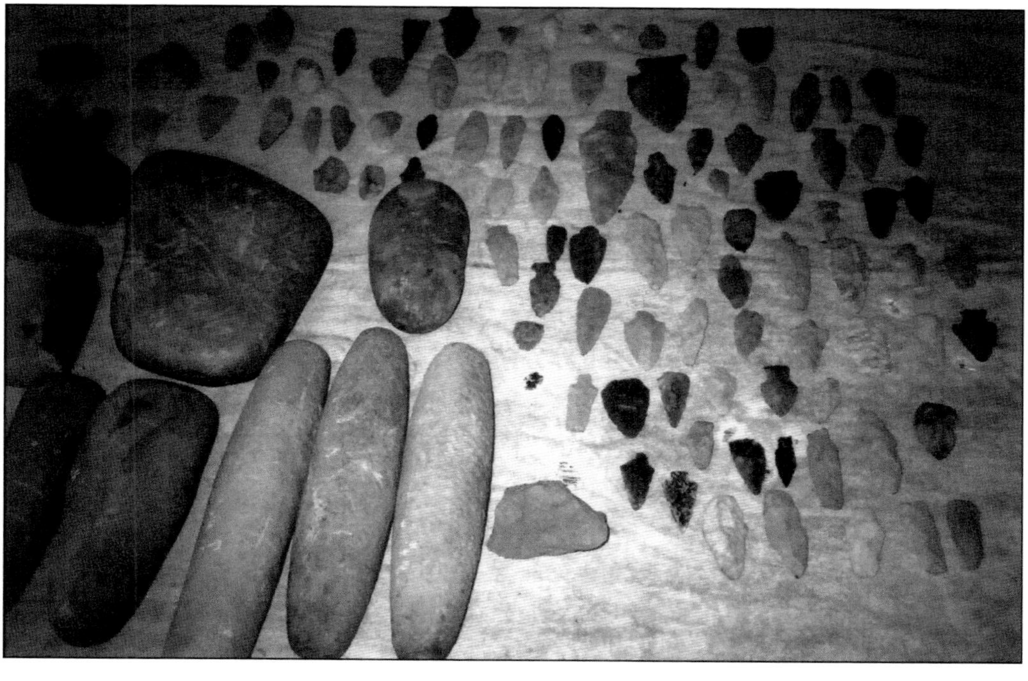

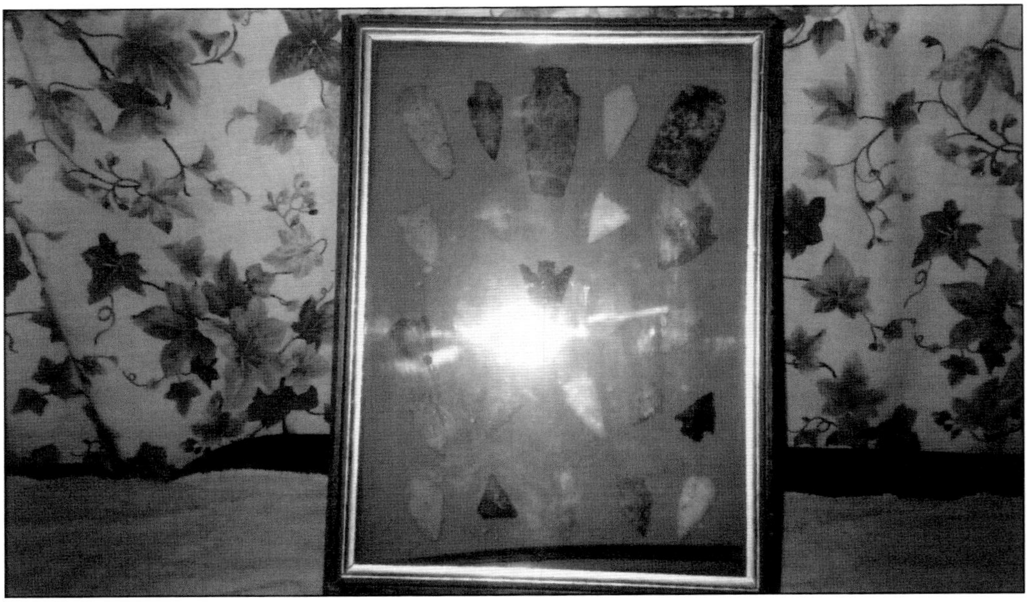

Pictured here is a frame of projectile points from the Leon "Dinkey" King collection. These comprise some of his best finds.

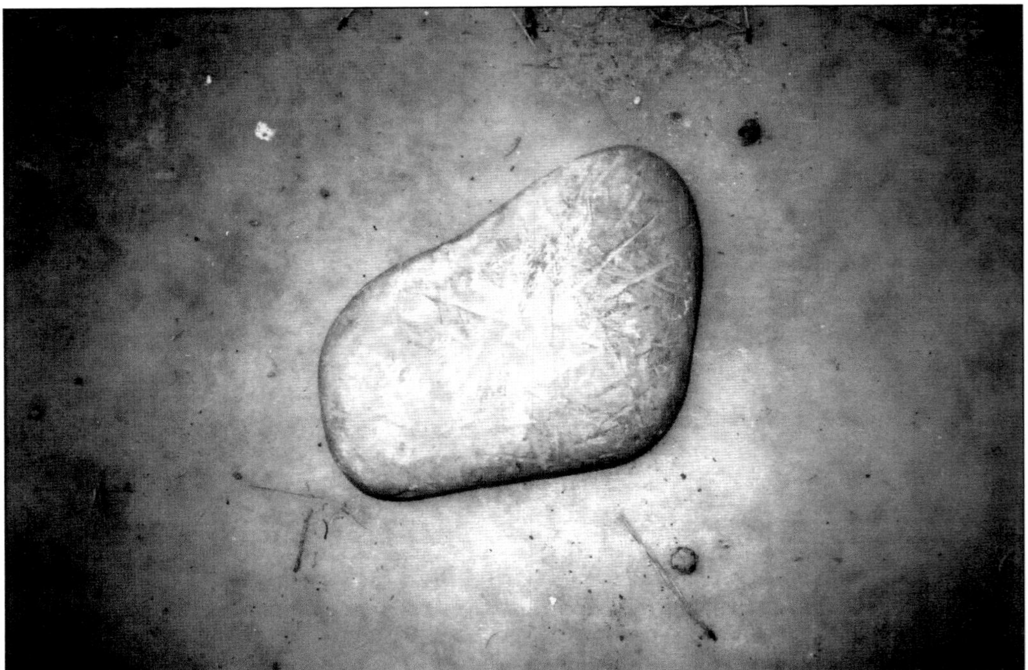

Seen here is an anvil or working platform of natural stone. Projectile points and other stone implements were made on slabs like this, which provided a working surface for the flint knapper to practice his skills.

Two

The Brotherton Reservation

During the formative years of Colonial New Jersey, many changes were occurring. Every effort was being made to obtain the land from the aboriginal population by barter and trade goods. In spite of the colonists good intentions, many thousands of Native Americans fled the state and headed into Pennsylvania and further west. Many more succumbed to the dreaded disease smallpox, on which native cures had no effect. By the mid-1700s, the native population had been reduced to less than 1,000 persons. By 1750, those natives that remained south of the Raritan River numbered only a few hundred.

Missionary efforts to Christianize the native population had been going on for many years. When the French and Indian War began in 1754, the warlike Munsee to the north of the Raritan River sided with the French, while the peaceful Lenape of central and southern New Jersey favored the English. Conferences were held with the remaining Native Americans to insure a peaceful coexistence. At one such conference held in Burlington in 1758, the Native Americans requested that a large tract of land be purchased for them as a refuge. The land they chose was known by them as Edgepillock or "place of pure clear water." It resulted in the first and only Native American reservation in New Jersey.

The reservation was named Brotherton by Royal Gov. Francis Bernard. He appointed Rev. John Brainerd to teach and care for the spiritual well-being of the Native Americans. A school, a meetinghouse, gristmills, sawmills, and log houses were erected for the natives to use. After the Revolutionary War, conditions began to deteriorate for the Native Americans. Funds from the state government were less than adequate. Failing health caused Reverend Brainerd to retire to pastor elsewhere. He died of a pulmonary ailment in 1781. Conditions at Brotherton worsened.

The Native Americans finally accepted an invitation from their cousins, the Oneidas, in New York State. In 1802, the reservation lands were sold at auction. The proceeds were used to transport the 83 surviving Native Americans to their new home. A noble experiment in humanity had ultimately failed.

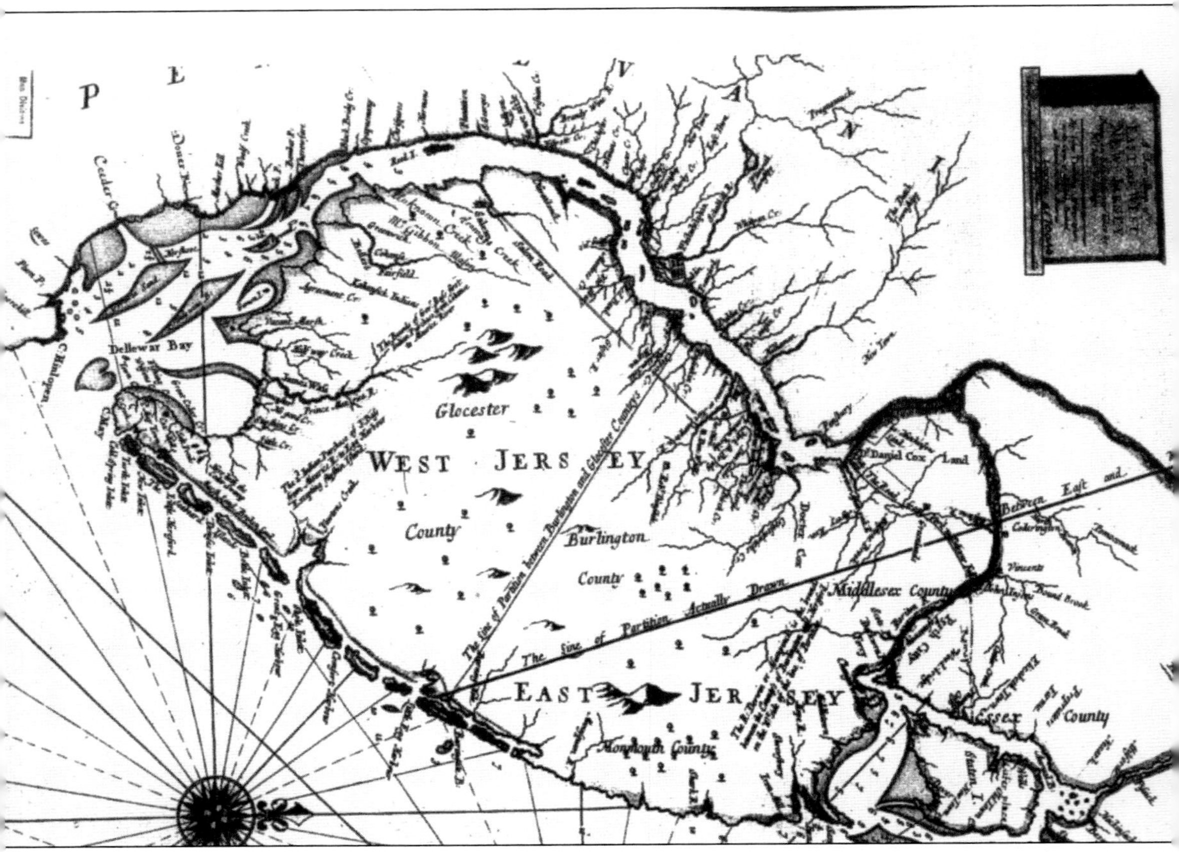

By a royal decree from England, the colony of New Jersey was divided into two parts. A survey line was drawn in a diagonal fashion separating East and West Jersey. Burlington County and all of southern New Jersey fell into West Jersey. The map above, dating from 1700, is from the Library of Congress. Many businesses, organizations, and societies still use the name West Jersey in their titles, harking back several centuries.

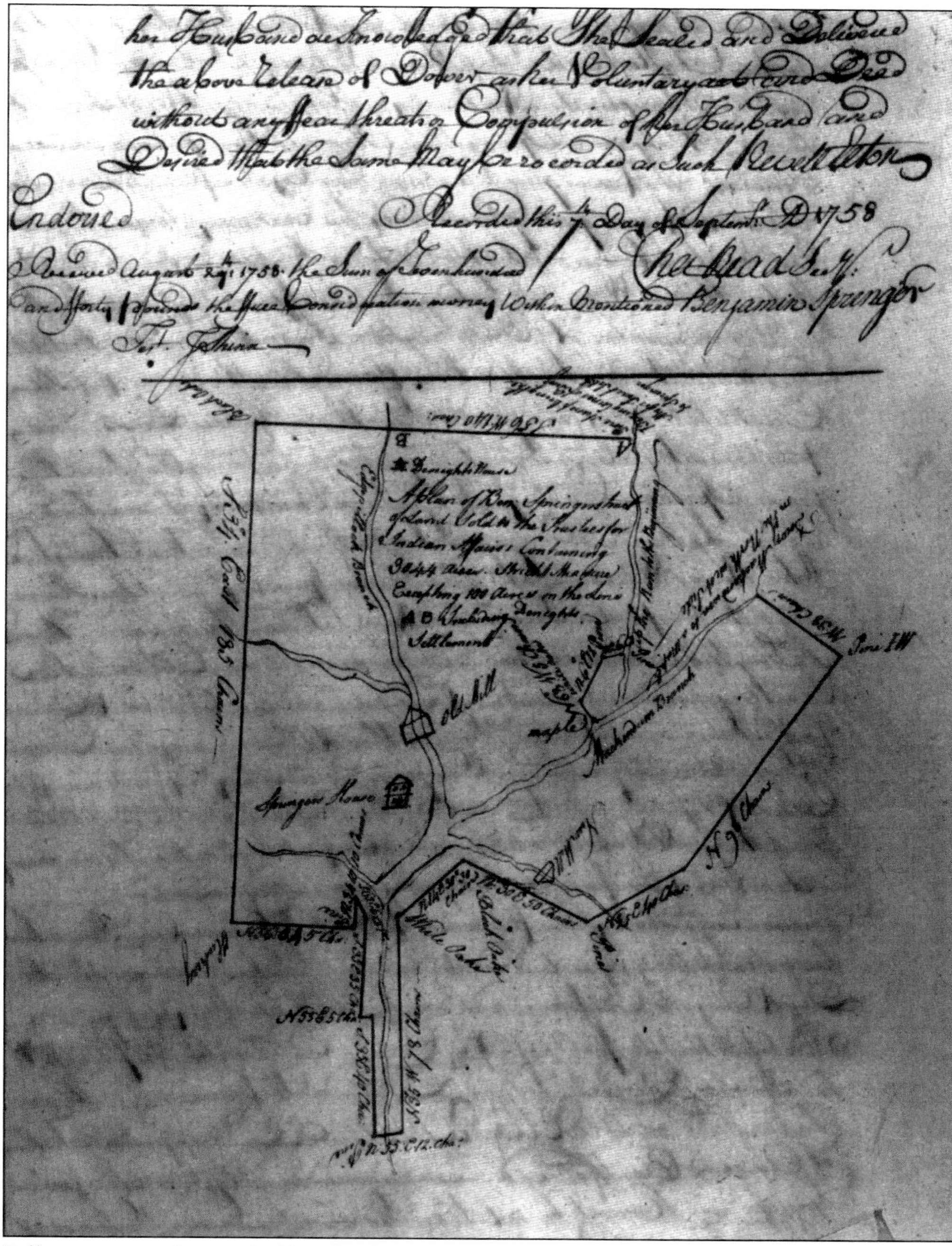

Following a conference held in Burlington on August 9, 1758, commissioners were appointed to purchase land to be used as a reservation for the remaining Native Americans, south of the Raritan River. The land was purchased from Benjamin Springer, who was then living on the property containing 3,044 acres. A clause in the deed provided that it would not be in the power of the Native Americans or anyone else to lease or sell any part of the land. A sawmill was already located there as well as the dwelling house of Springer that was soon occupied by Rev. John Brainerd. The deed above is from the New Jersey Archives.

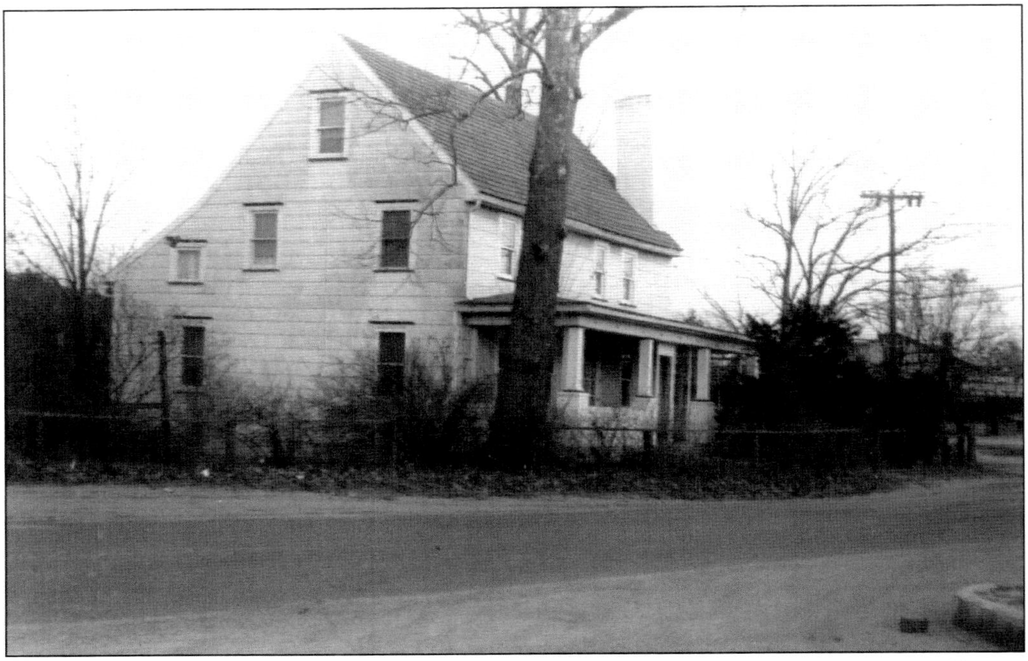

Charles Read, one of the Indian Commissioners, lived in this house from 1770 to 1773. He was the ironmaster of Aetna Iron Works at the time. It was demolished in 1959 to make way for a gas station. Read had also been the chief justice of the New Jersey Supreme Court, founder of the Atsion Iron Works in 1765, and also kept company with kings and royal governors.

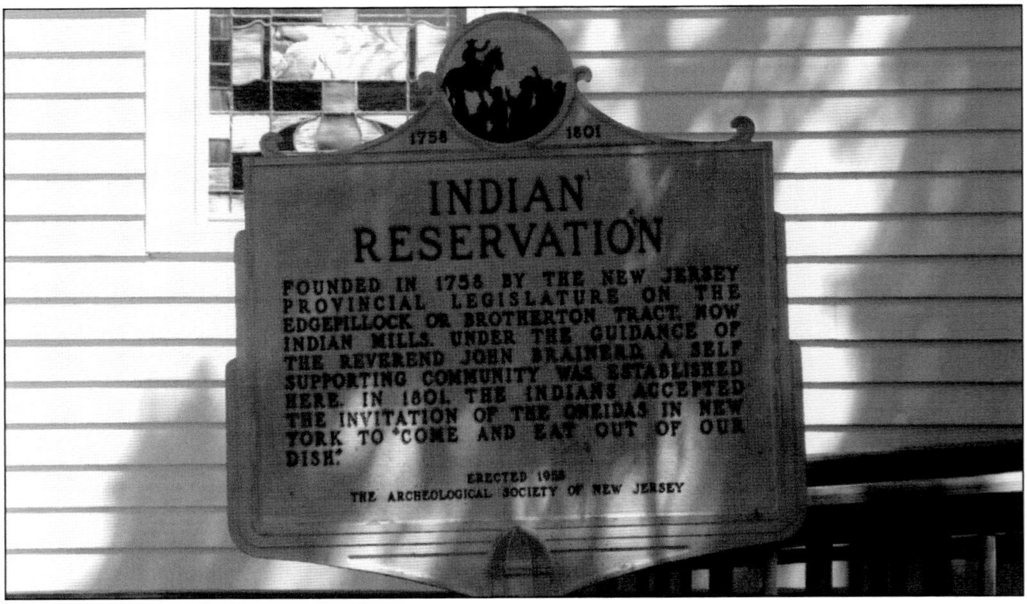

A historical marker was erected in 1958 to commemorate the 200th anniversary of the founding of the Brotherton Reservation. Over 300 persons attended the celebration. Many were descendants of the last full-blooded Lenape named Ann Roberts. The marker was erected by the Archeological Society of New Jersey. It previously stood on the front lawn of the Indian Mills Methodist Church but was moved to the side of the church due to lack of visibility at the intersection. It remains there today.

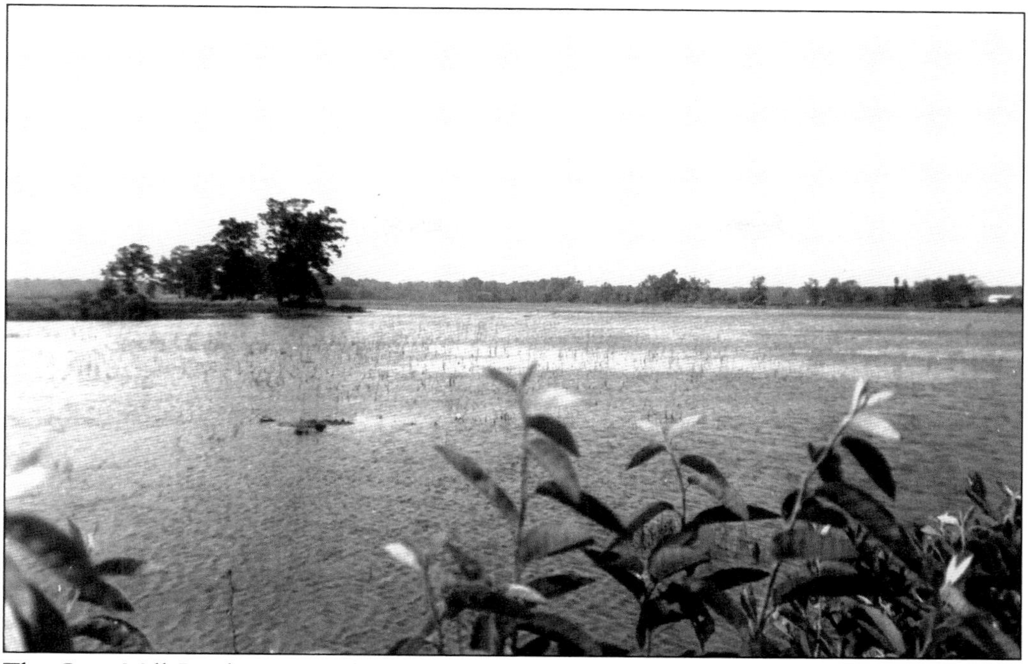

The Grist Mill Pond is pictured as it must have appeared during the reservation years. The Native Americans operated a gristmill at the head of the pond for many years. It burned in 1762 and was not rebuilt until around 1807 by subsequent white settlers.

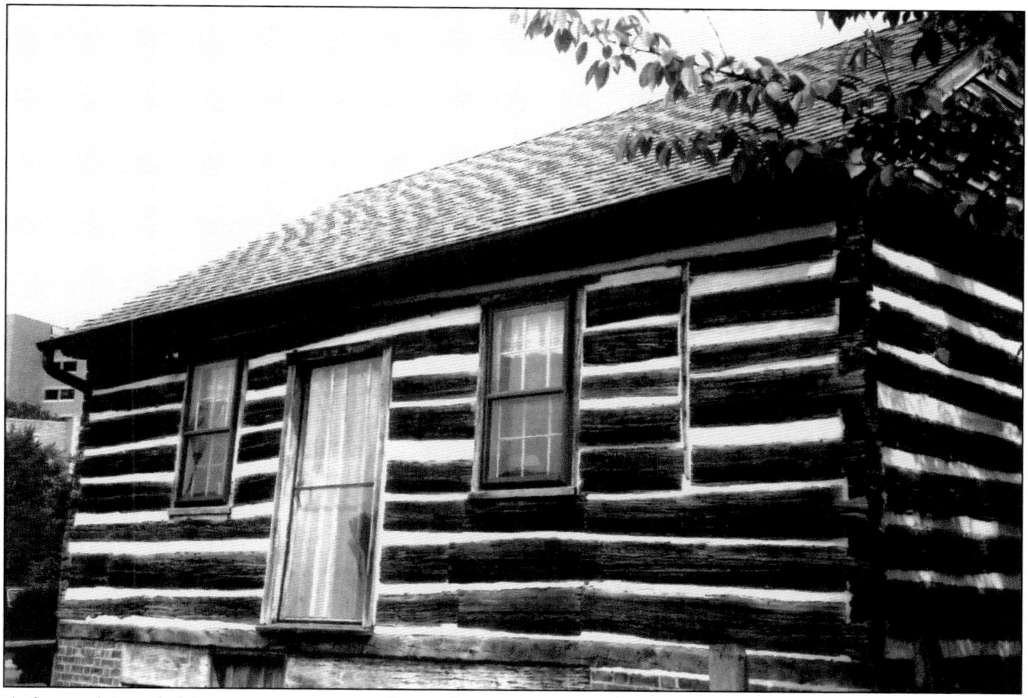

A log cabin of this type was erected on the reservation lands for use by the natives who lived there. Royal Gov. Francis Bernard visited Brotherton in June 1759 and was accompanied by three commissioners who laid out the plan of the town. There were to be 10 dwellings erected of this description. It was during this visit that the governor named the reservation Brotherton.

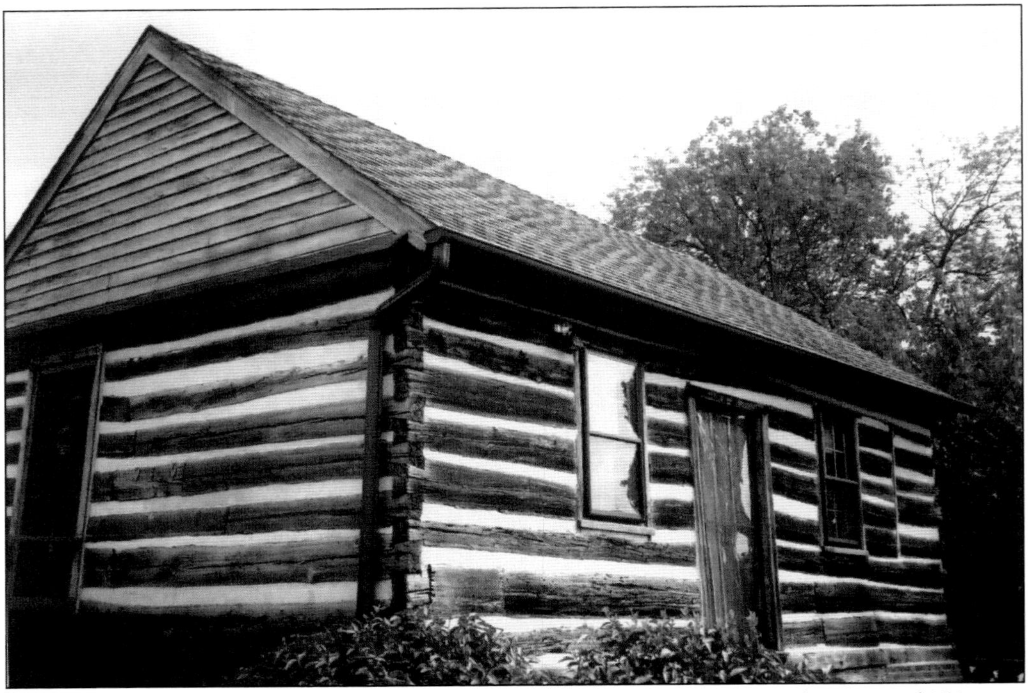

There have never been any remains of these log cabins found or uncovered in spite of 250 years of farming activity. There are eyewitness accounts that provide a description of them as late as 1795, shortly before the demise of the reservation.

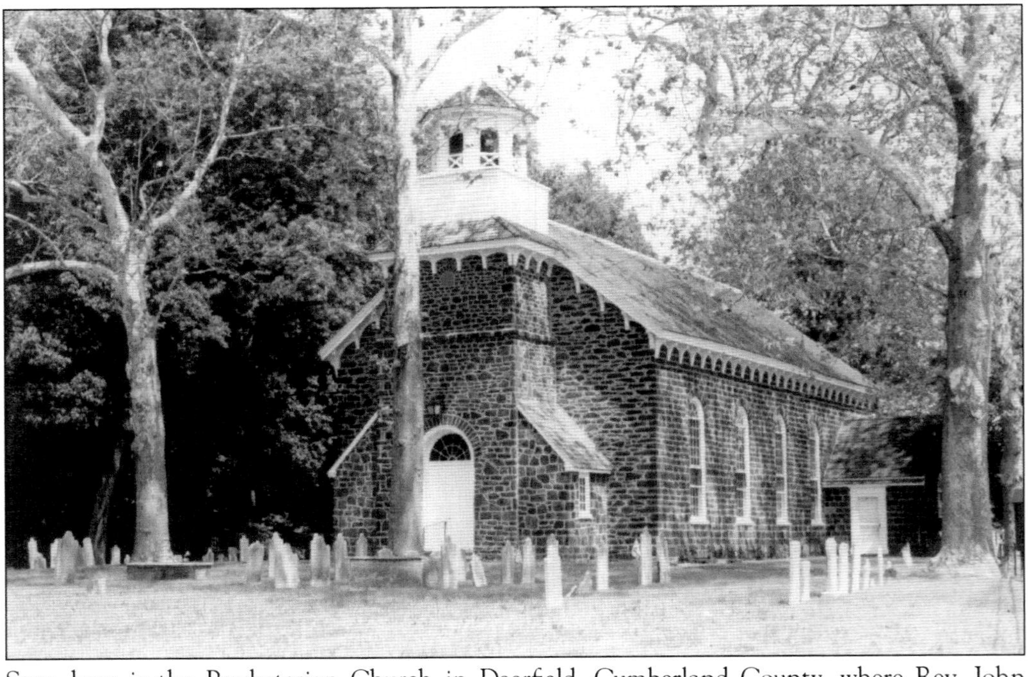

Seen here is the Presbyterian Church in Deerfield, Cumberland County, where Rev. John Brainerd began preaching in the early part of 1777. The previous pastor, Enoch Green had died in December 1776. The church is built of native Jersey sandstone and is still in active use today.

Reverend Brainerd died of a pulmonary ailment at the age of 61 on March 18, 1781. He was initially interred underneath the brick floor of the church in the broad main aisle. In 1907, a new heater had to be installed requiring his remains to be removed and reinterred just outside the right wall of the church. It is still visible there today.

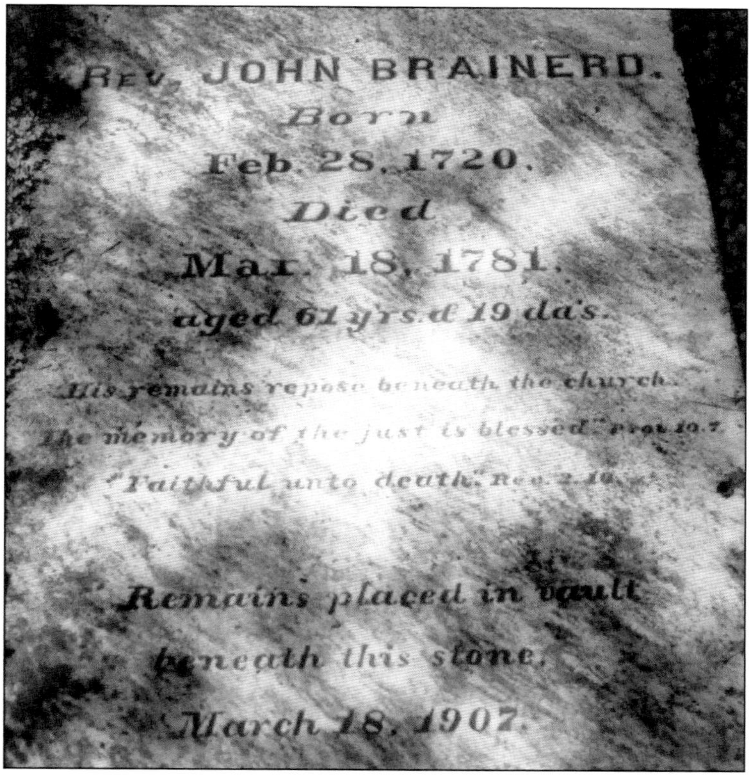

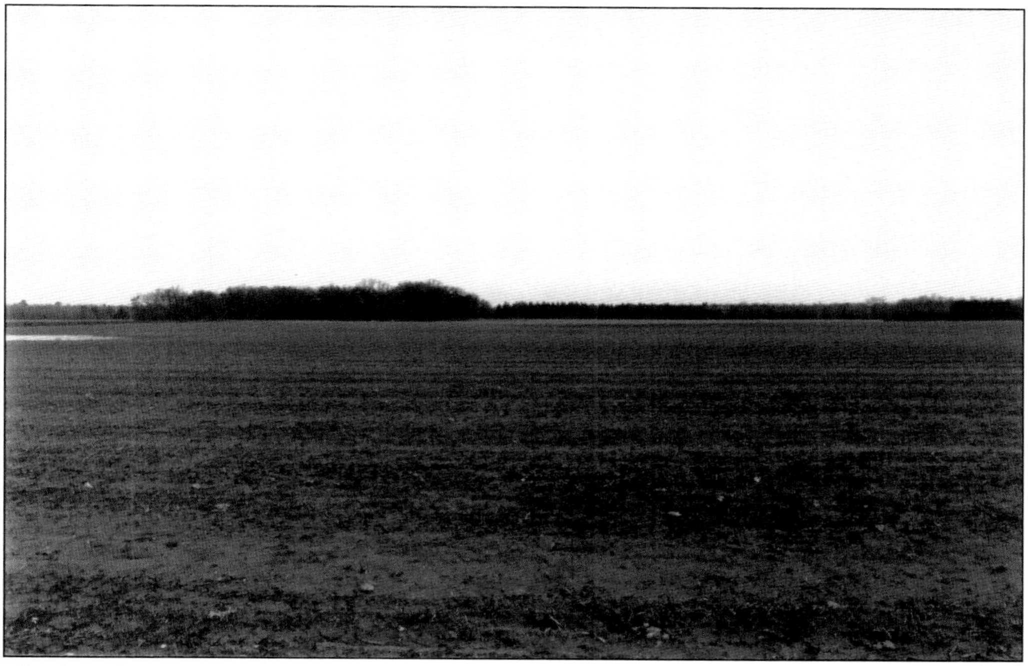

The broad expanse of the former Nathan Wright farm on Medford–Indian Mills Road is indicative of the many 100-acre plots of ground that were auctioned off in 1802. The auction of the Brotherton Reservation land took place at the Sign of the Buck Tavern nearby. The tavern was then owned by John Piper.

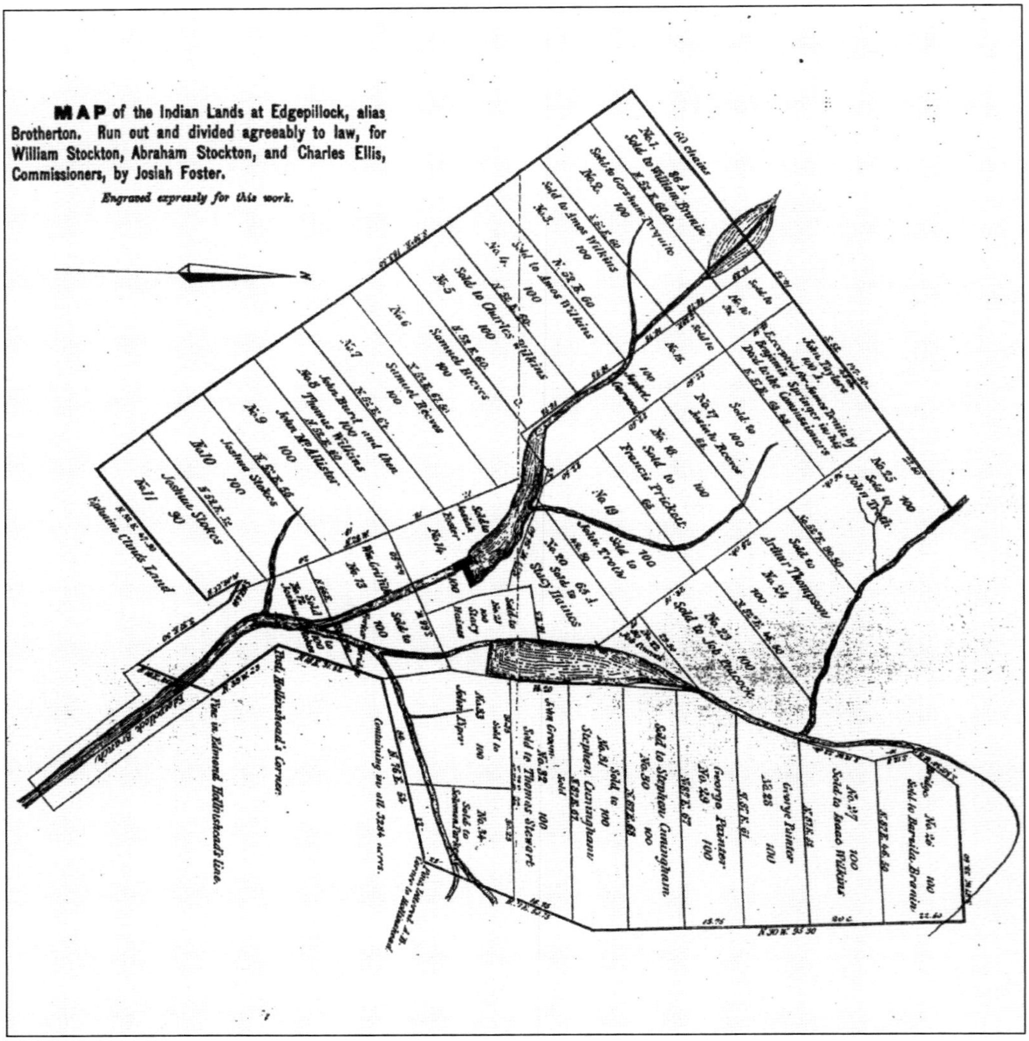

This map appeared in Major E. M. Woodward and John F. Hageman's *History of Burlington and Mercer Counties, New Jersey* in 1883. Many of these same 100-acre plots of land can be seen today on a modern tax map of the area. Although the original purchase of the reservation lands were deeded as 3,044 acres, it was found the reservation actually contained 3,284 acres. Many of these plots sold for as little as $2 to $5 per acre.

Three

The Village of Indian Mills

After the demise of the Brotherton Reservation in 1802, very little remained to recall the Native American presence. The home once occupied by Rev. John Brainerd lay in ruins. The log meetinghouse where the Native Americans (and later white settlers) worshipped burned to the ground in 1808. The log homes of the natives had fallen into ruin. Gradually settlers from surrounding towns began to populate and farm the 100-acre plots of ground they had purchased. Some too were speculators who eventually sold this land to others for a profit.

A gristmill and sawmill complex was erected about 1805 at the head of Grist Mill Pond. The Bedford family of Philadelphia had invested in the property, and John Murphy was hired to operate the mills and also erect a dwelling house. The present-day Indian Mills–Medford Road was once known as the Murphy Road on early deeds. During the reservation days, it was simply known as the "Road to the Indian Town."

Samuel Reeves rebuilt the old sawmill used by the Native Americans for over 40 years. In Dr. James Still's autobiography, he refers to his place of birth as the Native American mill of Samuel Reeves, where his father, Levin Still, was employed. Other than the mills and a few scattered farms, there was little else to recall an actual village. The earliest name for the crossroads that would eventually become Indian Mills was Hartford. The earliest public building was a schoolhouse erected by the Medford Quakers in 1805 and also called Hartford. Thomas Gordon's map of 1828 lists the village as Shamong.

In 1844, a church was erected in the village and known as the Methodist-Episcopal church of Hartford. In 1879, a larger church was built at the same location. By 1849, the map of Otley and Whiteford listed the village as Shamong or Hartford. A village store was erected at the crossroads in the 1860s, along with extensive wagon and livery stables. Scott's atlas of 1876 lists the village as Indian Mills. It has remained so ever since.

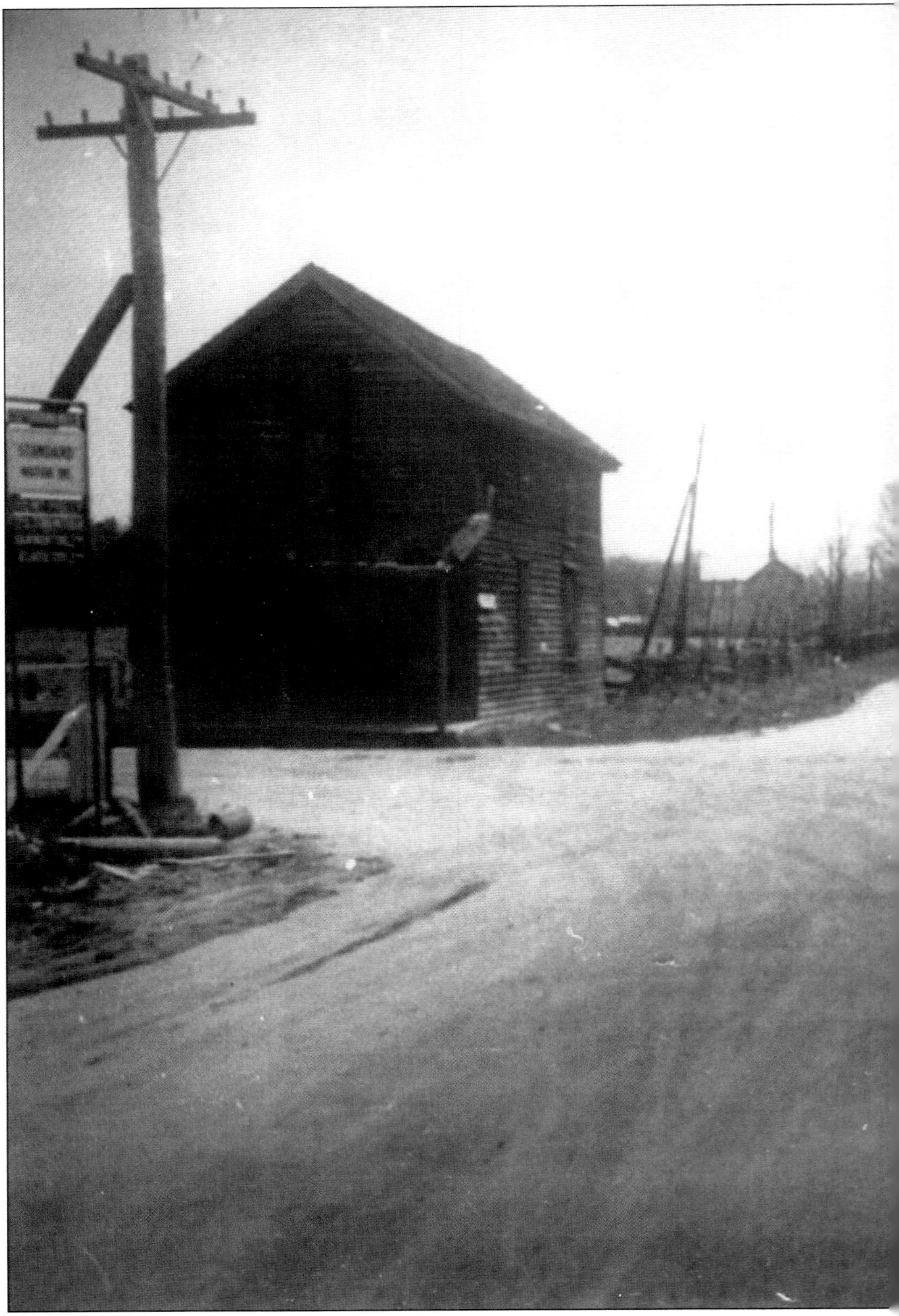

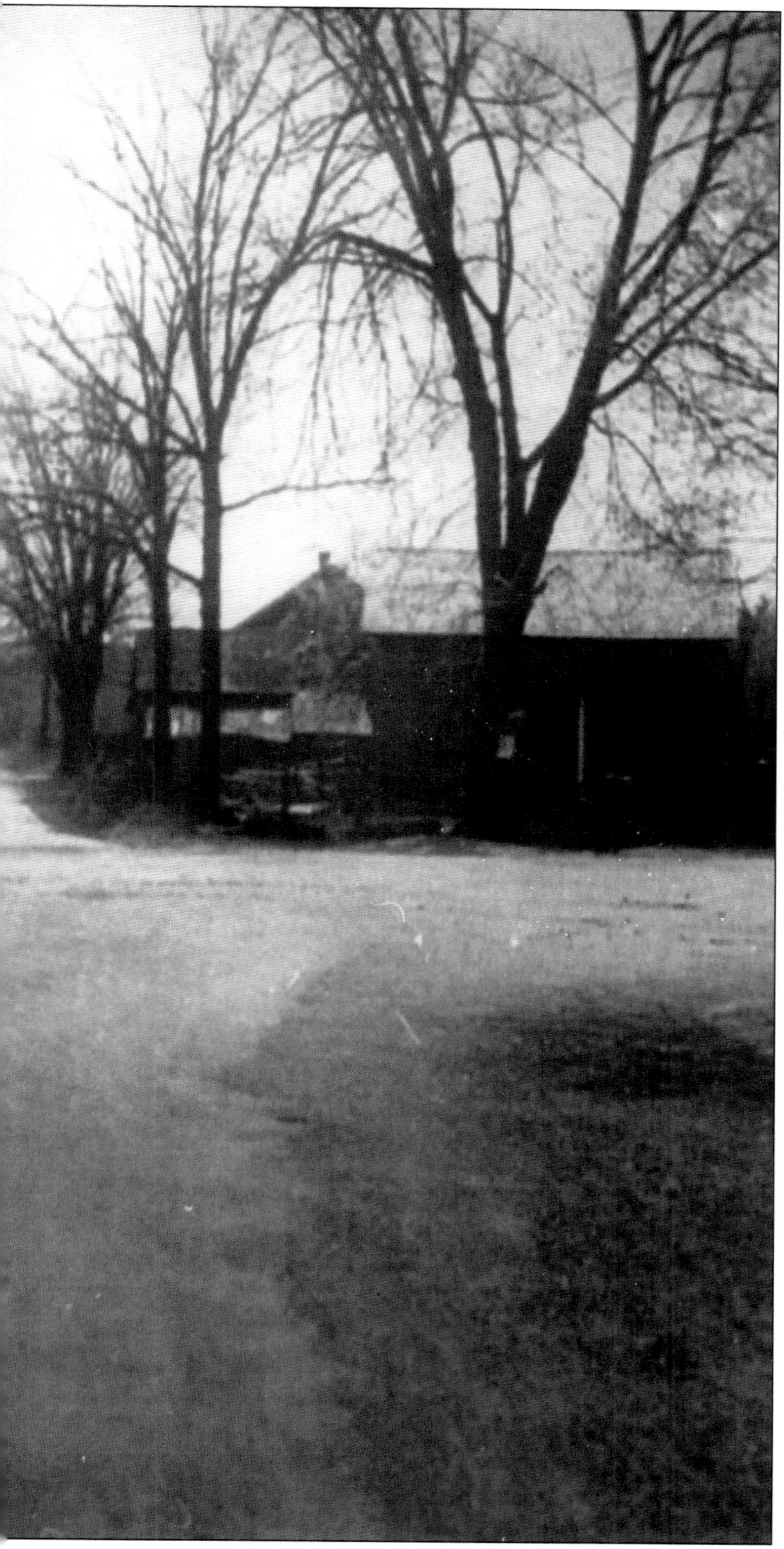

This is a scene of downtown Indian Mills from the 1930s. Many of the roads were still unpaved in the area. The general store is to the right of the photograph and not visible. The home to the right was the Amos Cotteral home, as shown in Scott's atlas of 1876. It is no longer standing. The building to the left is a former store and pool hall that was later moved to the rear of the farm, seen down the road to the left. This corner is now vacant. The road in the center of the picture is looking out Forked Neck Road to the east.

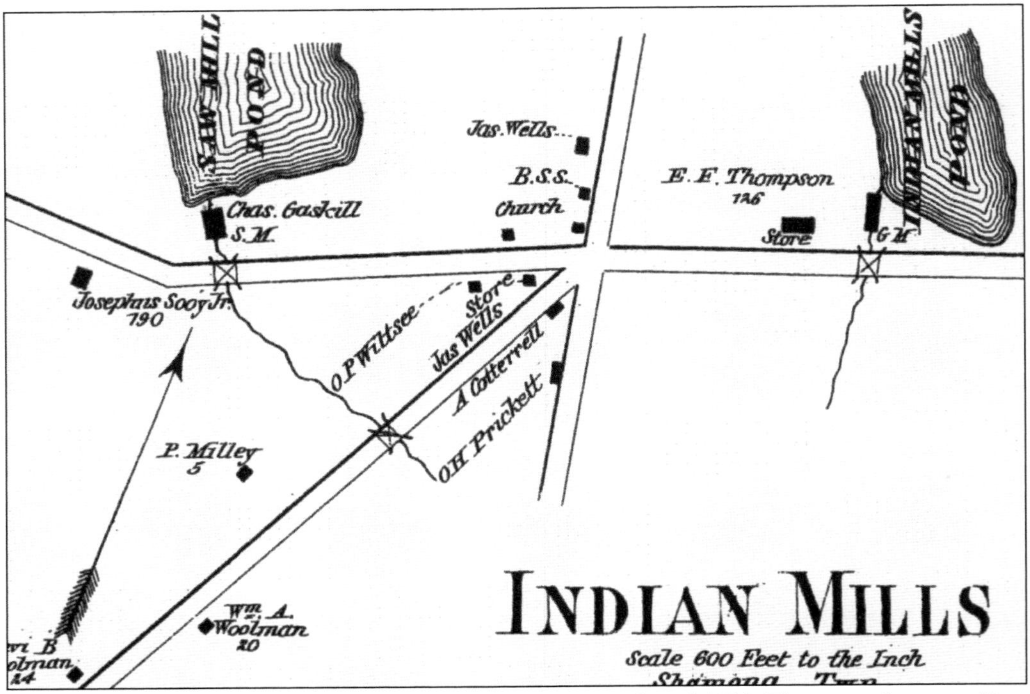

This is the village of Indian Mills as depicted in Scott's atlas of 1876. The store shown as "Jas. Wells" was actually spelled Wills. The store shown as "E. F. Thompson" was actually E. T. Thompson. The church depicted on the corner is the Indian Mills Methodist Church.

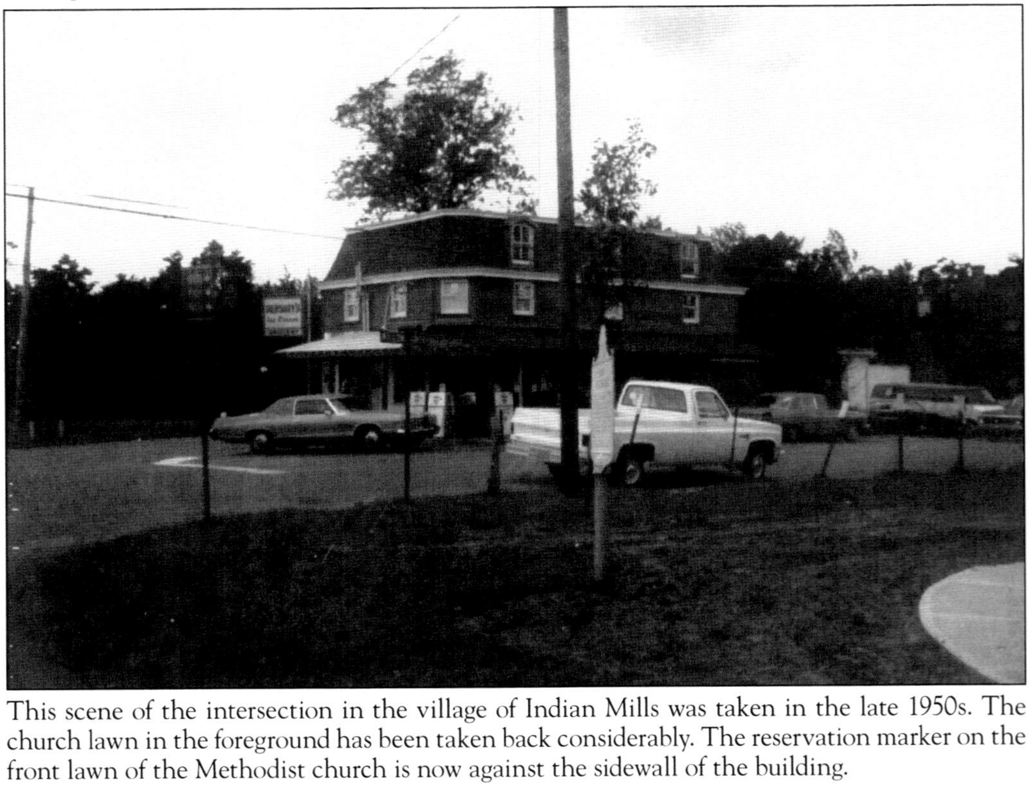

This scene of the intersection in the village of Indian Mills was taken in the late 1950s. The church lawn in the foreground has been taken back considerably. The reservation marker on the front lawn of the Methodist church is now against the sidewall of the building.

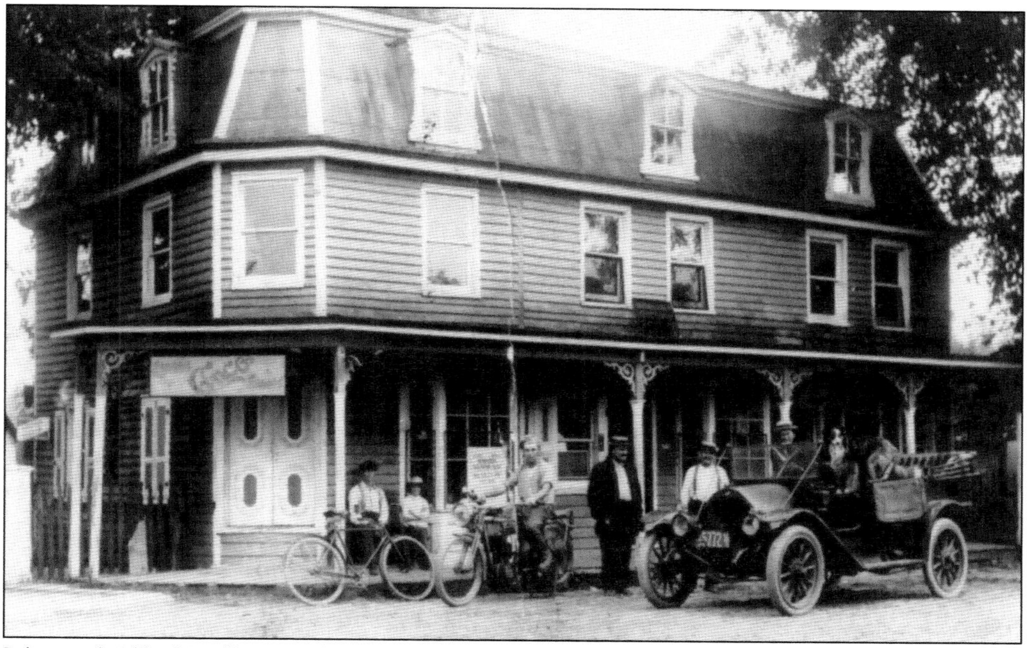

John and Alfred Wills were the owners of the store when this photograph was taken in 1908. They are standing next to the car. The store was built in the 1860s. Walter Batterson is seated on the bench to the left, and Raymond Crain is on the motorcycle.

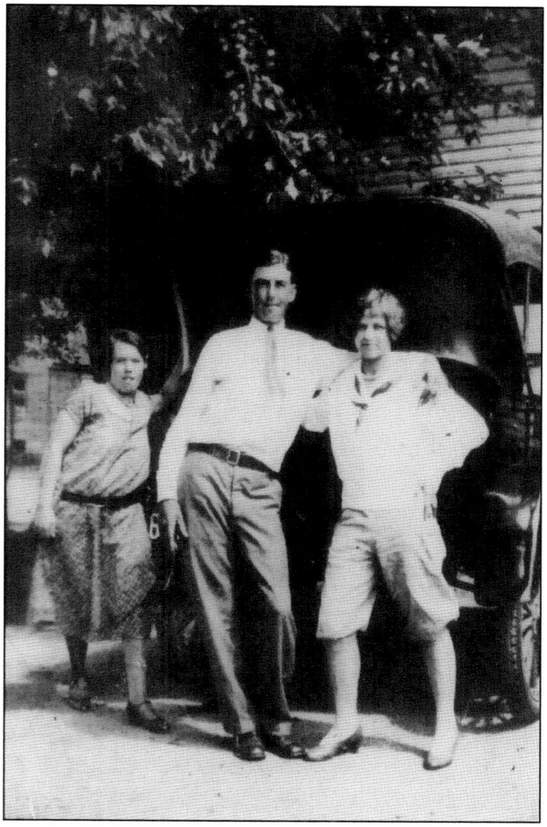

This is a photograph taken in the 1920s showing, from left to right, Reba Giberson, Bill Lemmon, and Marion Lemmon. They were all local Indian Mills people.

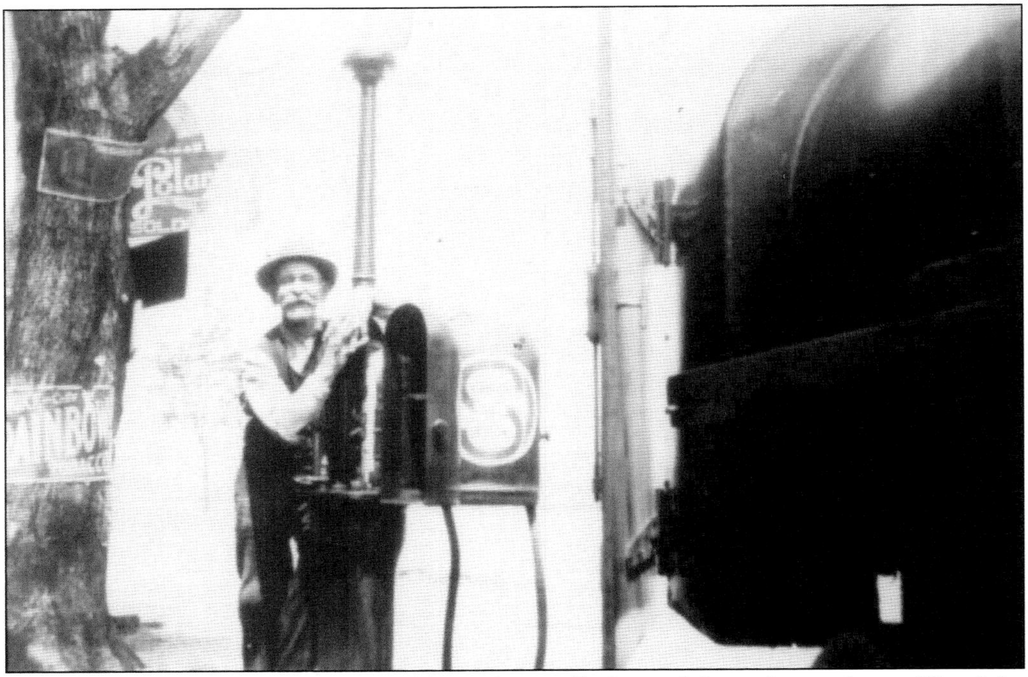

Mahlon Prickett was the proprietor of the Indian Mills General Store during the middle of the 20th century. This photograph was taken in the 1930s. He is seen pumping gas outside the store with a gas pump, which has been long since removed.

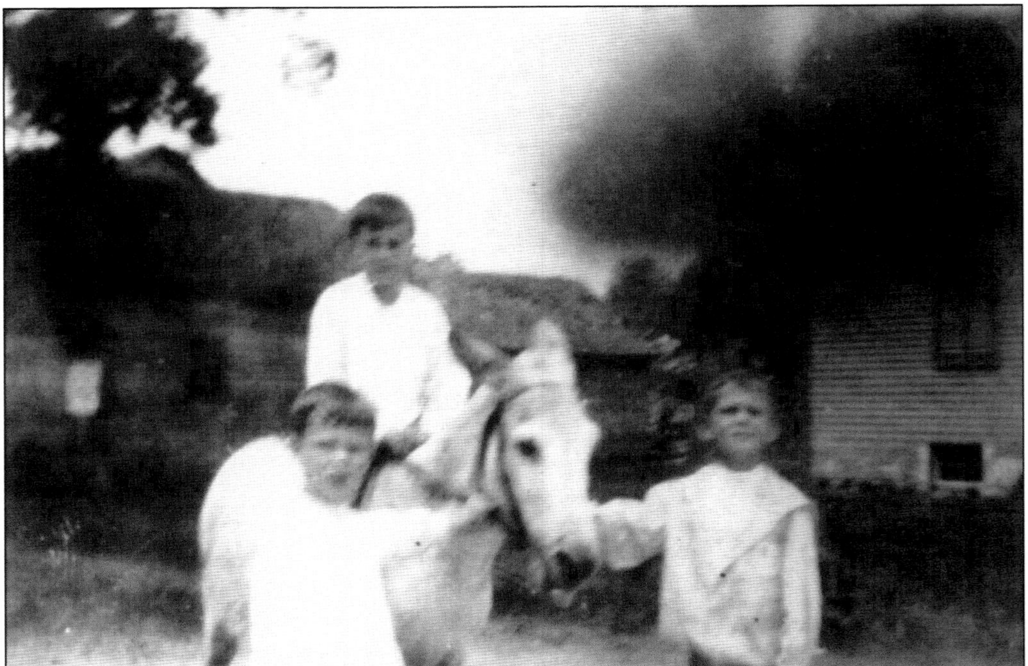

Merle Prickett is seen holding the pony on the right. The others are not identified. They are standing in front of the general store with the Methodist church seen at the right. The livery stables and storage buildings are behind the church. This photograph was taken in the 1920s.

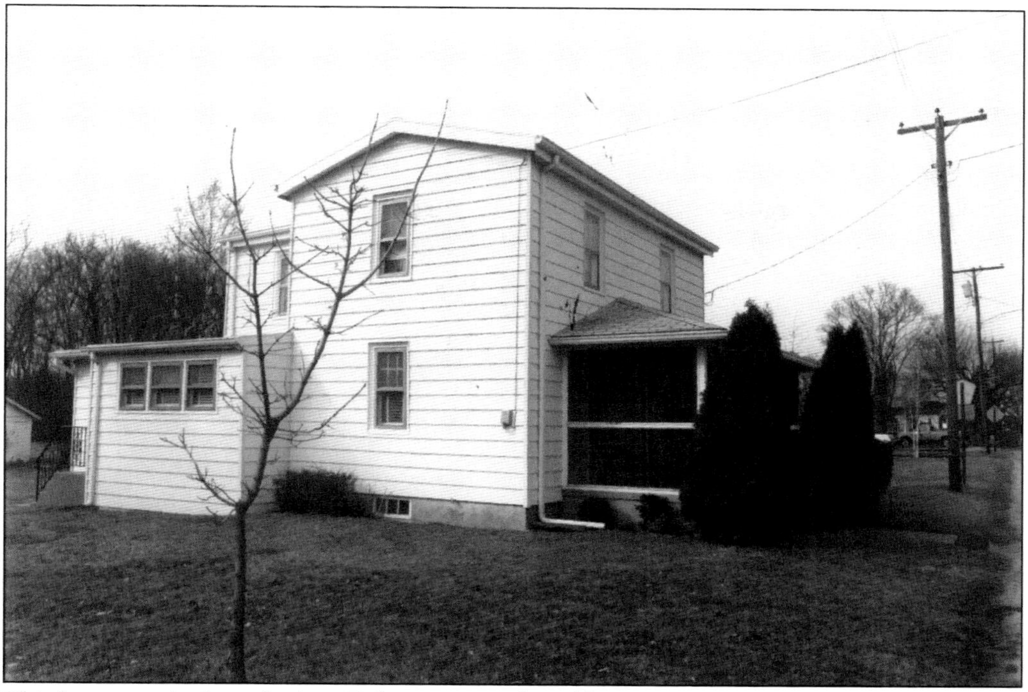

This home was built in the late 19th century and is of frame construction with Jersey sandstone foundation. Located a short distance from the Methodist church on the corner, it may have been the parsonage at some time in the past.

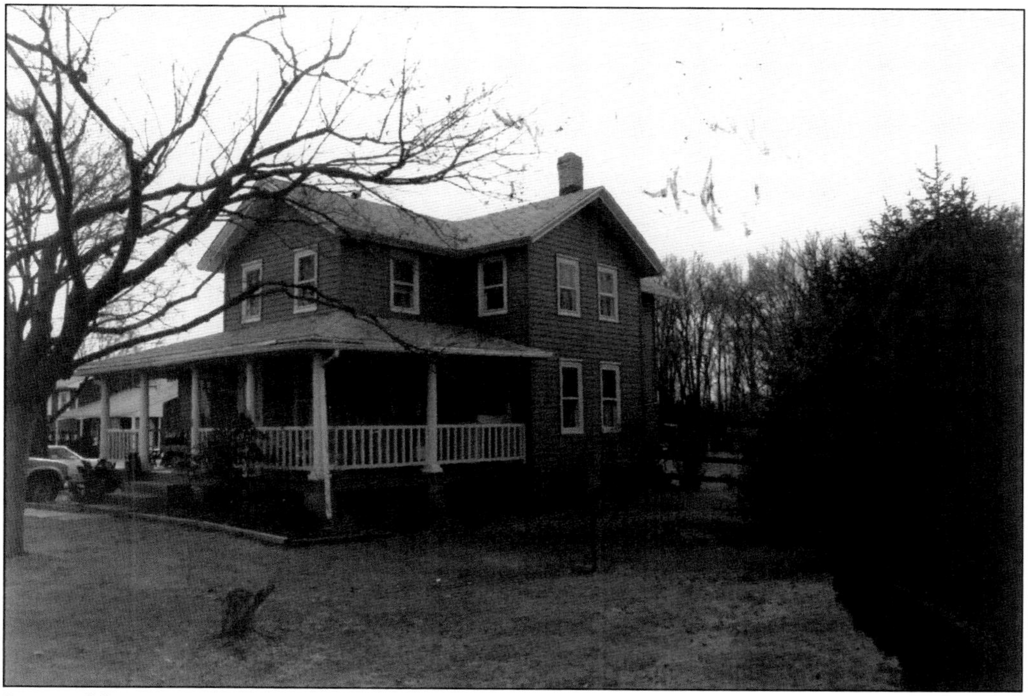

Pictured here is a two-story frame home with Jersey sandstone foundation still visible. It was built in the 1880s. This is one of the few homes still standing in the village area from over a century ago. It is in a good state of preservation.

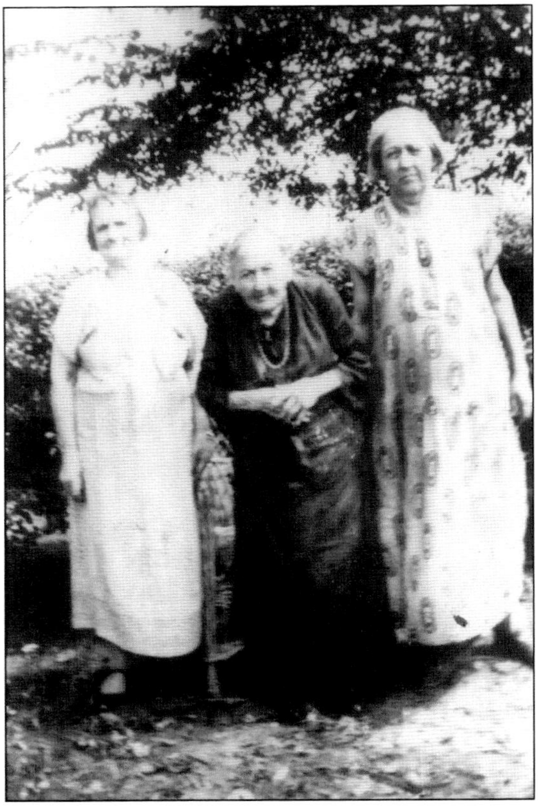

Seen here is a group of seniors in the 1920s. All are members of local farm families. From left to right are Mary Crain, Mary Gail, and Sara Giberson.

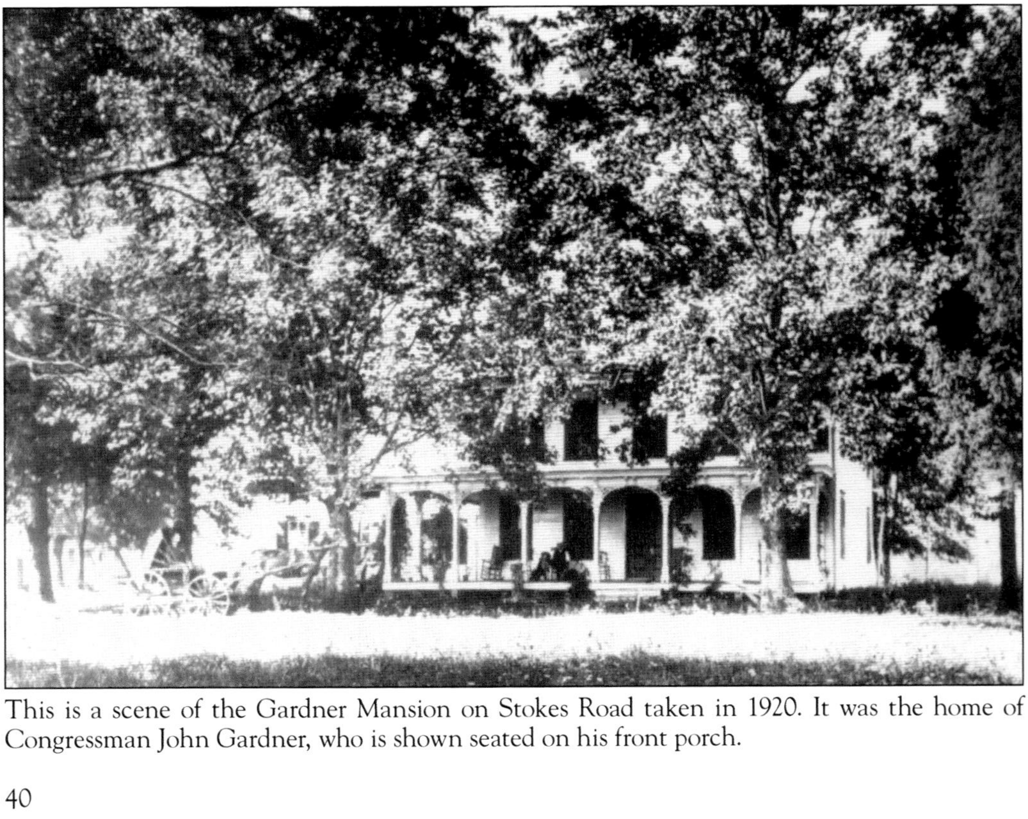

This is a scene of the Gardner Mansion on Stokes Road taken in 1920. It was the home of Congressman John Gardner, who is shown seated on his front porch.

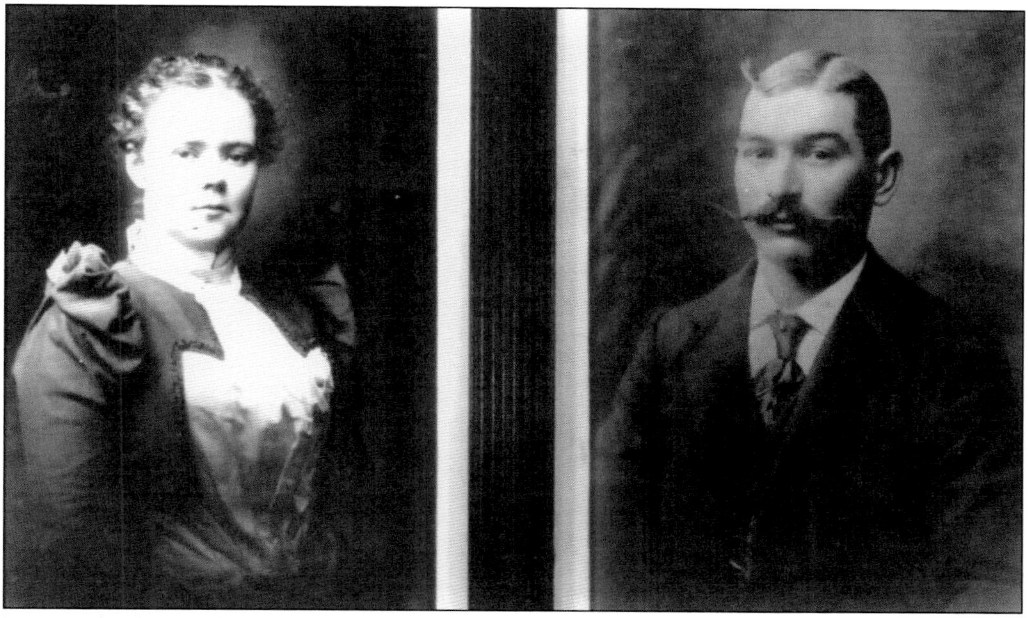

Lewis Schrider and his wife, Katherine, are pictured here in the early 1900s. They were a local farming couple. Their son Lewis Schrider Jr. became the mayor of Shamong Township in his later years.

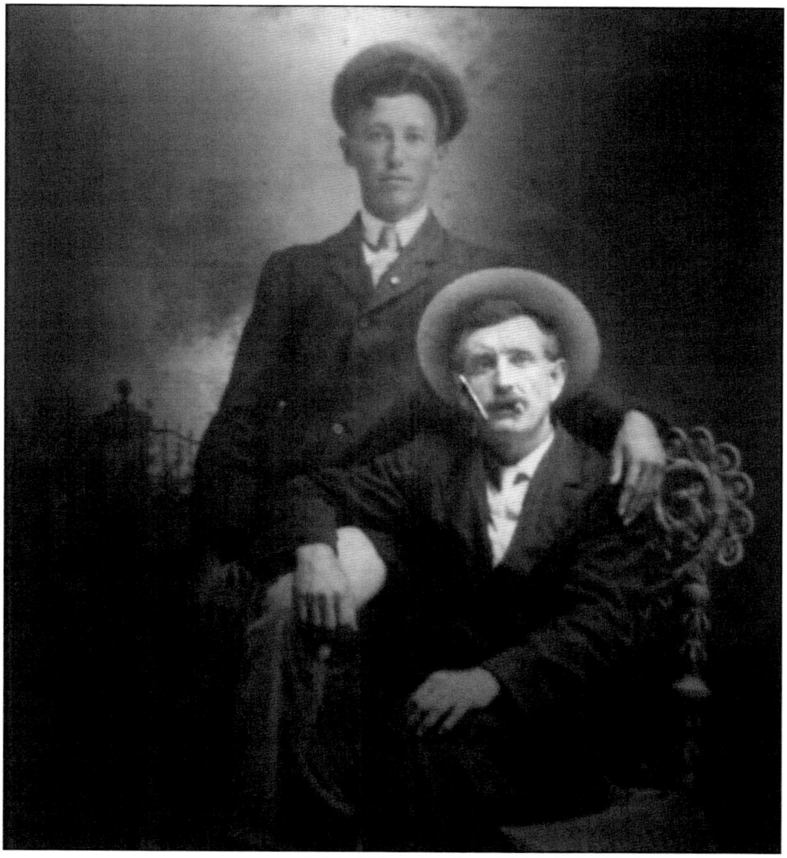

Ulysses Dellett is shown seated in the chair. His friend Joe Wells is standing behind him. This photograph was taken in the early 1900s when Ulysses still had his barbershop on Forked Neck Road.

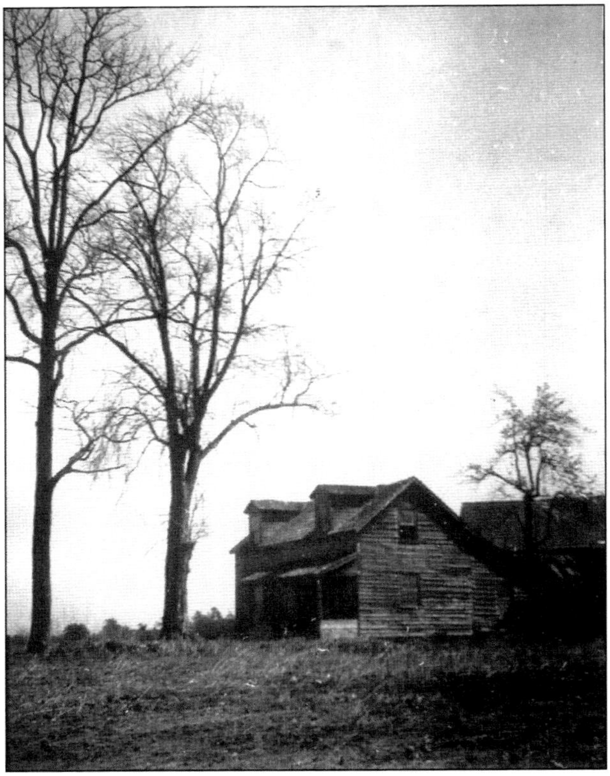

This saltbox-style farmhouse of the 1820s once stood on Forked Neck Road. A large barn can be seen behind the home. The scene is from 1939.

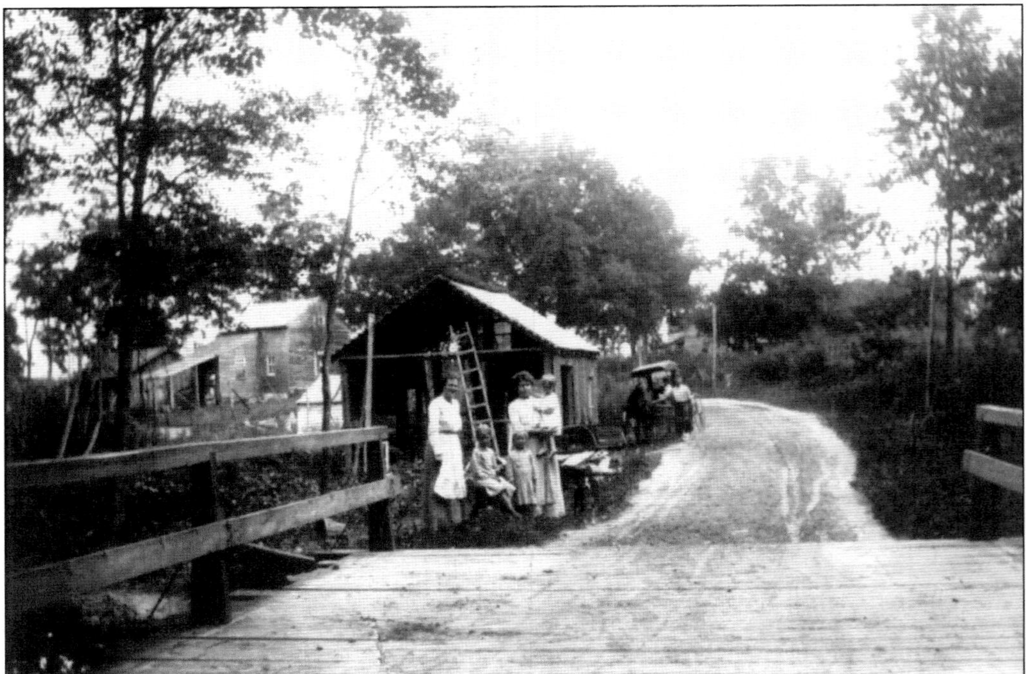

This scene is from the early 1900s looking east on Forked Neck Road. A blacksmith shop is shown just over the wooden bridge. Bertha Wood is standing with her two daughters Julia and Olive Wood. Her husband is the blacksmith. Elizabeth Batterson is holding her son George.

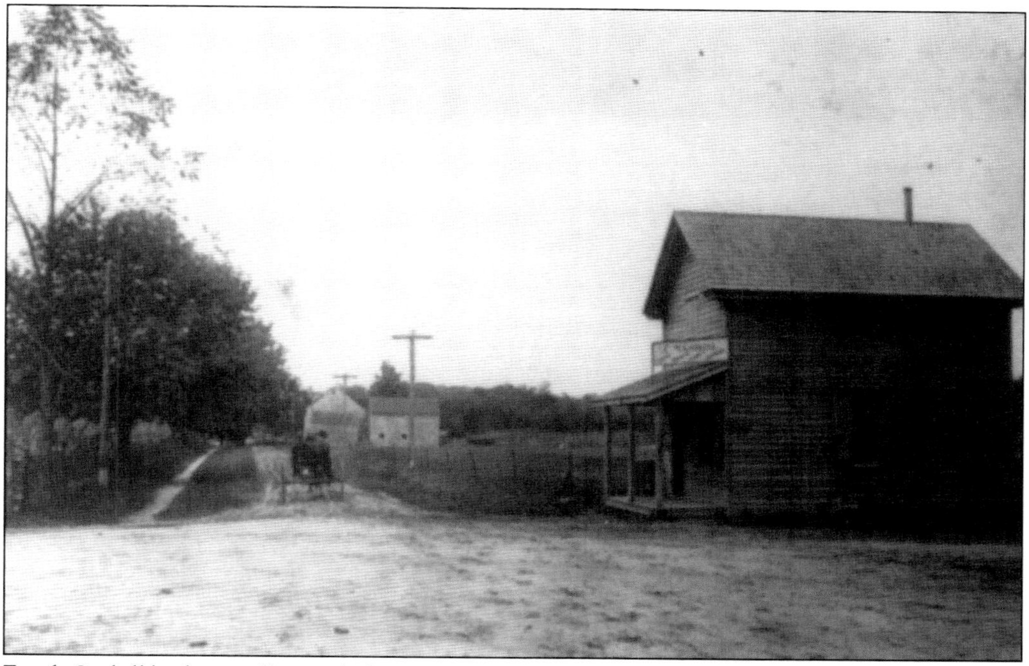

Frank Gaskill built a small store for his son C. Marriott Gaskill. He sold candy and tobacco there. It was located on the corner of Forked Neck Road and Willow Grove Road. The business continued until his death in 1910. His brother Alva "Duff" Gaskill made a pool hall on the second floor. He also sold groceries and men's clothing. For a short time, a post office was also housed there.

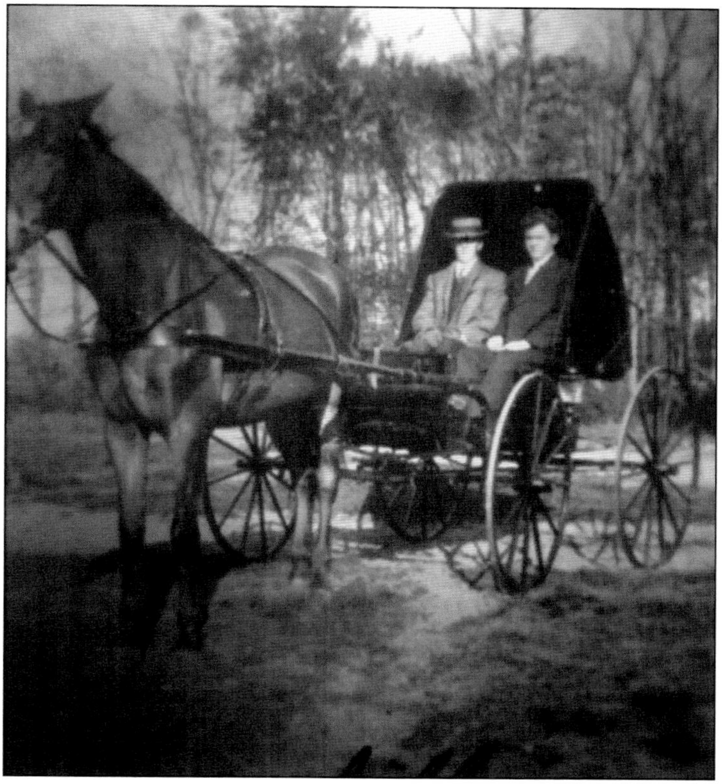

This is a photograph from 1908. Marriott and his brother Alva "Duff" Gaskill are near their home on Willow Grove Road. The roads were mostly unpaved at that time. Having one's own carriage was considered a great pastime.

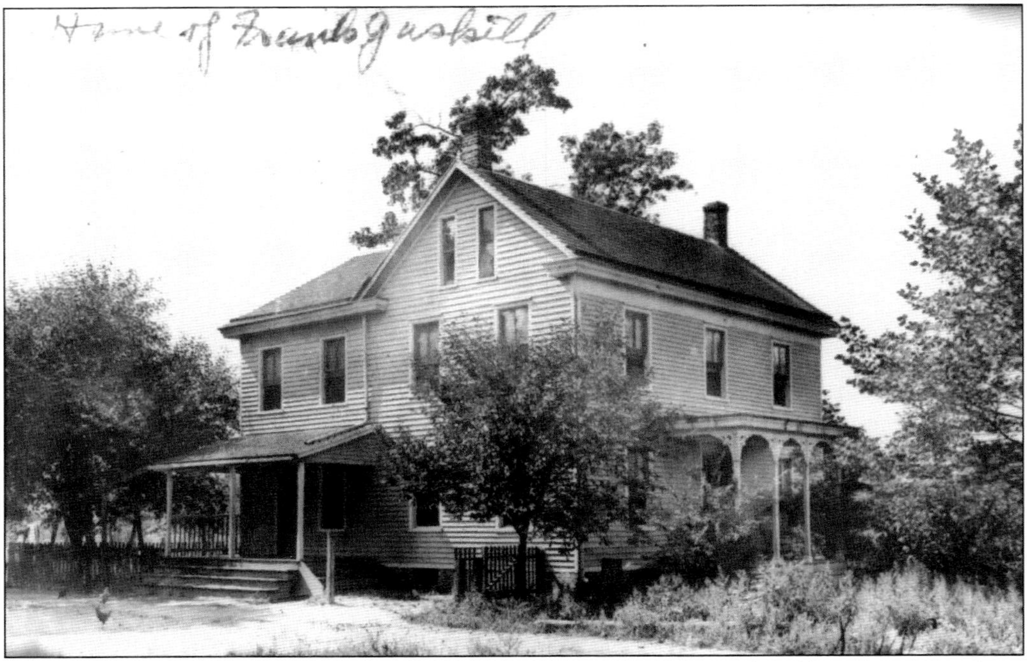

Pictured here is the home of Frank and Belle Gaskill that once faced Willow Grove Road. To the rear of this home and along the Muskingum Brook stood a steam-powered mill operated by Frank during the early 1900s. Nothing remains today.

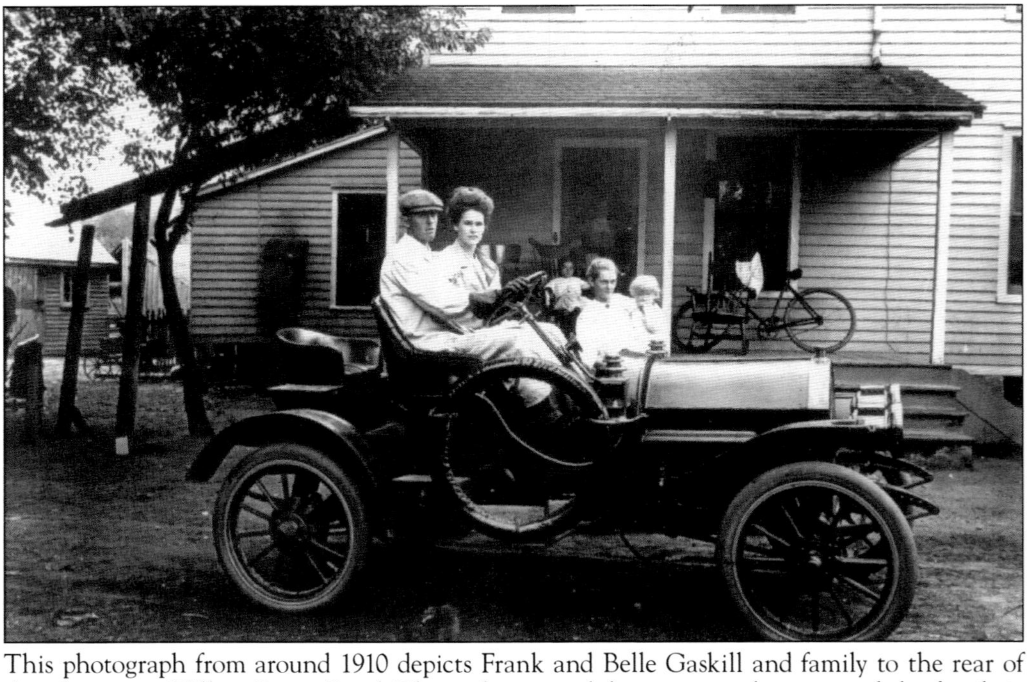

This photograph from around 1910 depicts Frank and Belle Gaskill and family to the rear of their home on Willow Grove Road. The early automobile appears to be new, and the family is proudly displaying it.

Cleveland Hagerthey is seen on the left and Marriott Gaskill is on the right. They appear to be posing next to this unusual bush. The picture is dated about 1910.

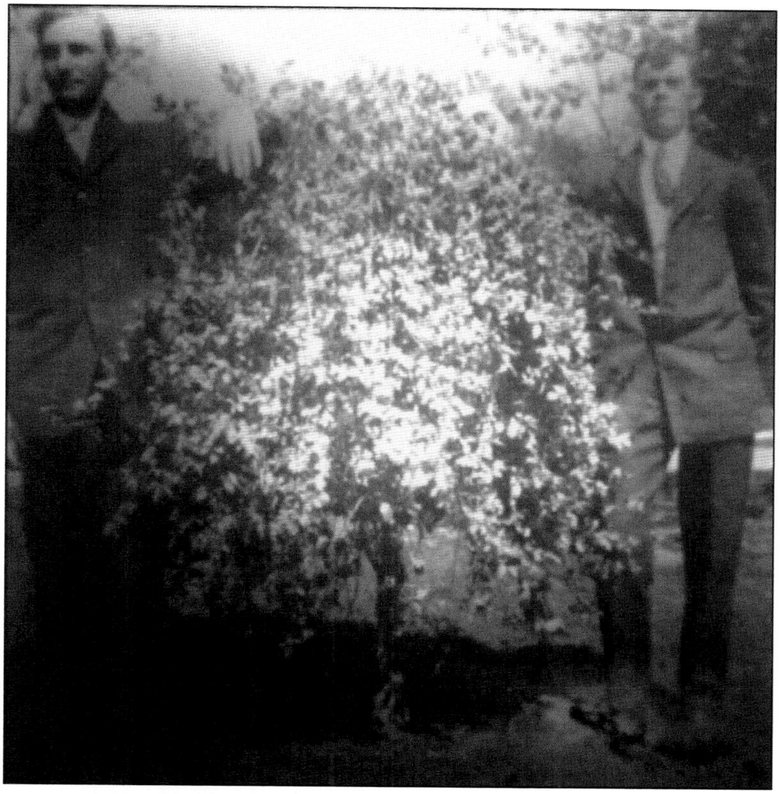

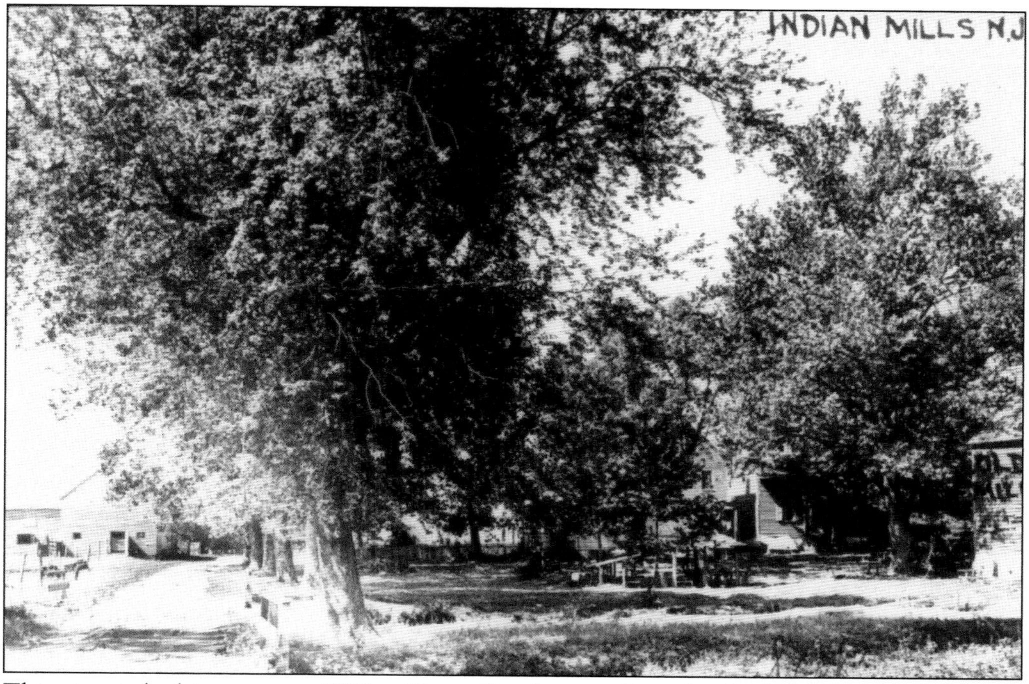

This view is looking west on Willow Grove Road across from the Gaskill home. The barns to the left belong to Benjamin Mingin. The Mingin home is to the right. A corner of the Mingin Gristmill can be seen at the far right, as it appeared in 1908.

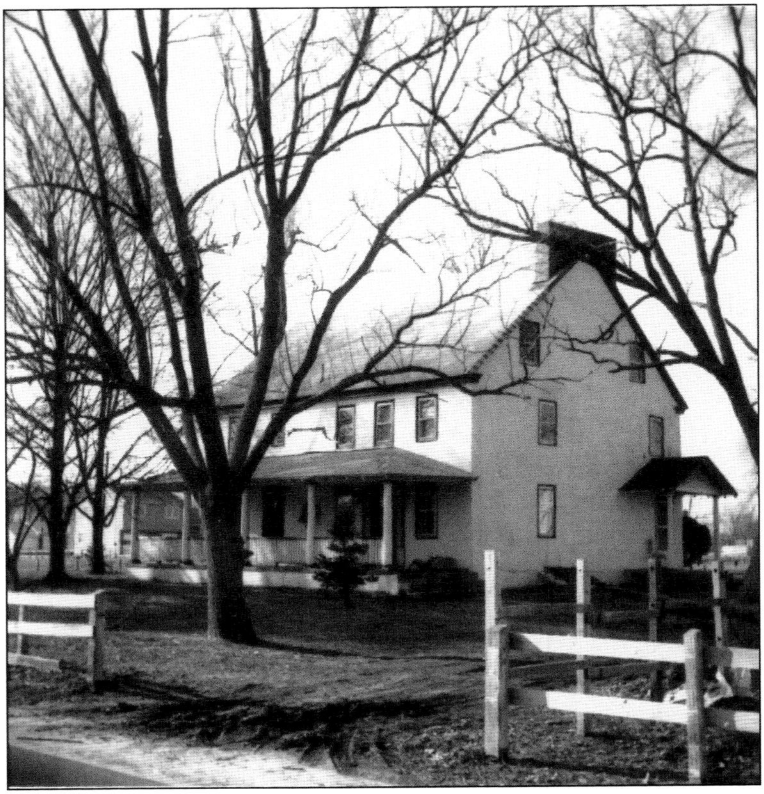

The left-hand side of this home is the oldest in Shamong Township. It was erected by the Bedford family in 1805. Many others lived in this home over the years. The right-hand side, with the large chimney, was added in 1835 by Ebenezer Engle. Edward T. Thompson was living here when he was a New Jersey State assemblyman during the 1870s. He ran the gristmill and had a store with a post office in the house.

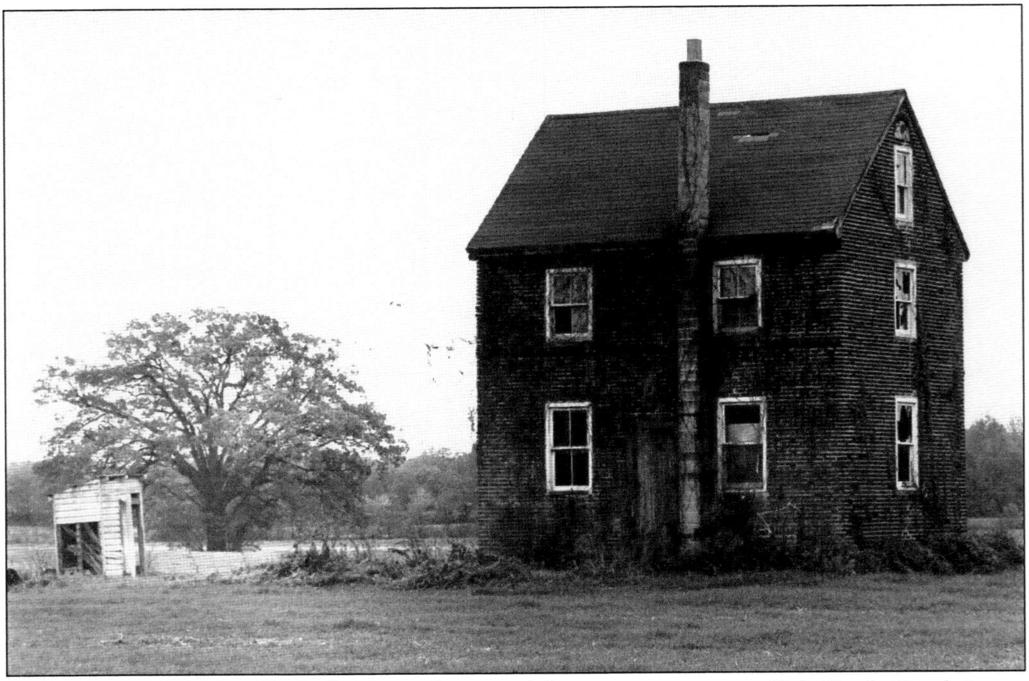

This is the venerable Old Brick House that stood for so many years on Oak Shade Road. It was originally built by Clayton Wilkins in 1809 on land left to him by his father, Amos Wilkins. John Sorden occupied the home in 1841 and lived here for many years.

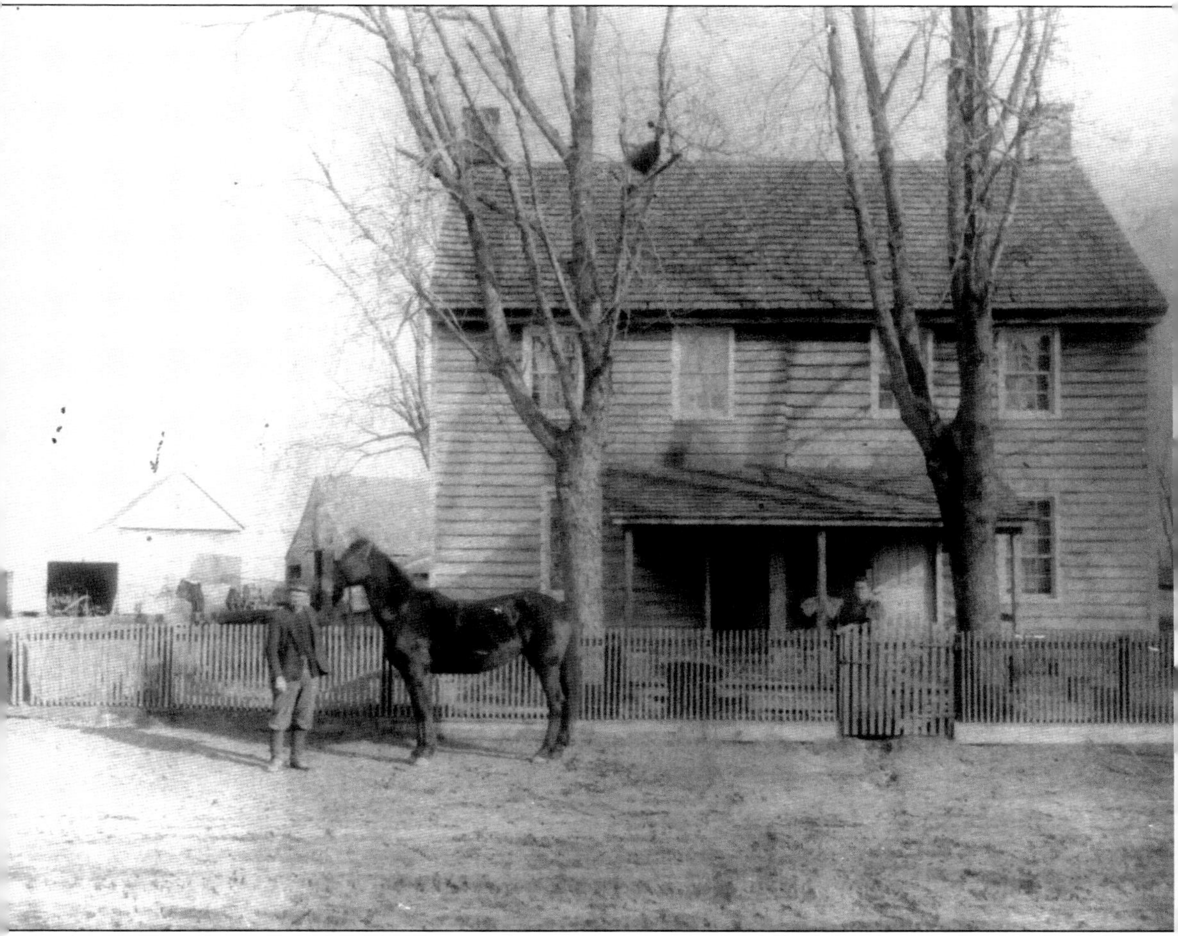

William H. Brown is pictured standing with his horse at his home on Old Indian Mills Road. His wife stands inside the fence. This scene dates from the late 1890s. The home was eventually purchased by Richard and Marie Giberson and moved to its present location on Tuckerton Road. It is still being used as a residence.

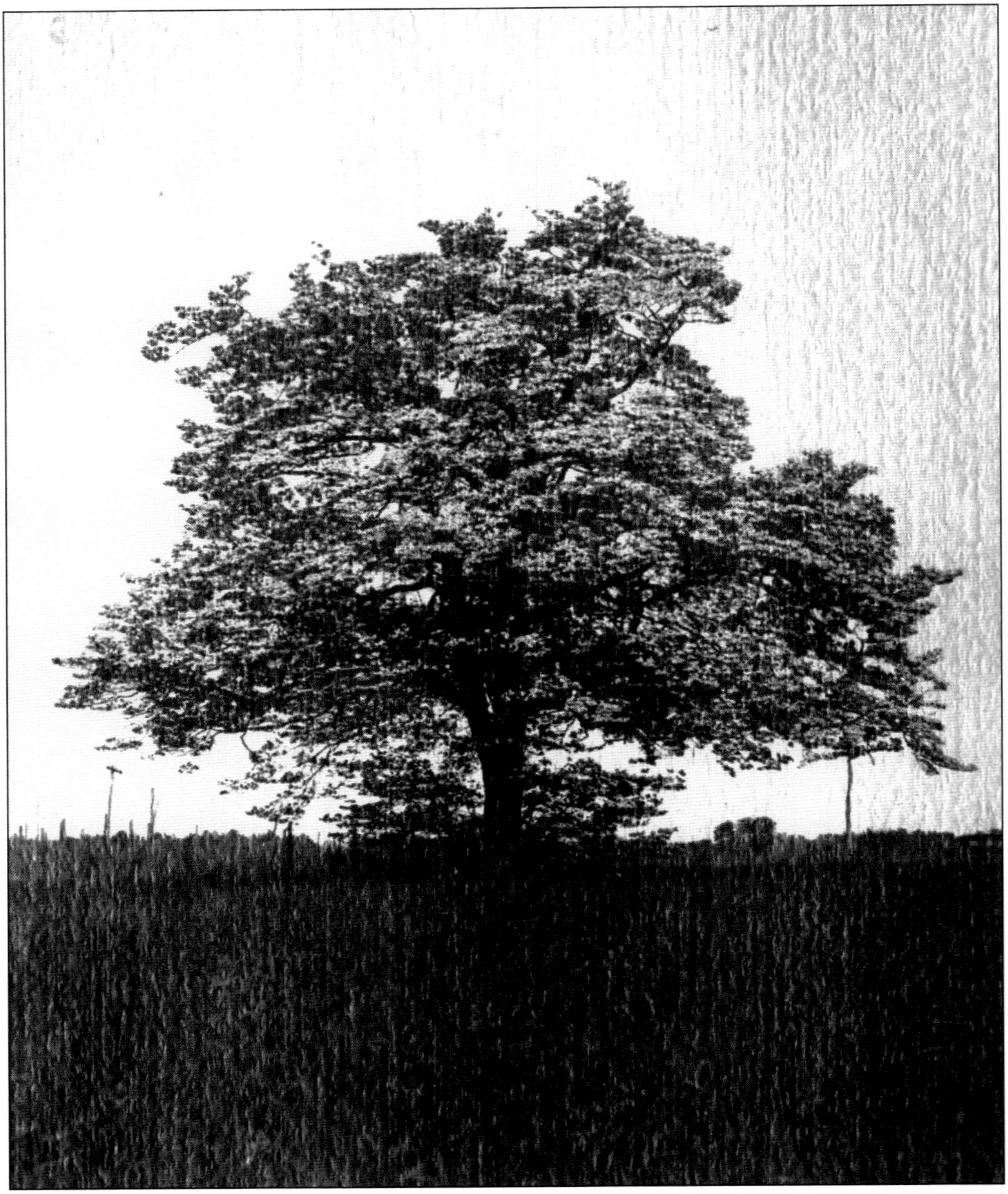

This tree was once known throughout Burlington County as the "Great Dogwood." It stood in the middle of the field between Old Indian Mills Road and Route 206, opposite the Texaco station. It was allegedly taken down to make way for additional farming area.

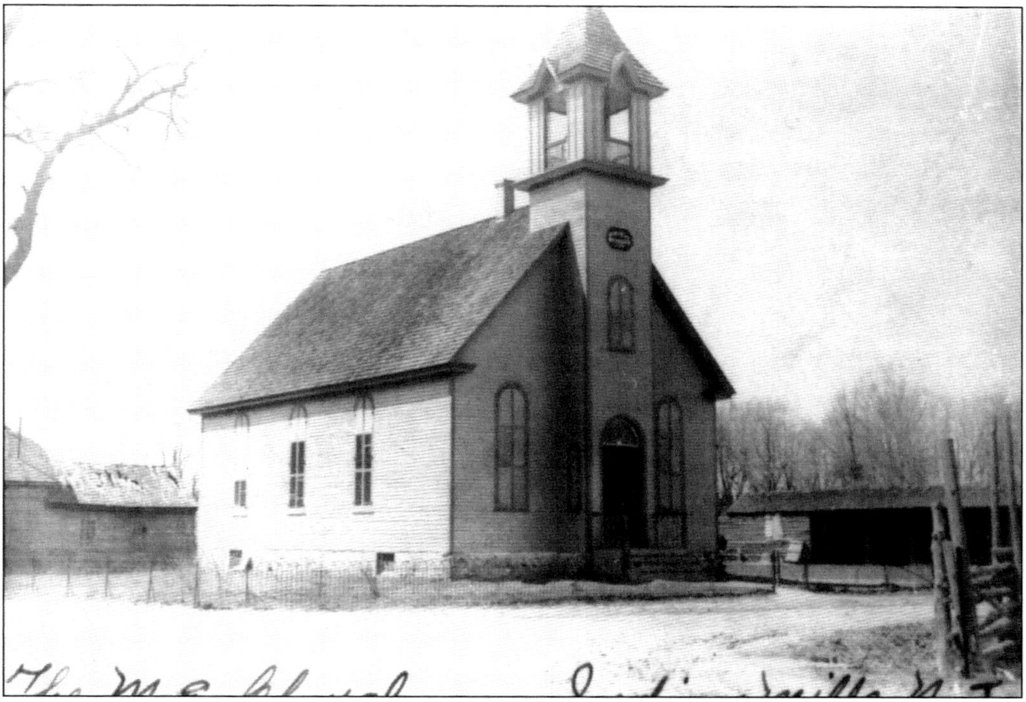

Here is the Indian Mills Methodist-Episcopal Church as it appeared in 1907. Note the carriage stalls to the right. Also note the extensive storage buildings to the rear of the church.

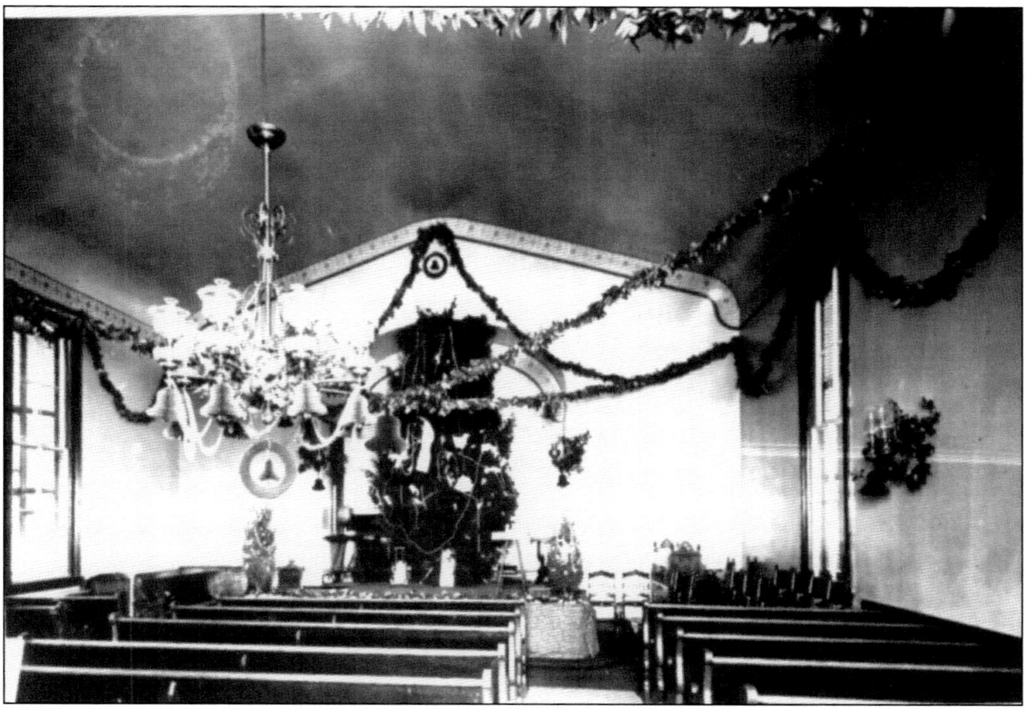

This is the interior of the church as it appeared at Christmastime. Note the antique chairs used for the choir at the front of the church. The picture was taken in the 1950s.

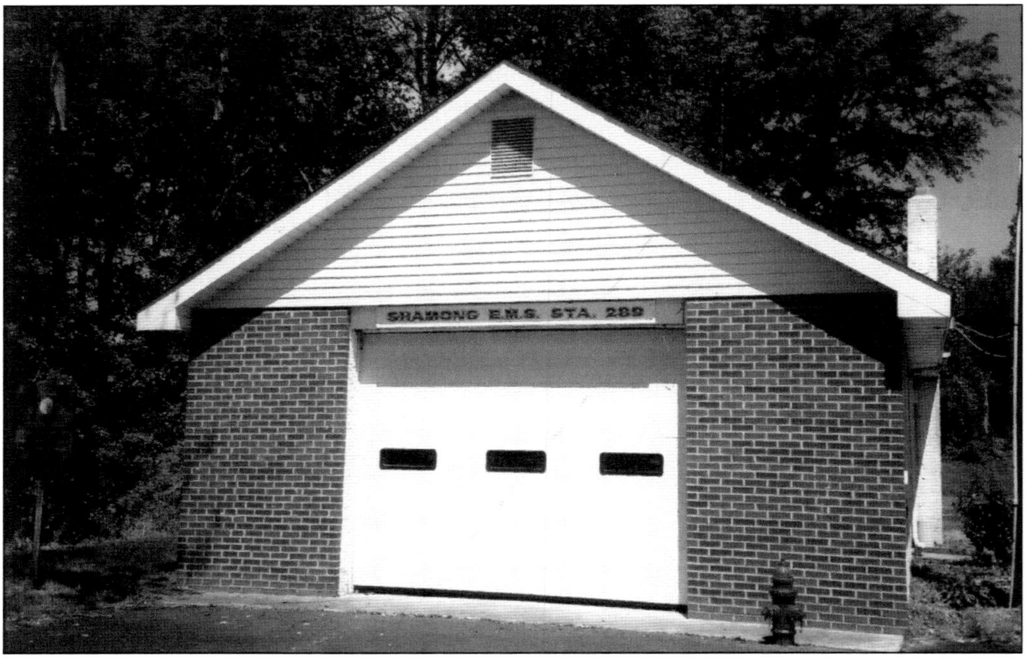

Pictured here is the first fire station to be erected in Shamong Township in 1942. It was in this same building that the founding of the Indian Mills Historical Society took place in February 1973. A small group had convened here to promote the preservation of the township history for future generations.

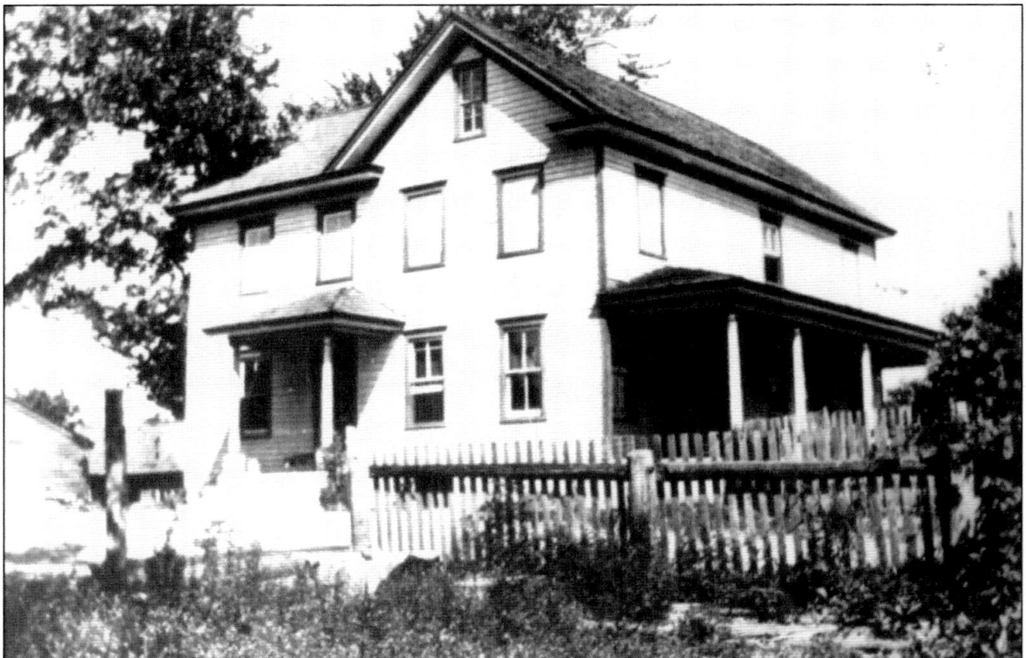

This was once the home of John Mingin, who farmed the land here for many years. It still stands today on Atsion Road but considerably changed in appearance. Mingin was also a talented violinist. He was born in Batsto in 1846 and was the son of Franklin Mingin and Sarah Cline.

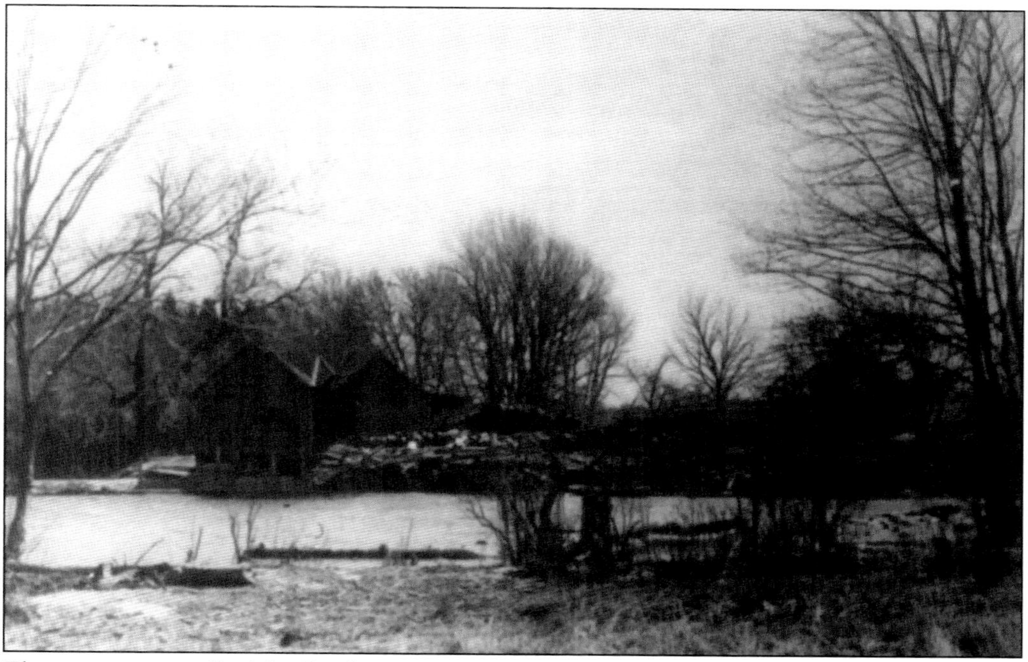

The ancient sawmill of the Brotherton Native Americans was located here. After 1802, it had a succession of owners. Samuel Reeves was the pioneer sawyer in 1812, then came Eber Engle in 1824, Godfrey Hancock in 1841, William Woolman in 1847, Josephus Sooy in 1863, Charles Gaskill in 1876, and Benjamin Mingin in 1920. It was during Mingin's ownership that the mill burned to the ground and was never rebuilt.

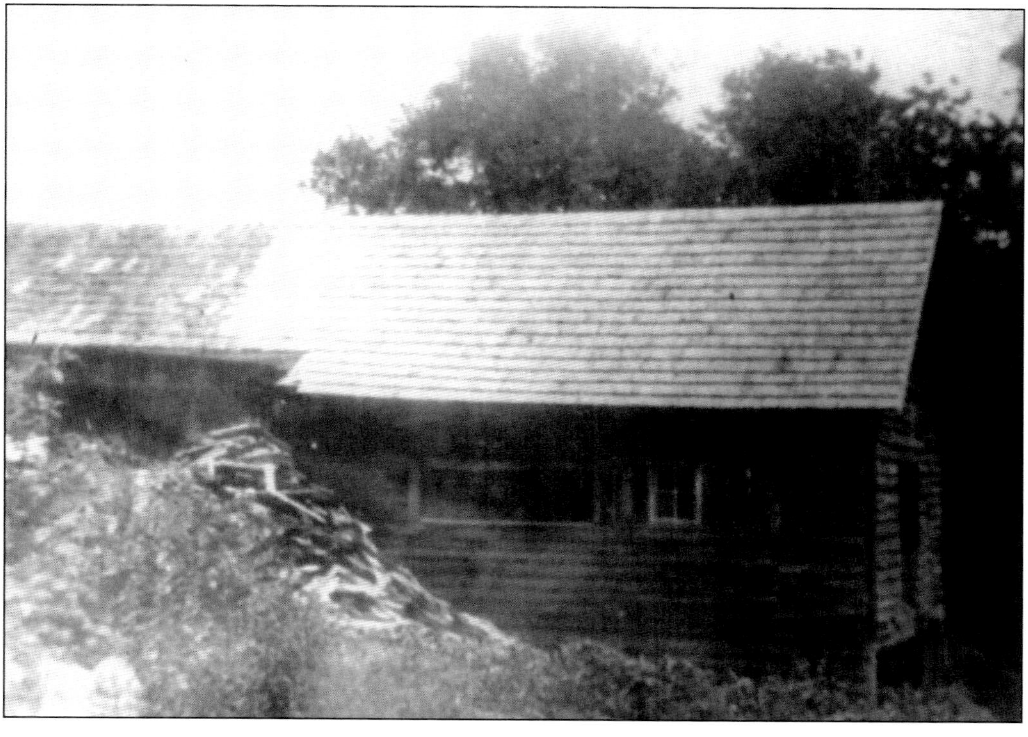

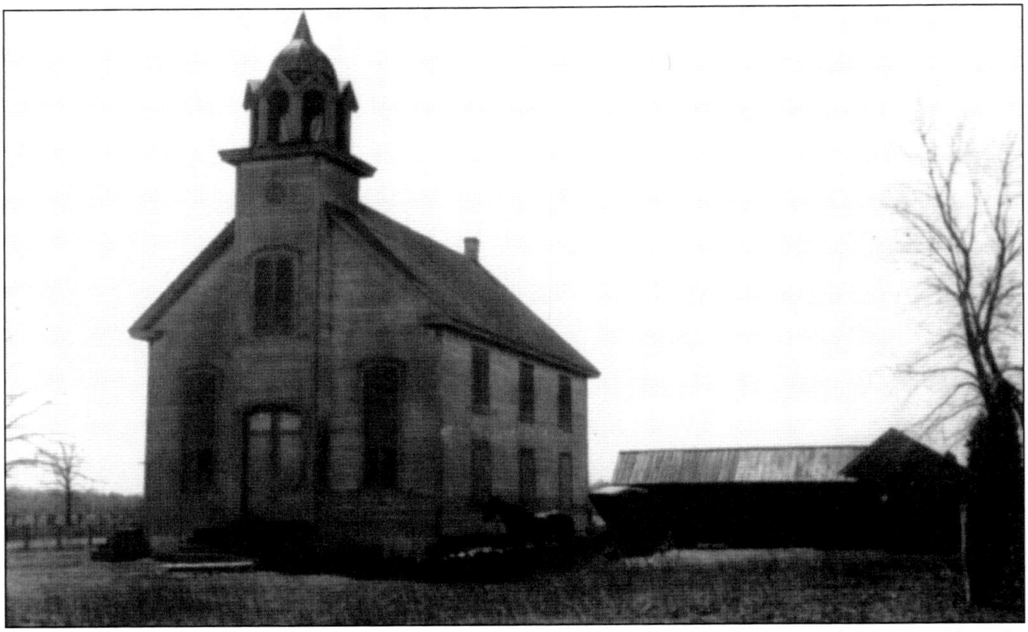

This building was originally constructed in 1876 and named the Centennial Baptist Church. Its use as a church was short lived. By 1881, it was being used by Edgepillock Tribe No. 168, Improved Order of Red Men. It then became known as Red Mens Hall and was used by the lodge as well as for social gatherings, dances, and as a polling place. Township meetings were also held here.

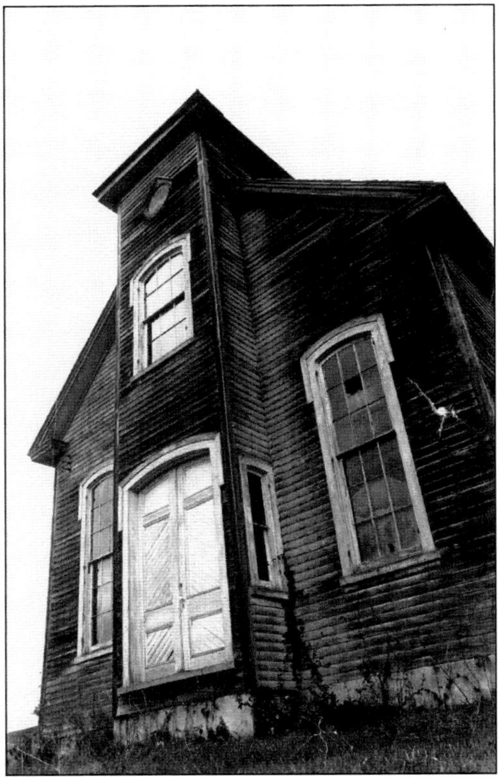

This view of the venerable Red Mens Hall was taken in 1967 shortly before its restoration by the Schauman family. It was originally constructed as the Centennial Baptist Church in 1876. For many years, the Red Mens Lodge used it as a meeting place. The township also conducted many of its functions here. It remains a local landmark to this day.

Four

The Village of Tabernacle

The area today known as Tabernacle is located completely within the Pinelands National Reserve. It has always been primarily a farming community and remains so today with limited residential growth due to Pinelands restrictions. There remain vast fields of truck crops, as well as extensive fields of blueberries and cranberry bogs. The surrounding forest also contributes greatly to the annual deer harvest. As late as 1887, the village had a population of just 30 persons. Today it has about 8,000 people in the township.

The area was first settled in the latter part of the 1700s. The Isaiah Bowker farmhouse, one of the oldest homes still standing, was likely built in 1780. There once stood a log meetinghouse near the old cemetery in the center of the village. One writer has alleged that Rev. John Brainerd had established a mission here in 1778 to preach to the Native Americans and early settlers. It was called the Tabernacle in the Wilderness. This log church was later used as a school until it fell into ruin and was taken down in 1885. In 1761, Reverend Brainerd did assist the Native Americans in building a log church known as the Coaxen Meetinghouse near a Native American village known as Wepink. He also maintained a log mission at the Brotherton Reservation. Both missions have been well documented in historical records of the area. There is however, no factual information to substantiate that Reverend Brainerd established a church in Tabernacle in 1778. By that time, Brainerd was in failing health. He had left the Brotherton Reservation in 1777 to become pastor of the Deerfield Presbyterian Church in Cumberland County, many miles away. He died there on March 18, 1781, of a pulmonary ailment.

The village of Tabernacle was once an integral part of Shamong Township. Many of the first families of the area are buried in the Tabernacle Cemetery as well as the Junior Mechanics burial ground nearby. The communities and their joint heritage are closely entwined. At the beginning of the 20th century, Tabernacle was formed as a separate township. This occurred on March 22, 1901, from parts of Shamong, Southampton, and Woodland Townships.

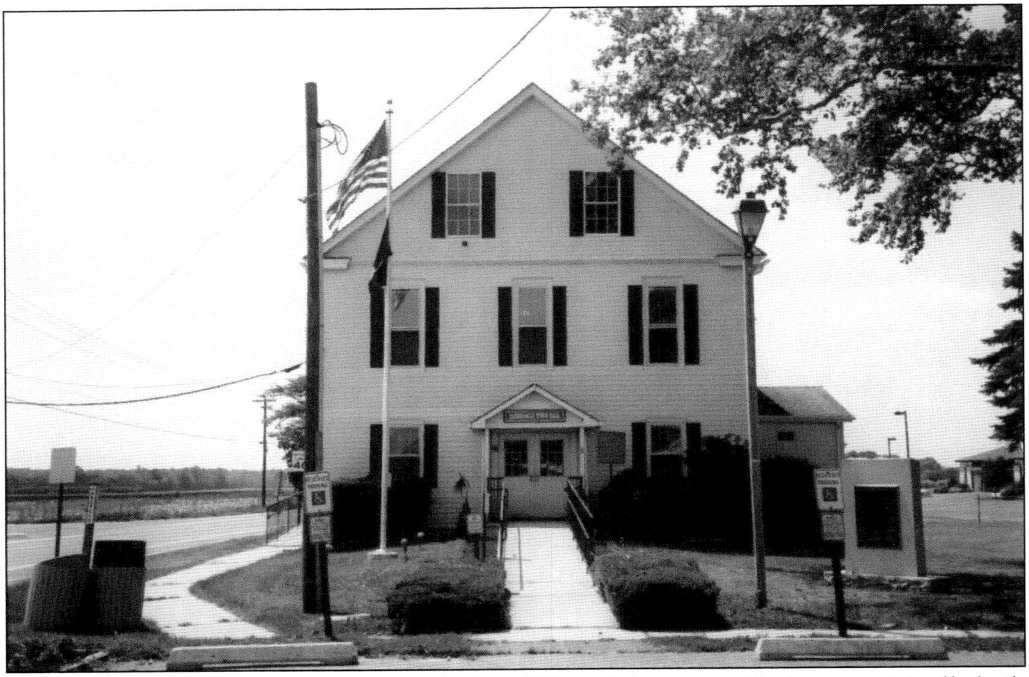

The Tabernacle Council No. 49 Junior Order of United American Mechanics originally built this as its meeting hall. The building was later donated to Tabernacle Township as a municipal building and continues as such today. It was, however, donated with the provision that they continue to be allowed to hold their meetings and activities there.

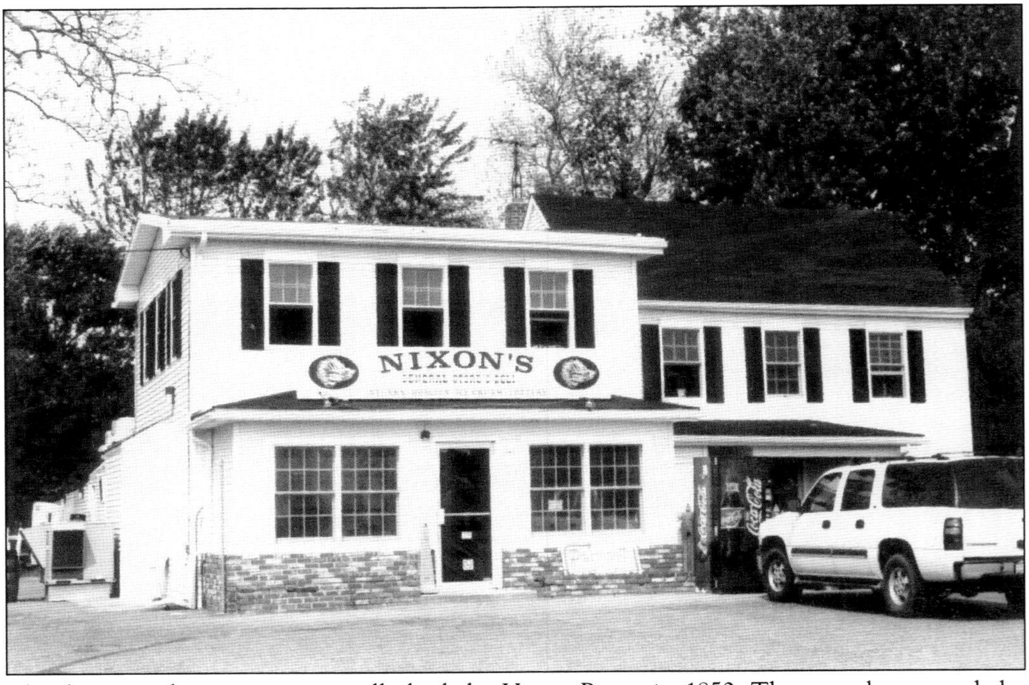

This home and store was originally built by Henry Peters in 1850. The store has served the people of Tabernacle and the surrounding area for over 150 years. It is now known as Nixon's. In 1877, it was also used as a post office.

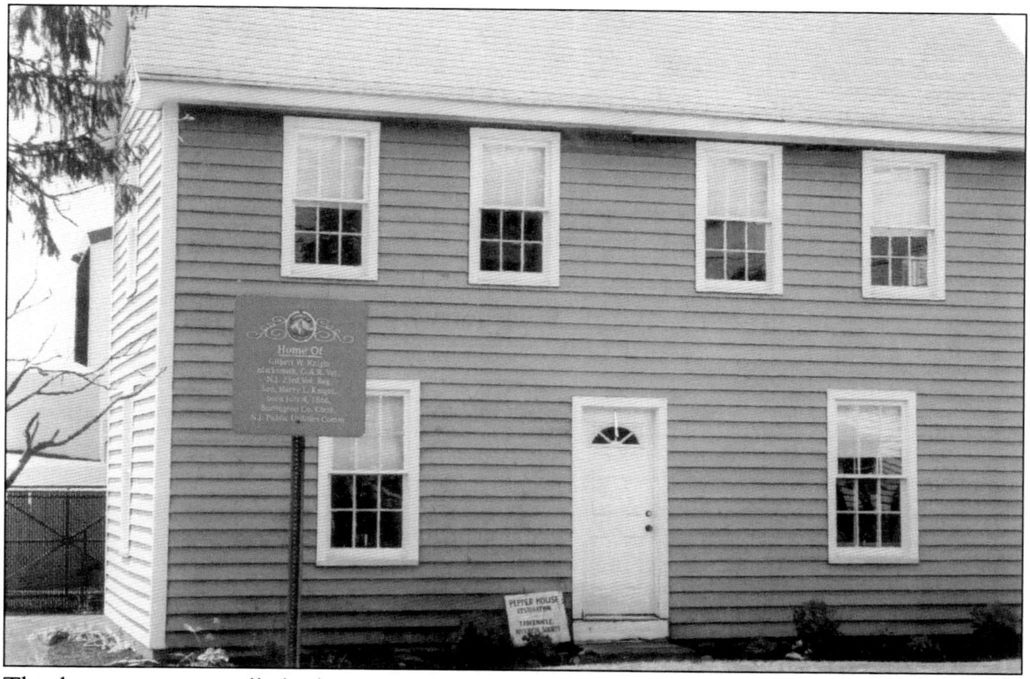

This home was originally built in 1860 by local blacksmith Gilbert Knight. He was also a Civil War veteran. He maintained his blacksmith shop near the premises. The home was last owned by Clara Pepper, who then sold the home to Tabernacle Township in 1987. It has been leased to the Tabernacle Historical Society who intends to use it as a museum and is actively restoring it.

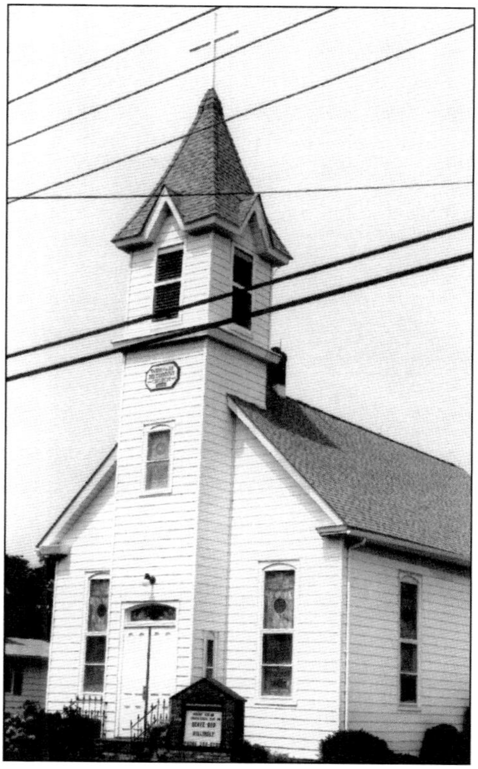

The Tabernacle United Methodist Church was erected in 1880 on land donated by Joseph Mathis. It is identical in outward appearance to the church in Indian Mills, and most likely the same builder was used. The church remains a prominent landmark in the village of Tabernacle.

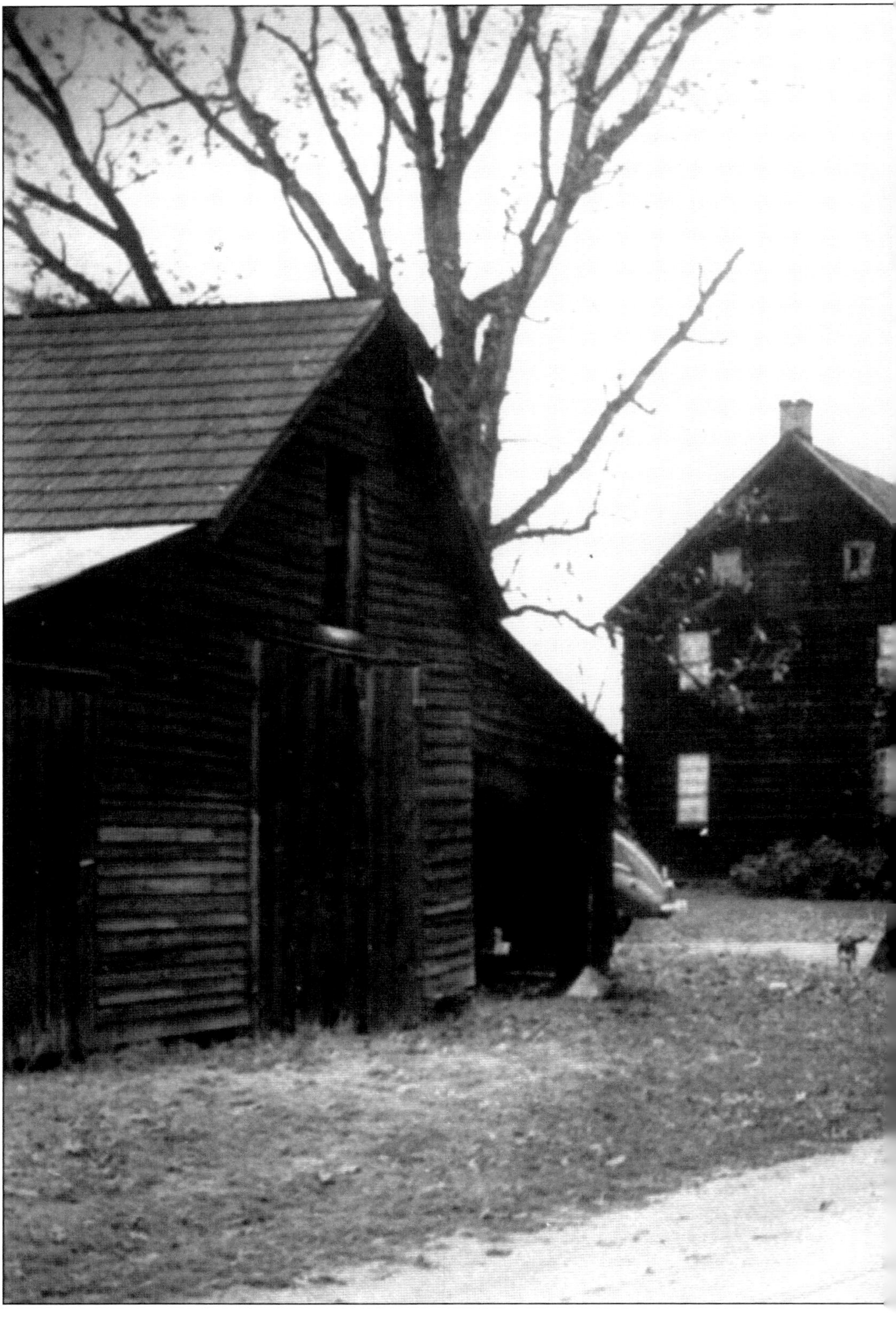

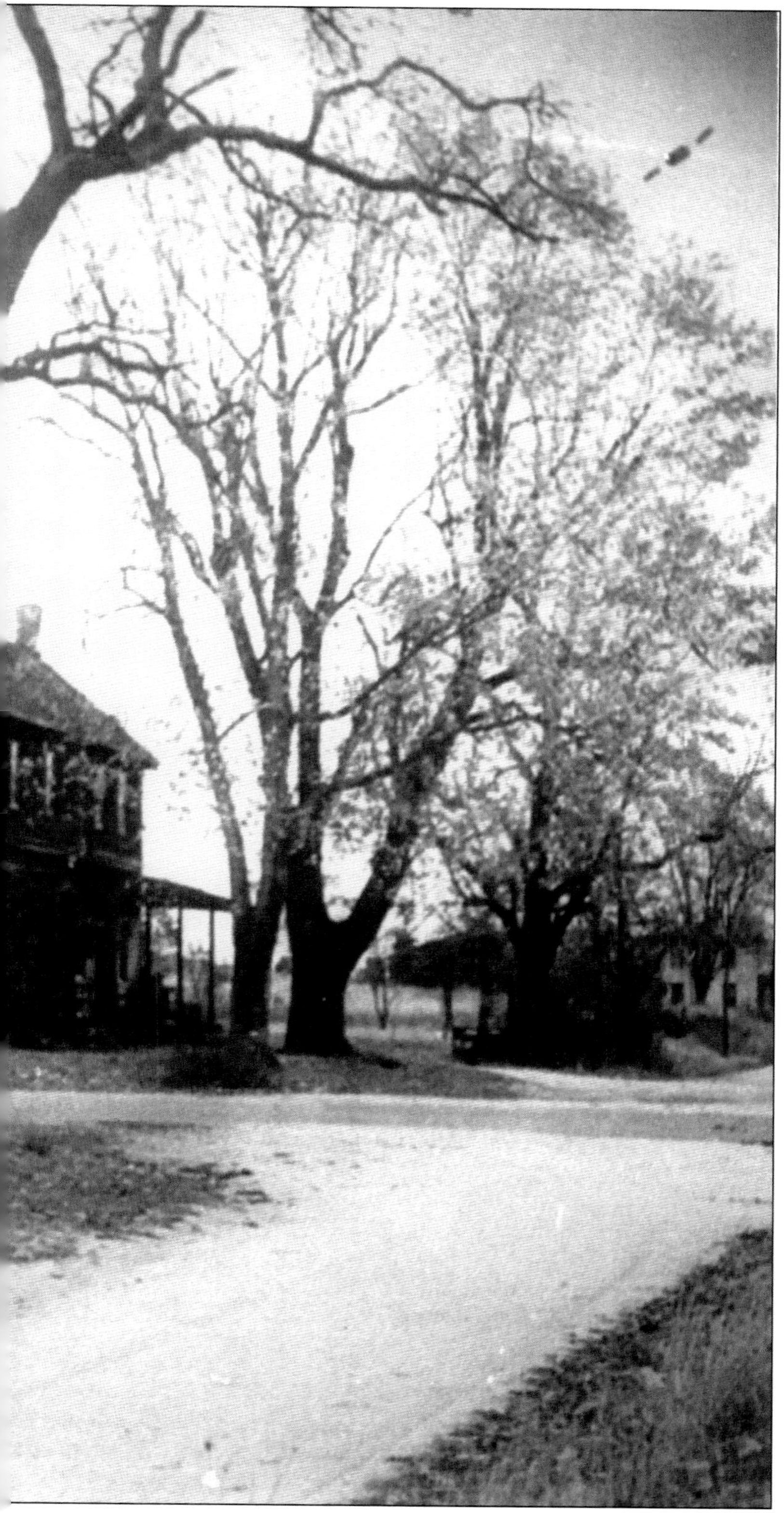

This crossroads is on the Tuckerton Stage Road, where it intersects with Old Indian Mills Road. Stagecoaches once frequented Tuckerton Stage Road up until the last quarter of the 19th century. Joseph Naylor had purchased this property in 1825 from Isaac Wilkins, who in turn had purchased it from the Indian Commissioners in 1803. It has long been known as Naylor's Corner. It has also been called Oriental.

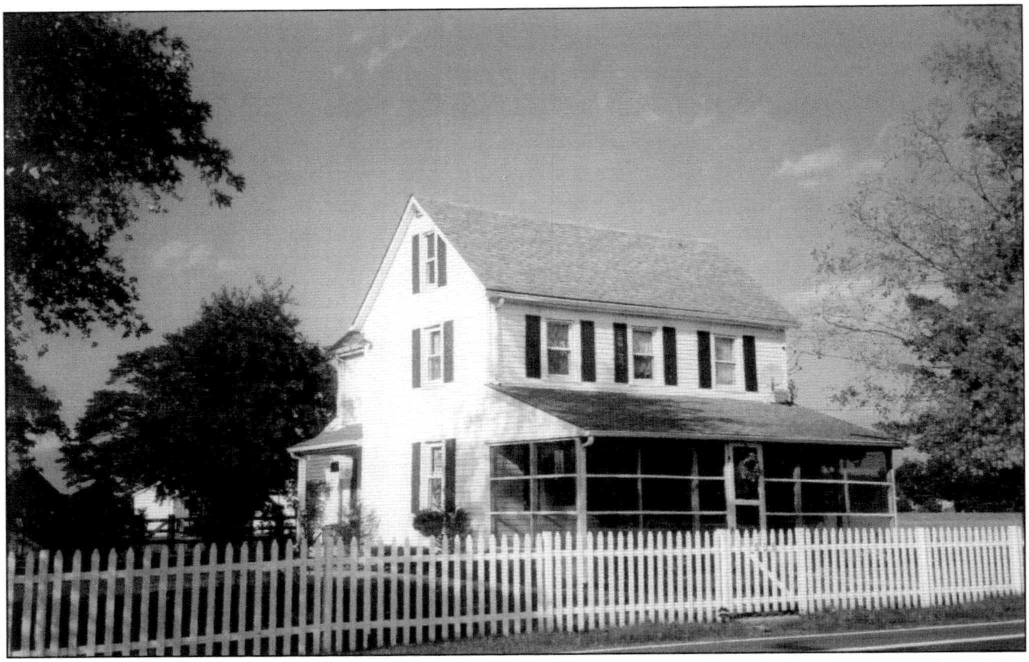

This quaint farmhouse with the white picket fence was built around 1860. It has been faithfully restored by Raymond and Bea Worrell. It is located on Chatsworth Road just outside the village proper.

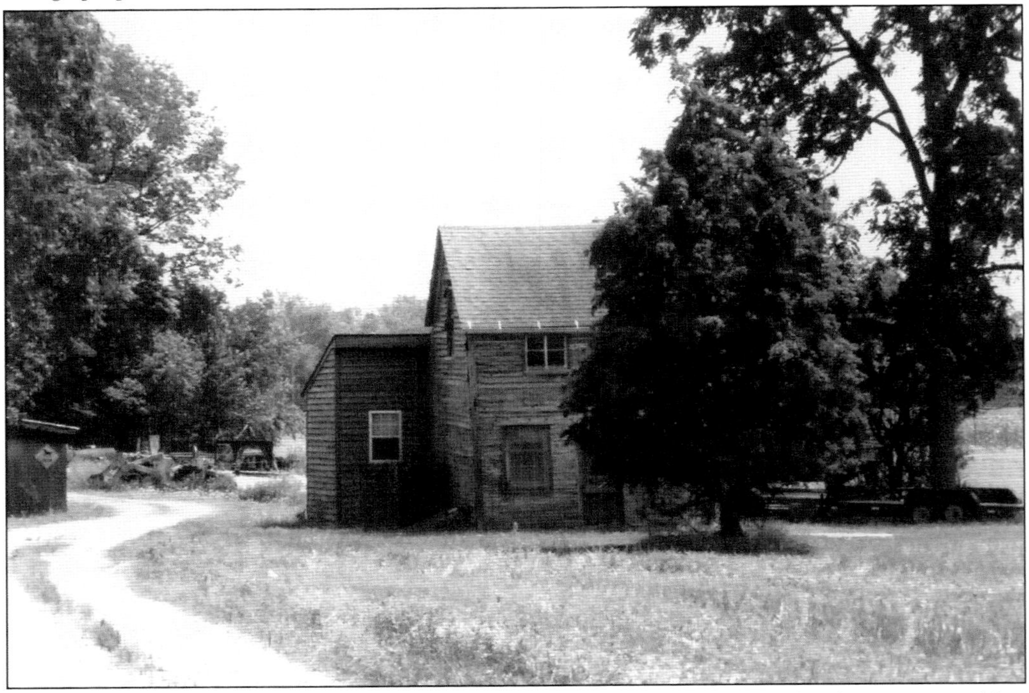

Joseph Yates came from Philadelphia to this wilderness area of the Pinelands. He erected his home in 1875. Several generations of the Yates family have lived in this home. The last member of the family to live here was Carlton Yates. The home has been standing for 115 years and never had electricity or indoor plumbing. These were luxuries that the Yates clan could do without.

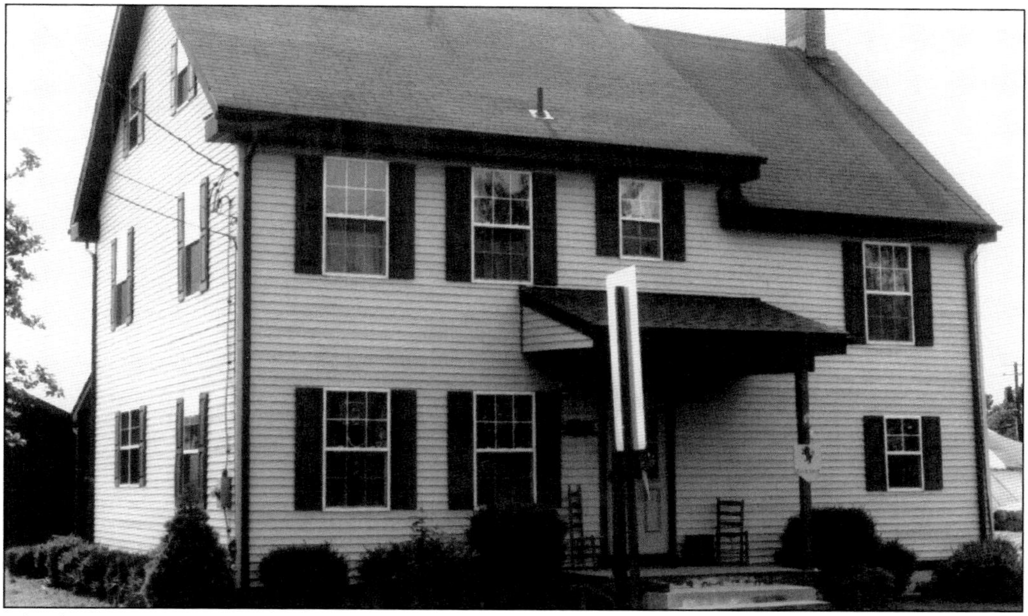

The former hostelry, known as Kemble's Inn, operated here in the mid-1800s. It was located on the main stage route from Mount Holly known as the Great Road to Little Egg Harbor. The owner, Charles S. Kemble, was a farmer and blacksmith. He was on the Shamong Township Committee from 1860 until 1863. He served in the New Jersey Assembly from 1855 to 1859. At the time of his death, in 1869, he was serving as the Burlington County sheriff.

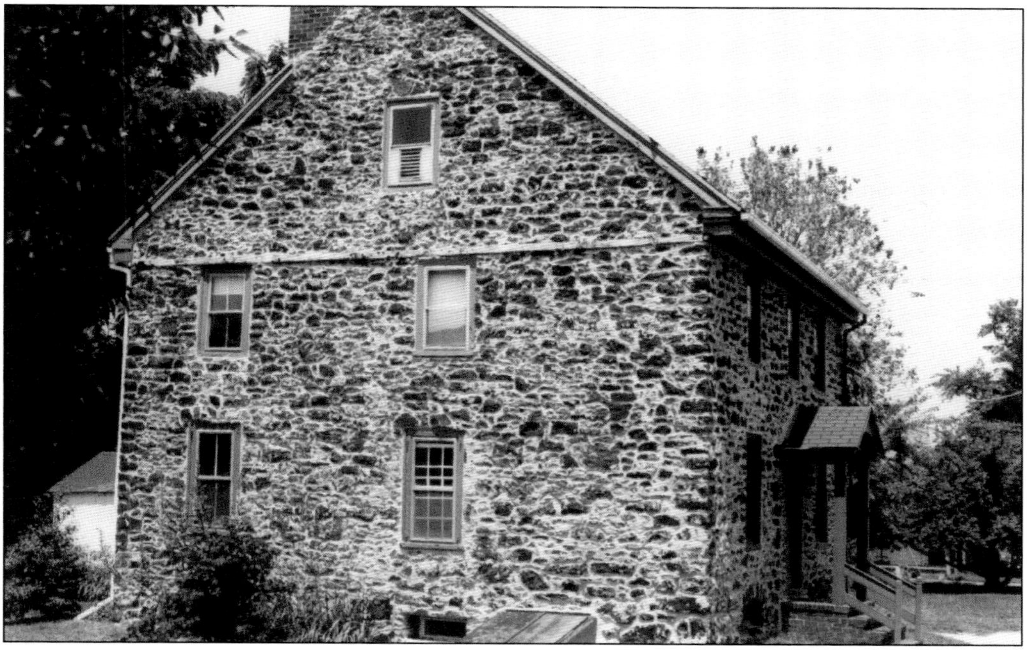

The tavern known as the Gate was located at the entrance to Hampton Furnace. It stood near the base of a land feature known as the Stone Hills. No doubt, the tavern was constructed from the Jersey stone found here. David Cavileer was the innkeeper in 1812. An advertisement appeared in the *New Jersey Mirror* in 1838 describing the large stone house built for a tavern. It was on the main stage road to Tuckerton and must have appeared similar to the tavern house above.

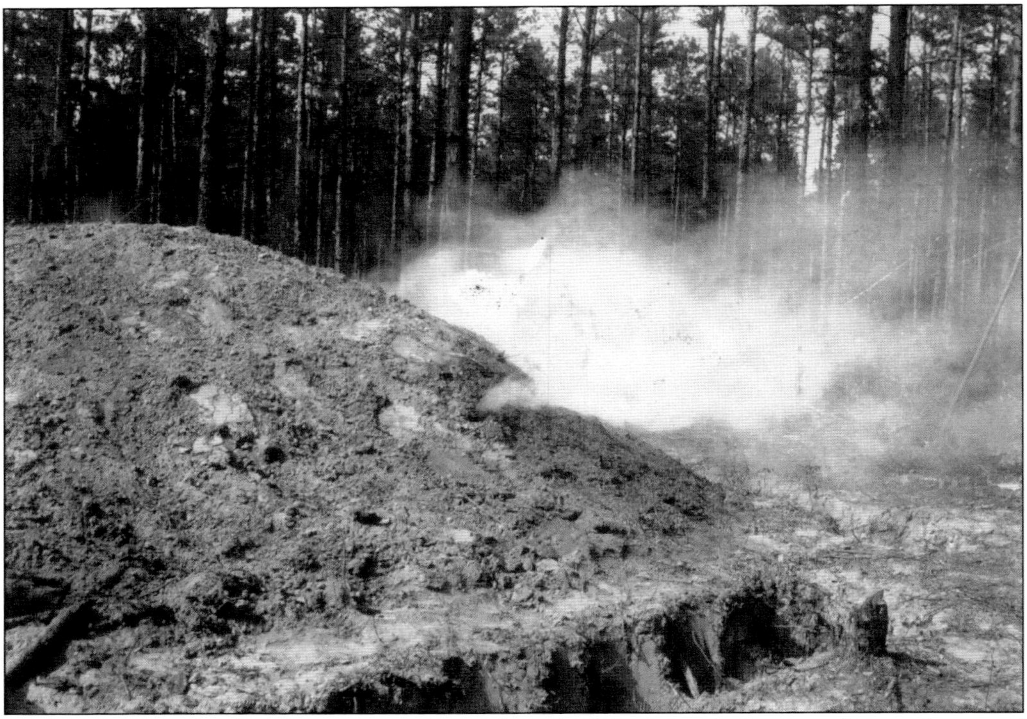

Deep in the Pinelands, an ancient industry flourished for several centuries. It was the art of making charcoal. The men who engaged in this endeavor were called colliers. It was an industry that was most prevalent during the days of the bog iron furnaces. It continued even after the iron-making days well into the 20th century.

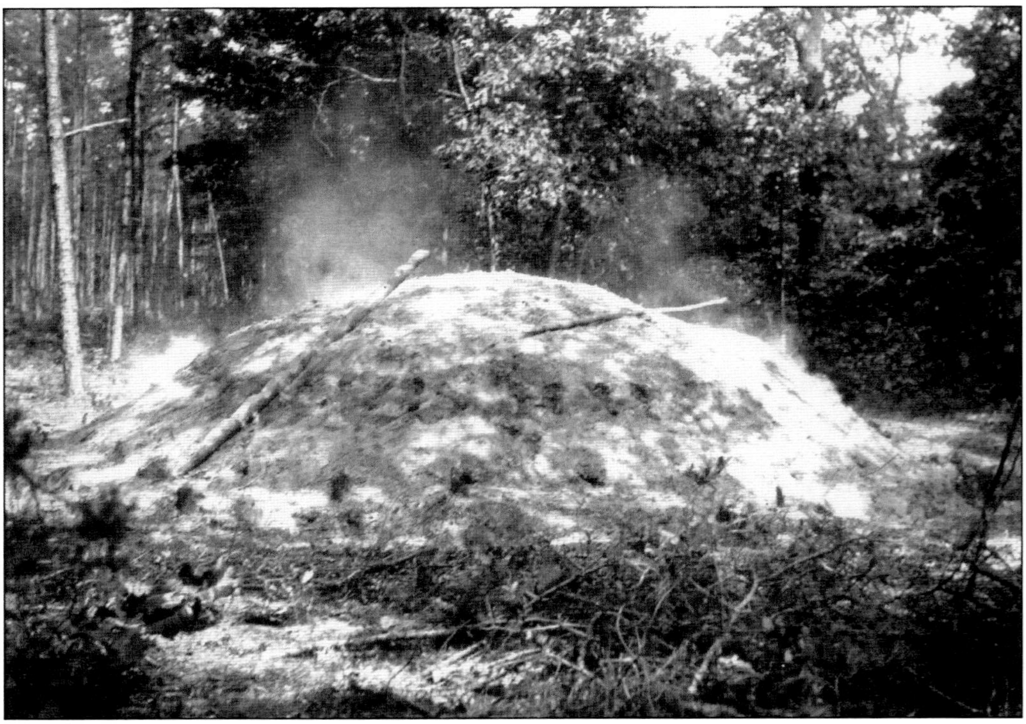

Five

THE VILLAGE OF ATSION

Atsion Village dates back to the era of the Brotherton Reservation in 1758. Charles Read had purchased large tracts of land surrounding the reservation as early as 1755. He had held places of prominence in the early colony of New Jersey, rising to chief justice of the New Jersey Supreme Court. He was also one of the commissioners involved in the purchase of land for the Native Americans to live on.

In 1765, in partnership with David Ogden and Lawrence Saltar, Read erected a forge and named the place Atsion. Read had suffered financial reverses and sold his interest to Henry Drinker and Abel James. Ogden sold his interest to Saltar. A new company was then formed. In 1774, the first bog iron furnace was erected by Drinker and Saltar. In addition to the forge and furnace, there were also three sawmills and a gristmill erected. The Revolutionary War had begun, and the ironworks was engaged in supplying camp kettles but no products involving munitions for the Continental army. Drinker was a Quaker and as such was a pacifist. The ironworks continued to prosper. Drinker's son-in-law Jacob Downing bought out the Saltar interest. By 1815, the iron works was failing, and by 1823, it was in ruins. It was then purchased by Samuel Richards, who rebuilt the entire community. It then prospered for many years until 1842, when Richards died.

His son-in-law William Fleming erected a paper mill, and this failed as well. The Richards estate was finally sold to Col. William C. Patterson in 1861. He changed the name of Atsion to Fruitland. He declared bankruptcy in 1872. Maurice Raleigh purchased the estate and converted the paper mill into a cotton mill. Raleigh died in 1882, and the entire estate was then sold to Joseph Wharton who added it to his other vast holdings in the Pinelands. In 1954, the State of New Jersey purchased the extensive property, and it became part of the Wharton State Forest. It has remained so to the present day.

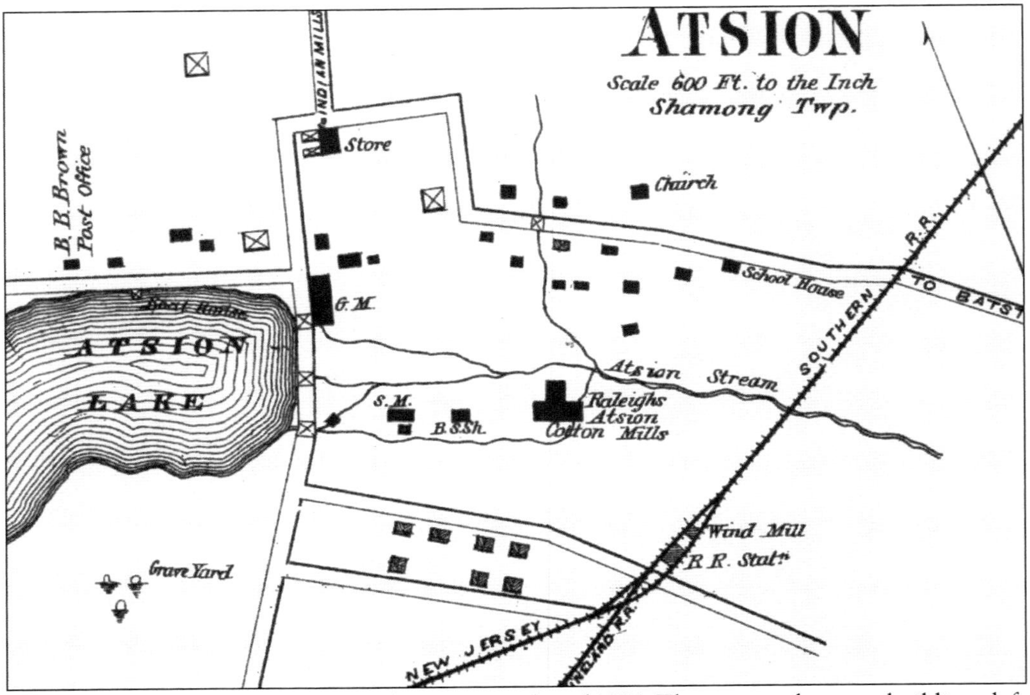

Here is Atsion Village as it appeared in Scott's atlas of 1876. There are only seven buildings left standing today. Ruins of many buildings can be seen. They have been destroyed by vandalism, arson, and neglect. The village was once the hub of activity. Its industries employed over 100 workers and hundreds more were dependent on it.

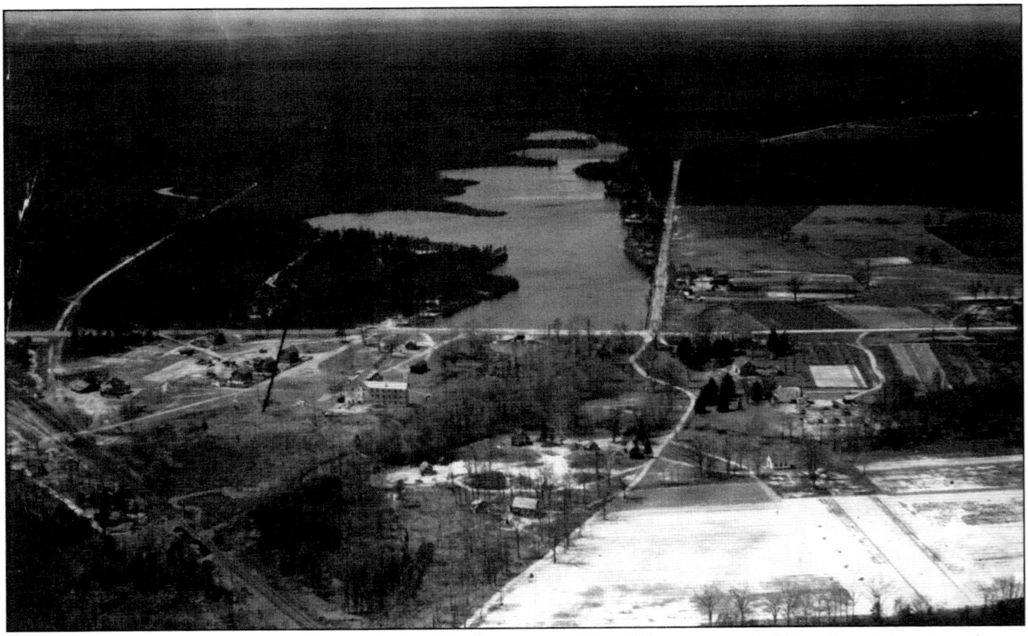

This aerial view of Atsion Village was taken in 1954. The open fields of cultivation have disappeared. All is now dense forest. Most of the buildings have disappeared except two houses along the lakeshore, the Richards Mansion, a one-room schoolhouse, the village store (now a ranger station), a gun club, and a small church.

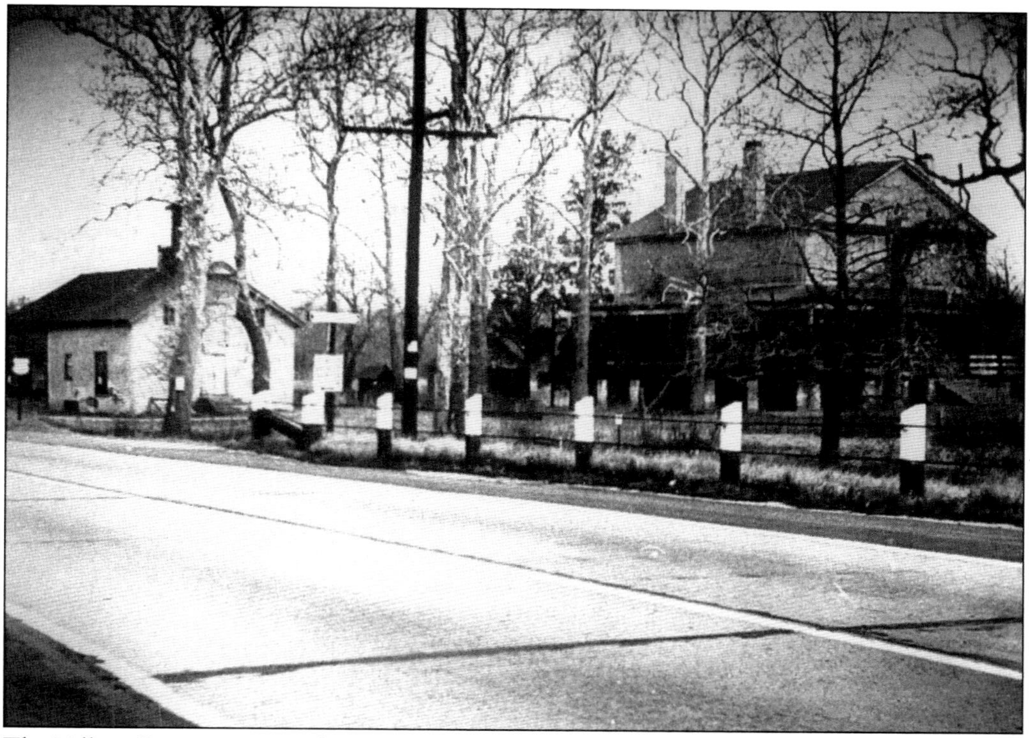

The Village Store was erected in 1827 by Samuel Richards. The Richards Mansion to the right was erected in 1826. The photograph was taken in 1939. Newly constructed Route 39 (now Route 206) passes in the foreground.

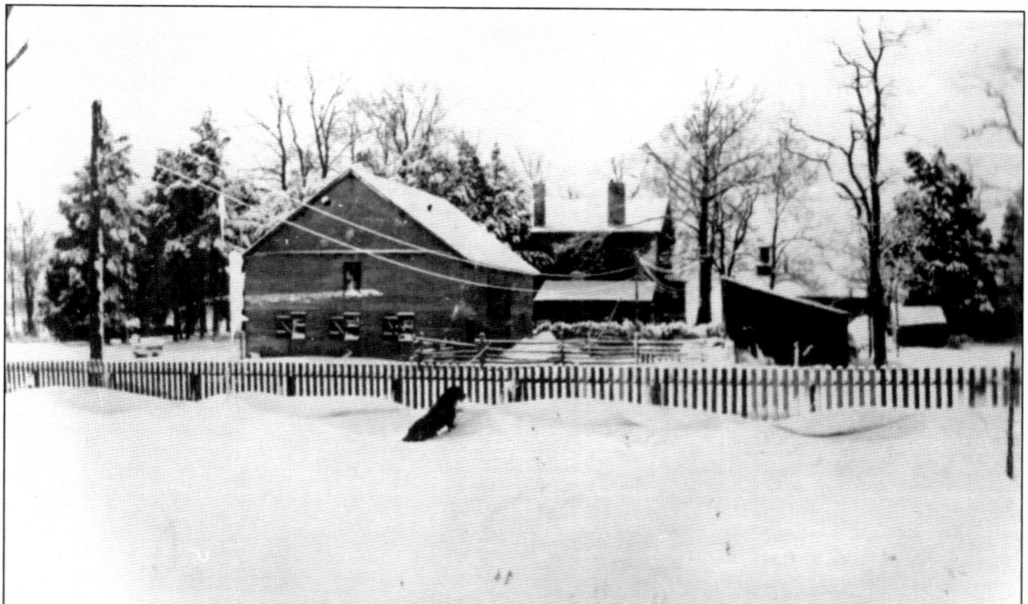

A winter scene in the 1930s shows the Richards Mansion from the rear. The concrete barn of the Wharton era is in the foreground. It is now in ruins. The other buildings seen are no longer standing.

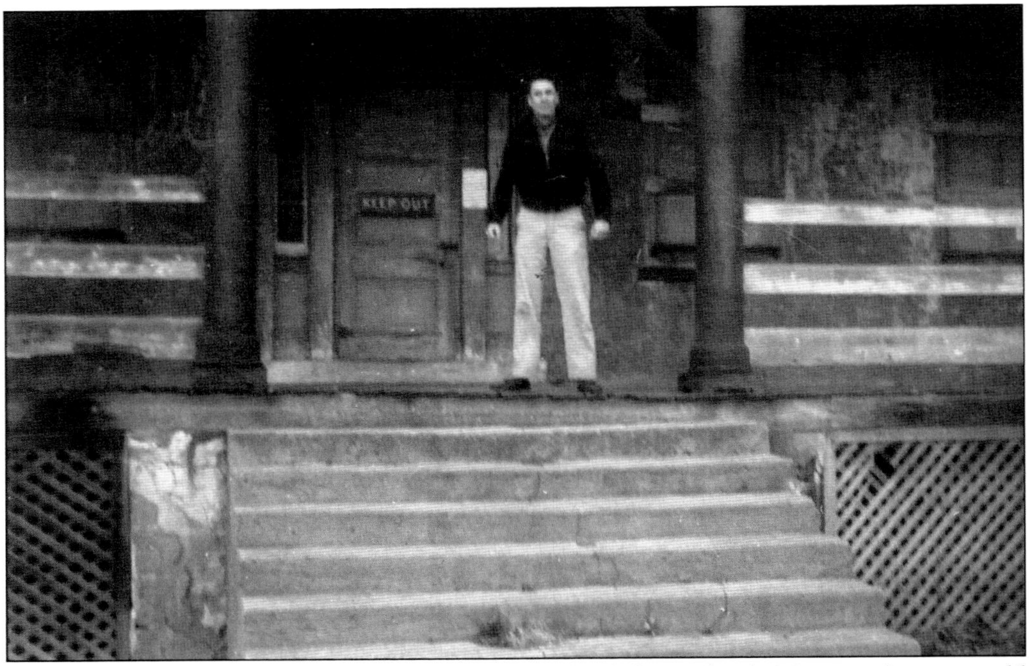

Seen here is the author standing on the front porch of the Richards Mansion. It was a cold wintry day in January 1957. The condition of the mansion had deteriorated considerably since 1948. The village store was still vacant. All was quiet in the former village of Atsion, where so much activity had once been.

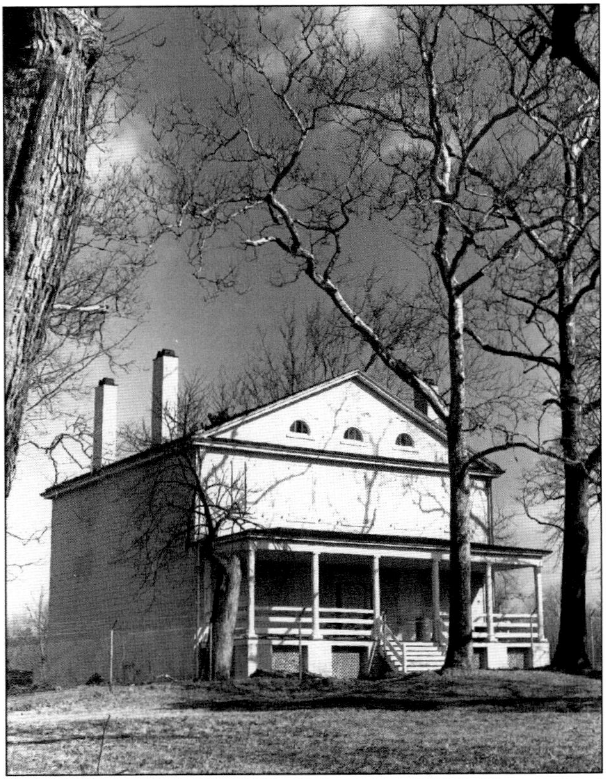

The State of New Jersey purchased the former Atsion estate in 1954. Plans were made to restore many of the buildings in the village. The mansion house of Samuel Richards was one of the first buildings restored but on the outside only. G. Edwin Brumbaugh was the restoration architect for the State of New Jersey. He decided to remove the porch and columns on the western side of the mansion. This was done in 1955.

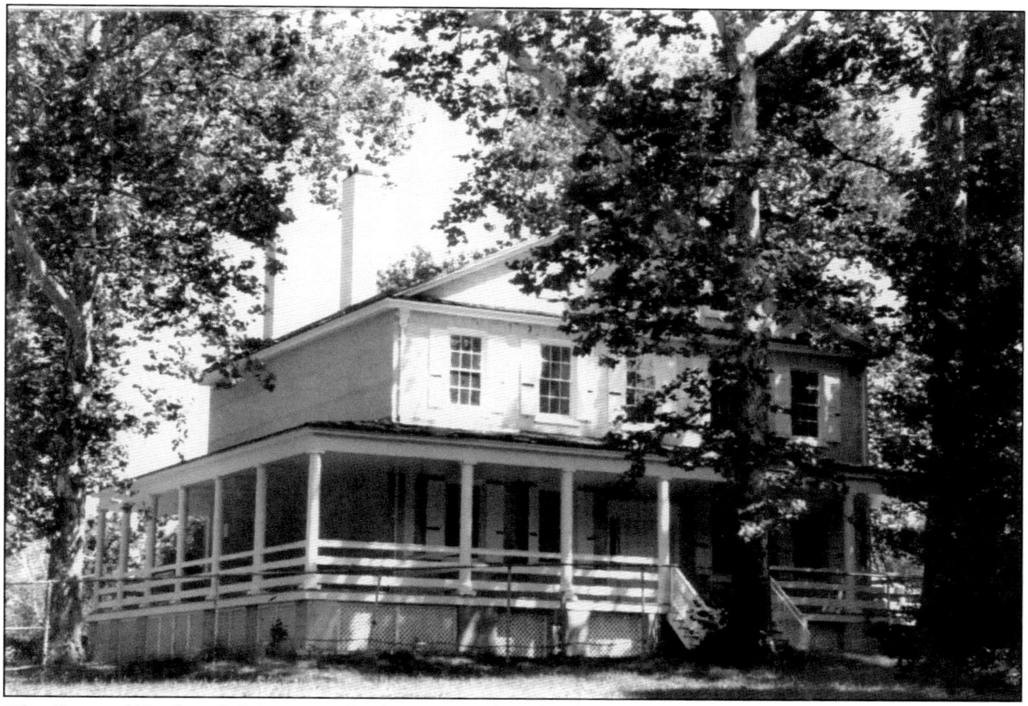

The Samuel Richards Mansion, built in 1826, has finally been restored back to the classic Greek Revival style that was intended. A handicap ramp is concealed within the side porch. The interior of the mansion has also been restored. It remains the jewel of the Pinelands.

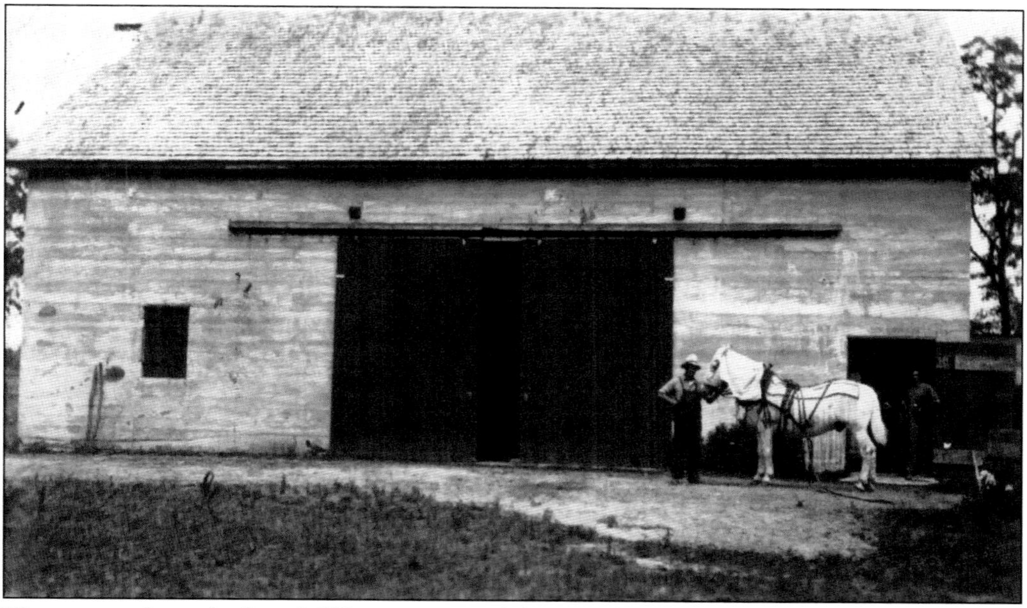

The scene is from the Joseph Wharton era and depicts a barn made of poured concrete. Sidney Crain is holding the horse bit with Ron Whitby standing in the doorway. There was a pair of dapple-gray horses used on the Atsion farmlands. The ruins of this barn are still standing to the east of the mansion.

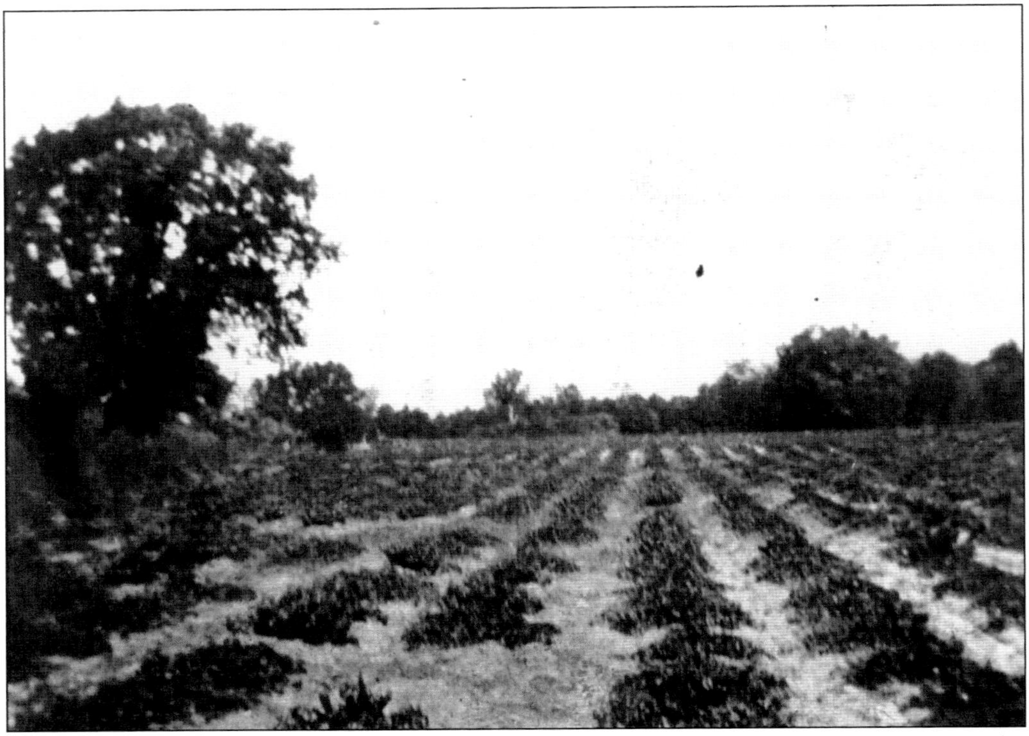

Fields of peanut plants were raised by Joseph Wharton as an experiment. He had imported a whole colony of German peasants to raise them. The venture was considered a success after he had spent thousands of dollars in the process. In the scene below, Wharton is in the foreground, wearing the derby hat and inspecting the peanut crop.

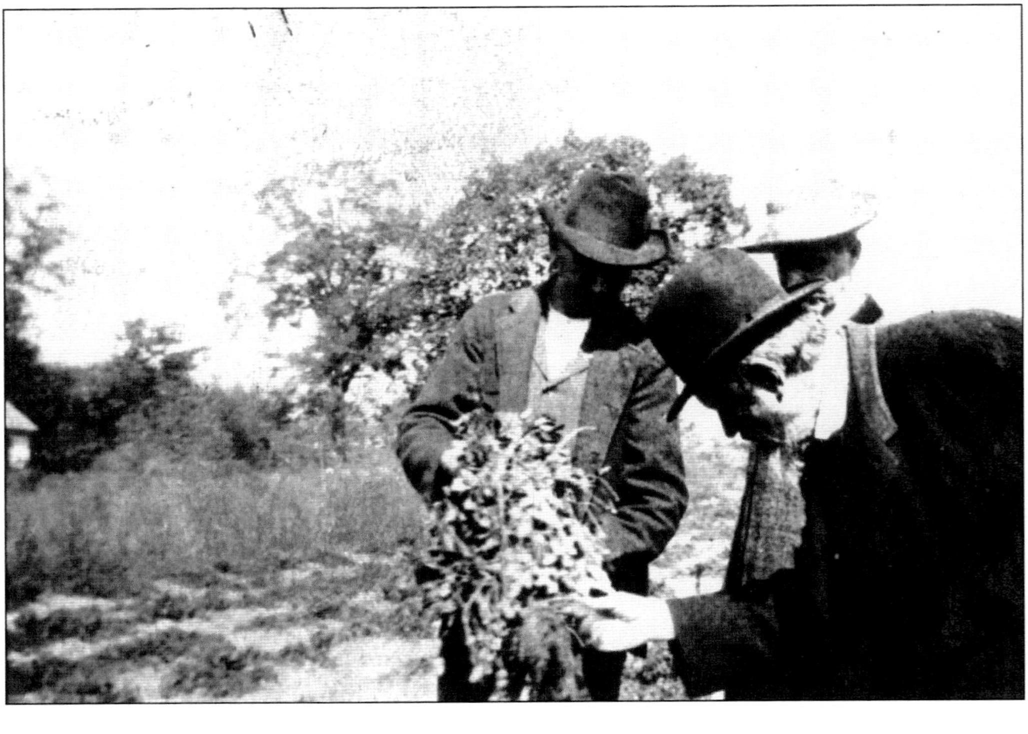

The former frame icehouse that once stood to the rear of the Richards Mansion's north side. Blocks of ice were cut from Atsion Lake by workmen and then packed inside the icehouse to be used as needed. Ice could be stored and kept in this fashion for many months.

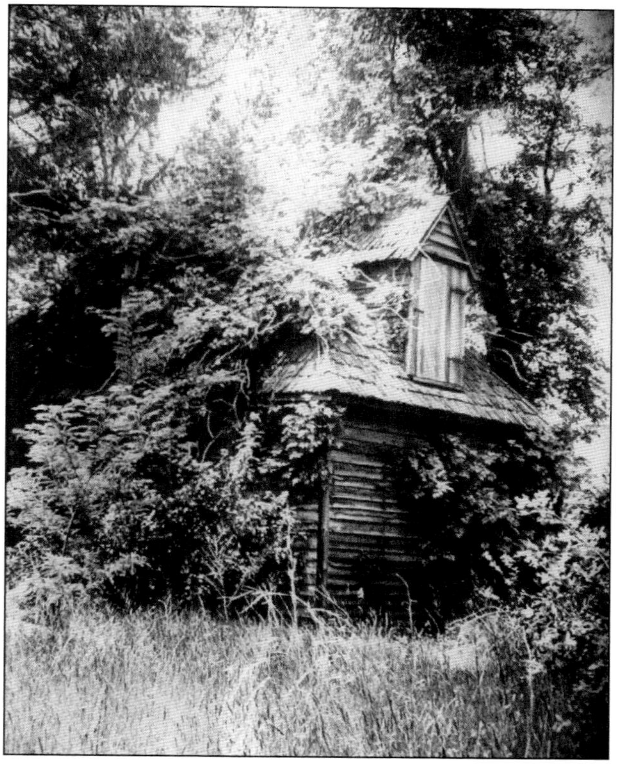

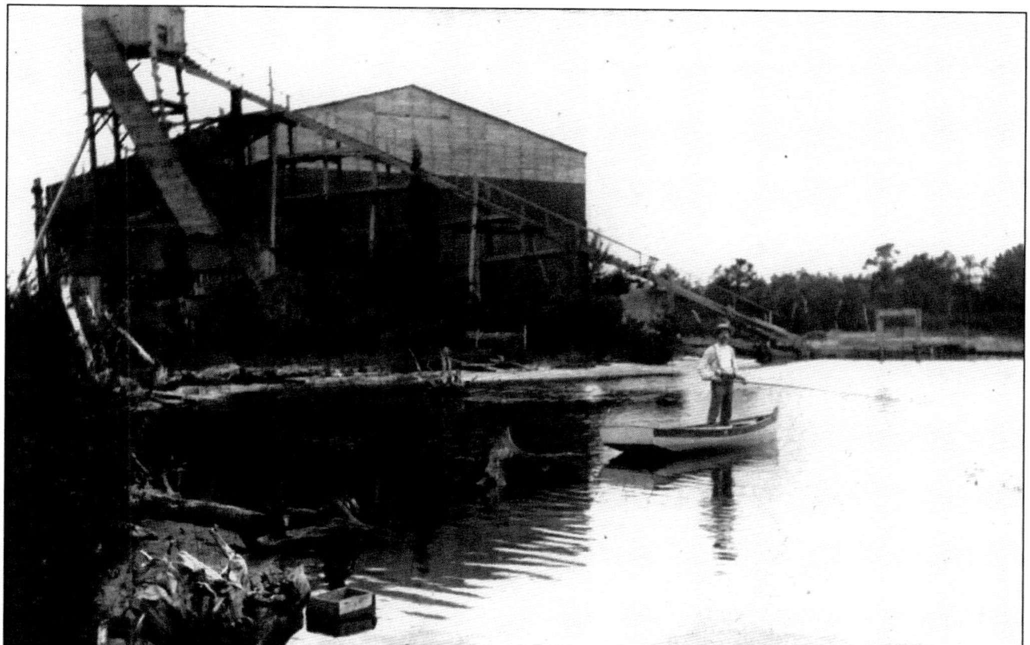

Seen here is the icehouse that formerly stood on the south shore of Atsion Lake in the early 1900s. It was located approximately where the present-day bathing beach and pavilion are located. In its heyday, ice was cut here, packed in sawdust, and taken by railroad cars to New York City and other cities, as well as being sold locally.

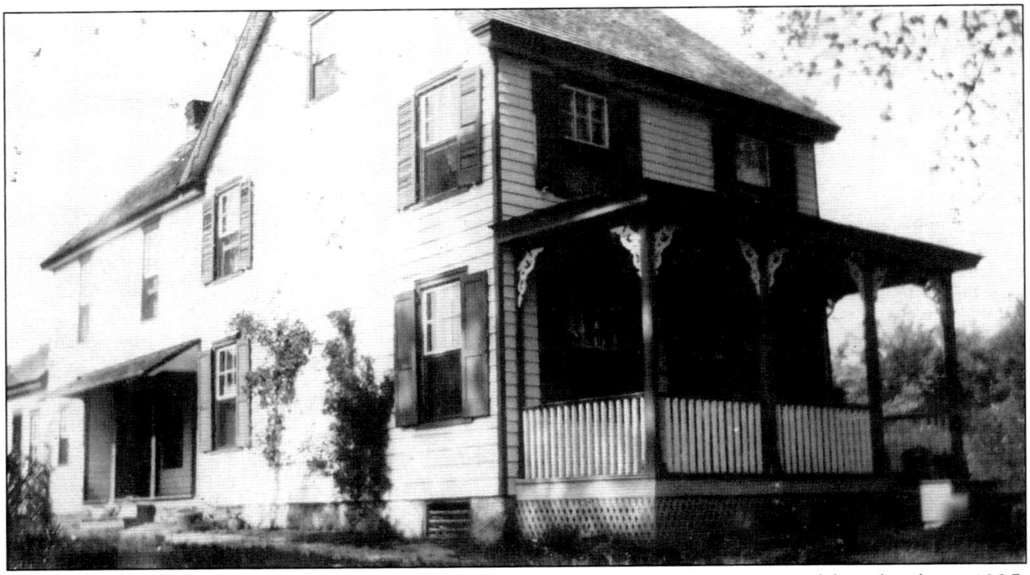

Andrew Etheridge was the manager of the Wharton estate from 1892 until his death in 1925. He lived in this home with his wife and family. They continued to live here until the Wharton tract was sold to the State of New Jersey in 1954. The home was then left vacant to be vandalized and finally to suffer the arsonists torch on March 1, 1998. This photograph shows how the home appeared in 1920.

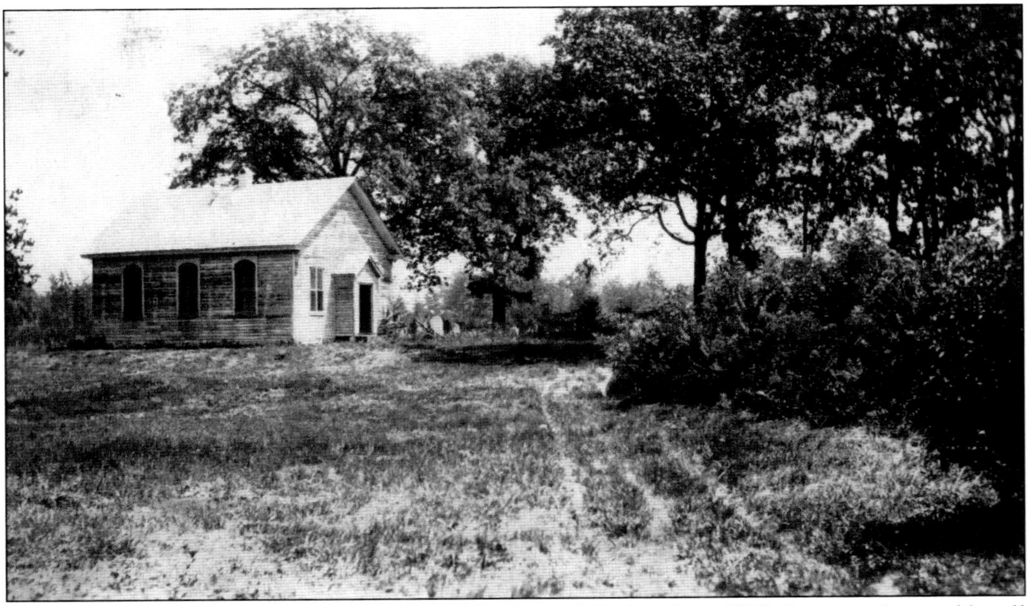

The Atsion community church was erected by Samuel Richards in 1828. It was to be used by all Christian denominations. This scene is how the church and adjacent burial ground appeared in the late 1800s. Church members to the present day are still using the church and burial ground. The building has been somewhat altered since 1828, but most of its original lines have been retained.

The tombstone of Manasses Dellett is located in the Atsion burial ground. He was a prominent local businessman and proprietor of Dellett's Hotel down the Atsion Road. He had also been the proprietor of Josiah Smith's Tavern on the northeast corner of Atsion Road. He made his home a short distance away on present-day Oak Shade Road and operated a grocery store there. None of these buildings are standing today.

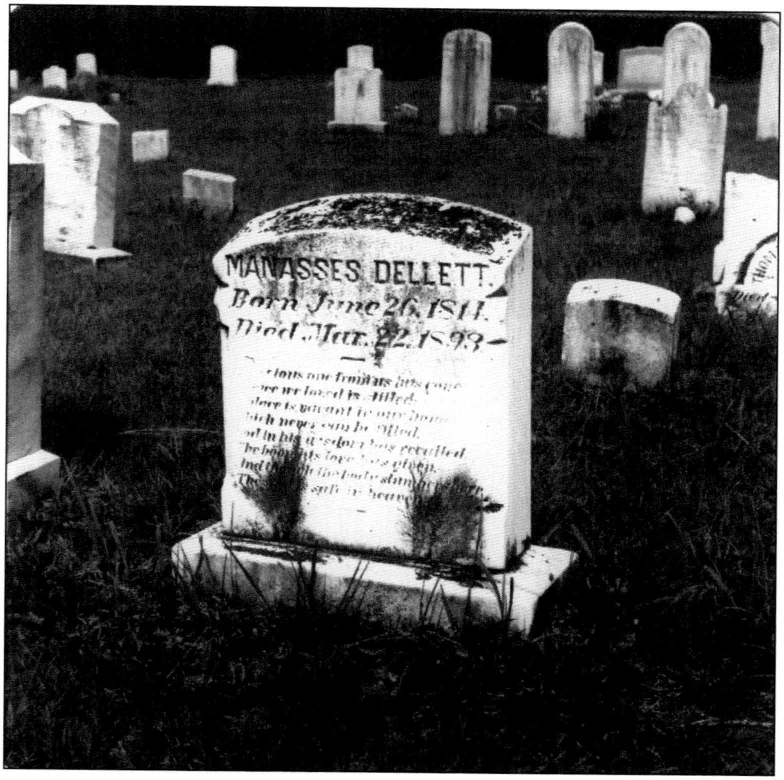

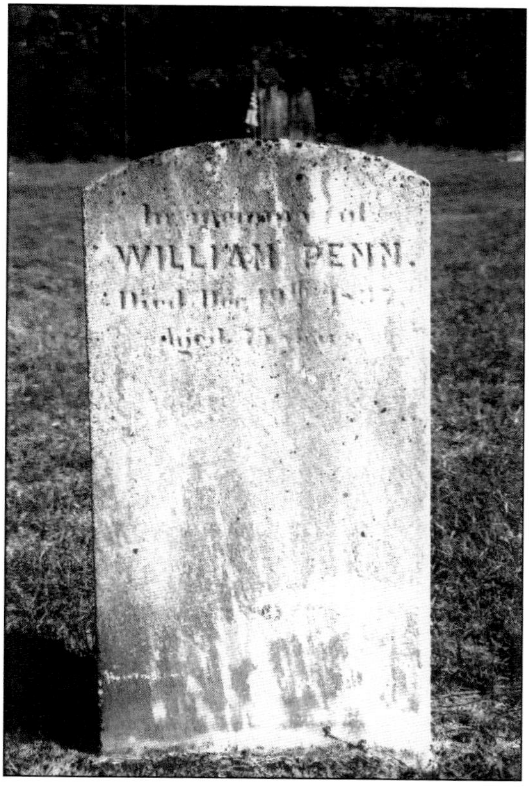

This is the interesting tombstone of one William Penn, who died December 19, 1837, age 75. His wife, Charity, who died in 1854, age 92, lies next to him. William was the son of James Penn Sr., born about 1729 in Cumberland County and died in 1814. James was the son of Edward Penn, who in turn was the son of another William Penn, a sea captain. This William Penn was born June 2, 1605, and died in 1696. He was not the famous William Penn of Philadelphia, but they may have been related. He was living in Maryland in 1678. There are many members of the Penn family in the Pinelands.

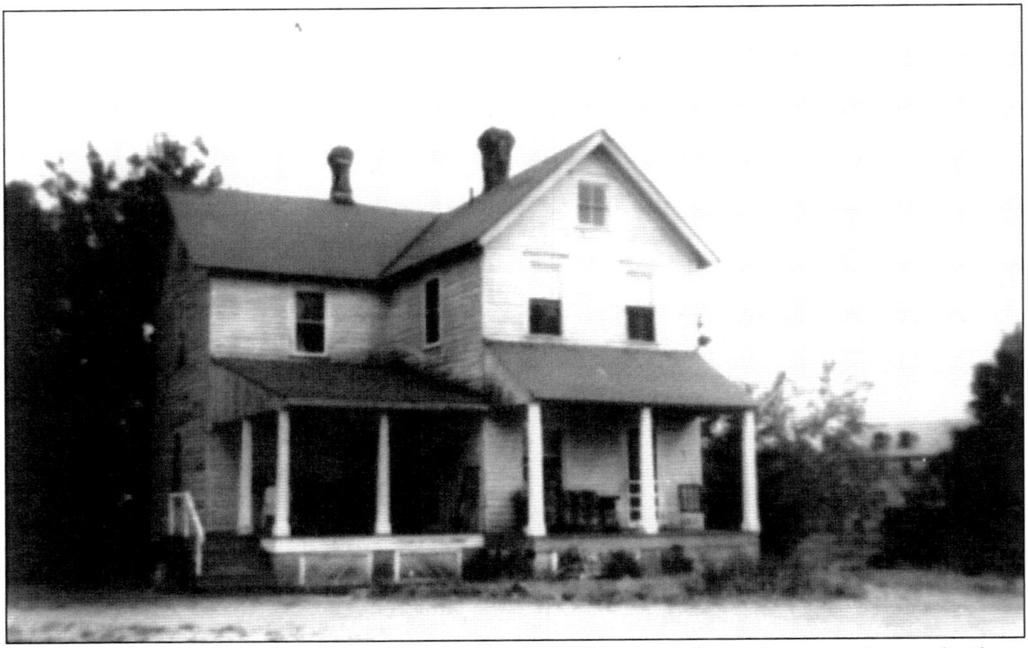

The Atsion Hotel once stood to the west of the railroad tracks and across the tracks from the train station. It was built in the late 1800s to serve passengers on the local Jersey Central Line that ran through Atsion. It was owned and occupied by the Hugh Phillips family during the 1930s. When the State of New Jersey acquired the property in 1954, the old hotel was taken down.

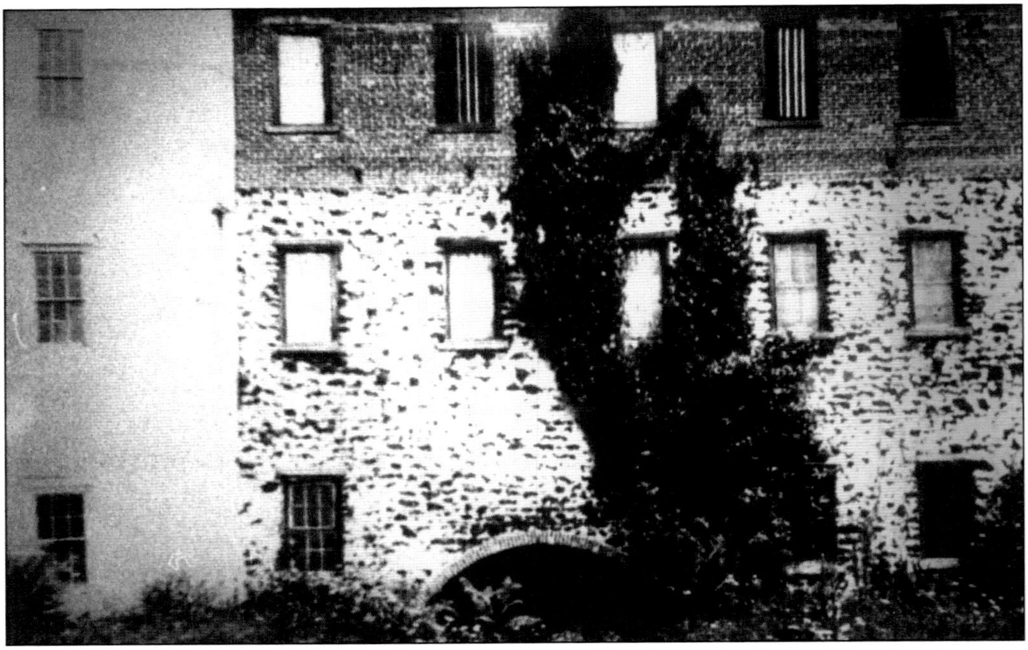

The scene dates from 1923. The oldest section is visible, dating back to 1852 when it was a paper mill and later converted to a cotton mill. Note the archway where the millrace water ran through to the Atsion River nearby. The old bog iron furnace was to the east of the cotton mill, and there is no doubt many of the furnace stones were used in the construction of the mill.

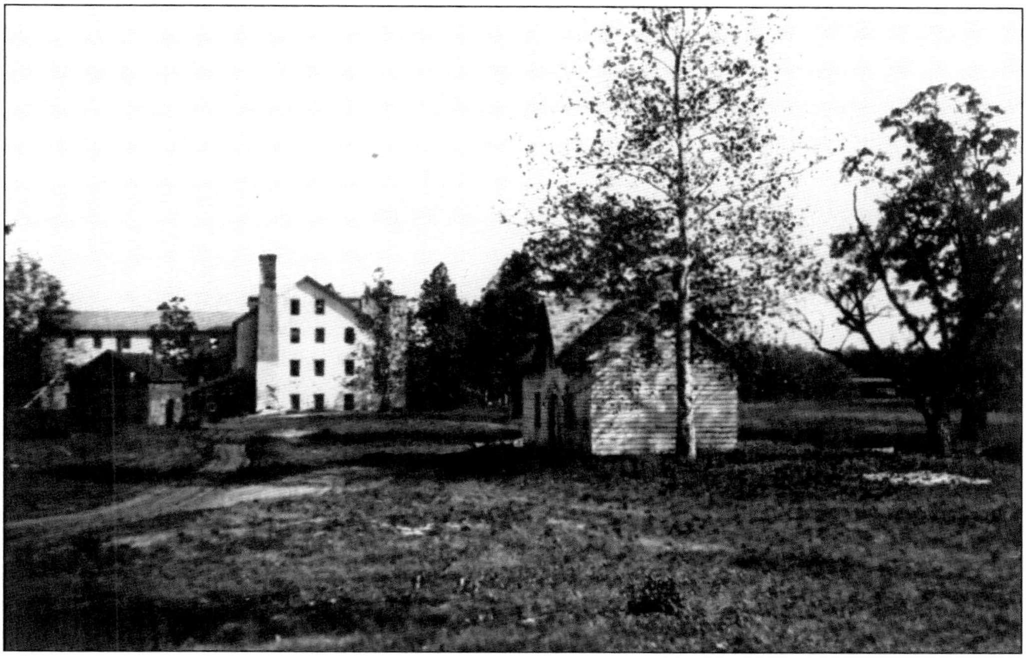

This is how the cotton mill and immediate area appeared in 1880. A blacksmith shop is the frame building to the left of the mill. The frame building to the right, sometimes known as the slab-sheathed house, stands along the millrace that runs behind the home. It was most likely erected in 1870. It still remains today, although vacant, boarded up, and awaiting an unknown fate.

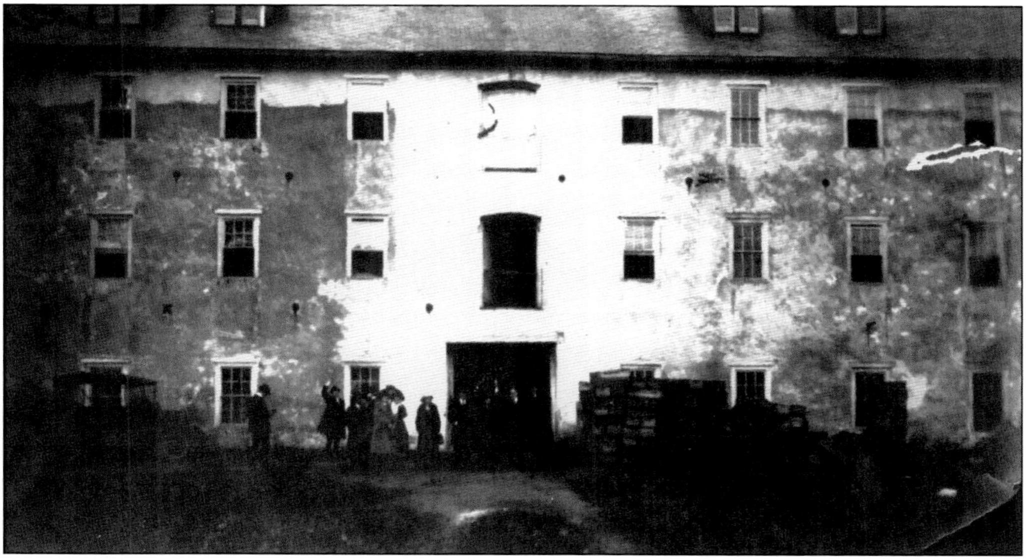

Joseph Wharton converted the old mill, once again, and in this image, it was being used as a cranberry sorting and storage facility. A group of friends of the estate stand in front of the mill. Stacks of cranberry storage boxes are piled in the front of the mill. The scene dates from 1920. Wharton had died in 1909, but his heirs continued to operate the various estate industries until 1954, when all was sold to the State of New Jersey.

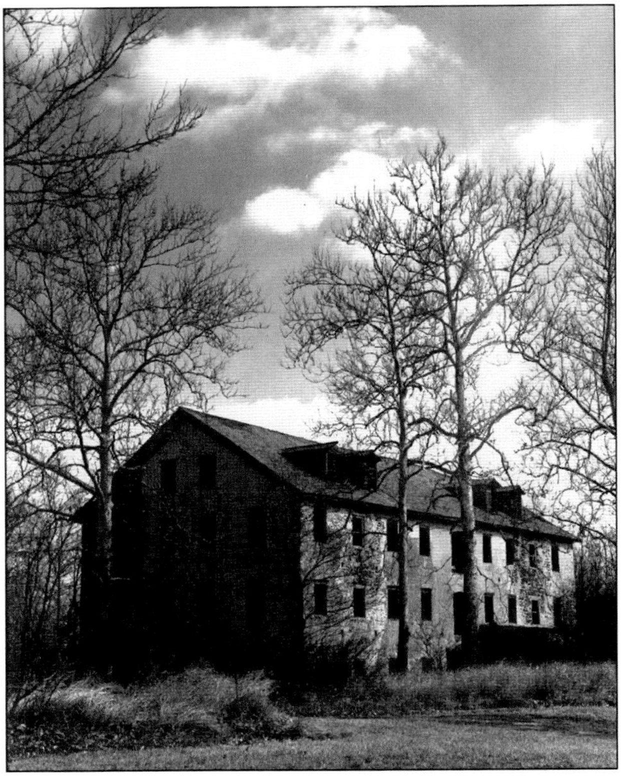

The mill that had stood as a landmark for so many years had finally come to the end of its existence. Once it had been suggested it could have been an excellent museum to house and display the history of the Pinelands, but this never came to fruition. An arsonist's torch once again struck Atsion during the night of March 27, 1977. By morning, the once-proud four-story structure that had endured for decades and employed many generations of workers was gone forever. This photograph was taken in 1974.

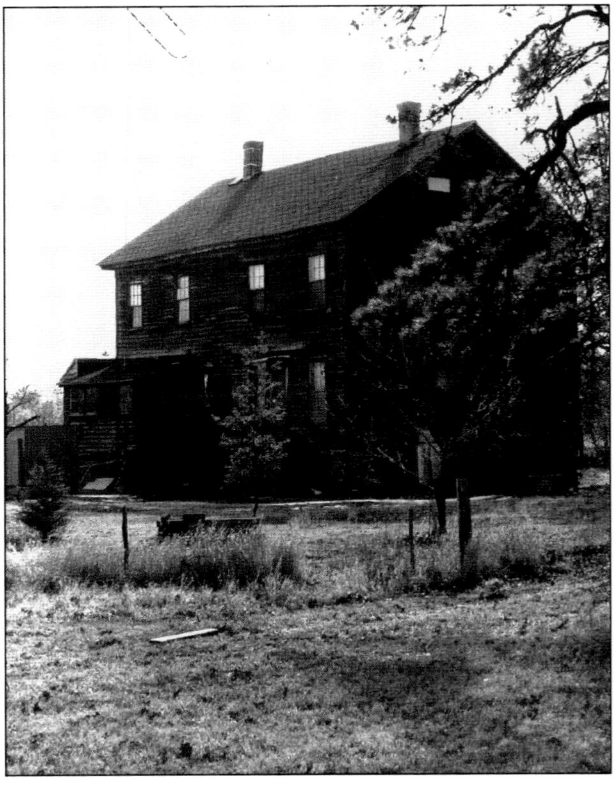

This is a classic example of one of seven double houses that were erected in the mid-1800s to house workers at the mill; it later housed those who worked for the Wharton estate. They too had felt the wrath of time, vandalism, and lack of interest in preservation. Many Shamong residents can trace their roots back to these double homes that had endured for so many years. All of them are now gone. The last one remained until 2007 when it too collapsed from lack of care. It had been enclosed by a cyclone fence to prevent anyone getting injured. It stands today as a pile of ruins, still inside the fence.

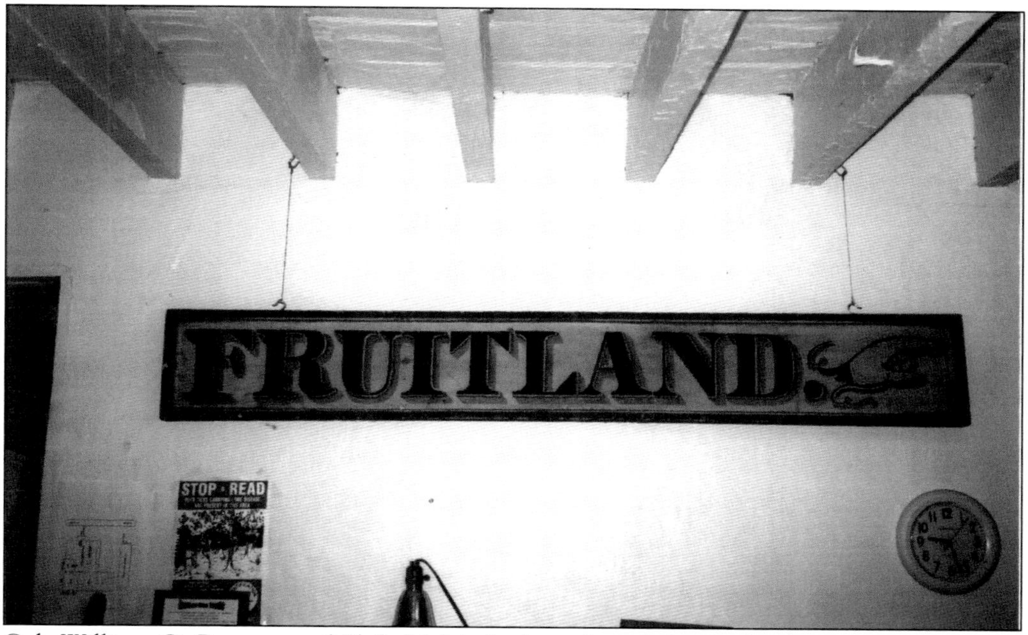

Col. William C. Patterson of Philadelphia had purchased the Richards estate in 1862. He planned to rebuild the area into a glorious farming community, which he named Fruitland. Even the post office was changed from Atsion to Fruitland. Many years ago, this sign was found in a storage area inside the old village store, which is now a forest ranger's station. It is now on display inside the building.

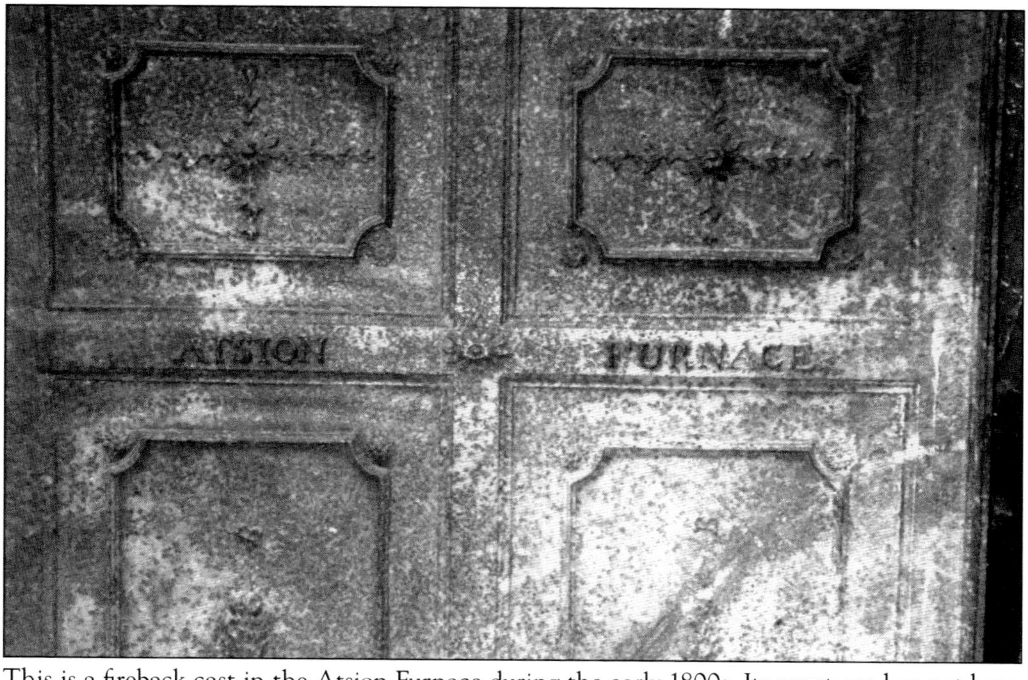

This is a fireback cast in the Atsion Furnace during the early 1800s. Its exact age has not been determined. It is presently owned by the Indian Mills Historical Society. The society plans to publicly display it once appropriate quarters are found to house it. For now, the fireback remains in storage under the care of a society trustee.

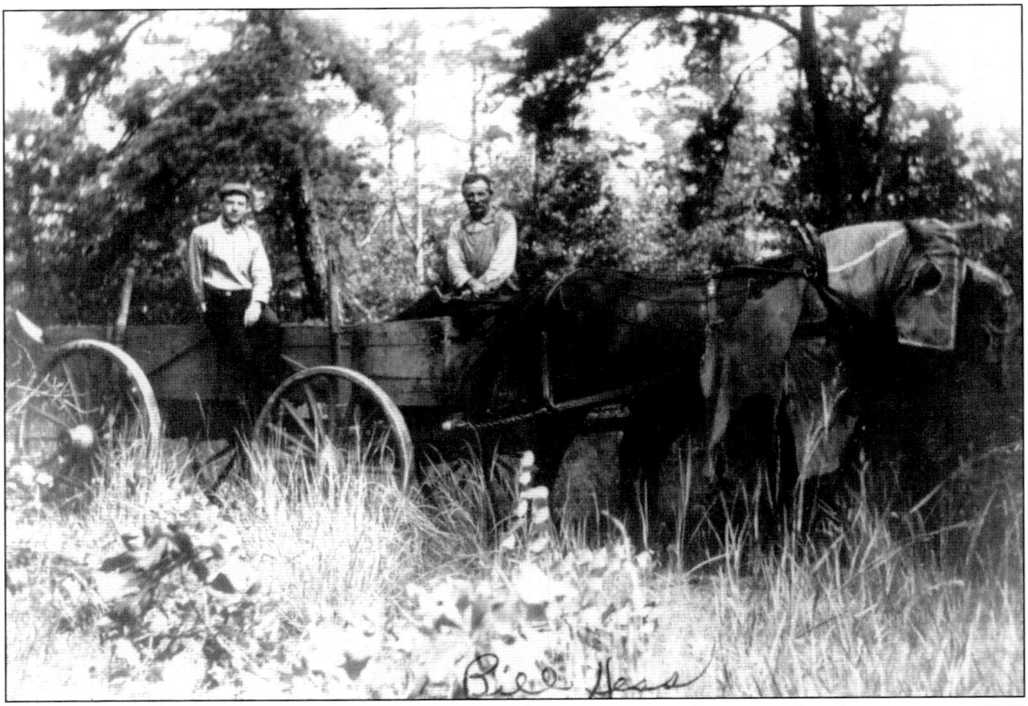

This is a scene at Atsion in the early 1900s. Both mean are workmen at the Atsion estate. Bill Hess is driving the team of horses.

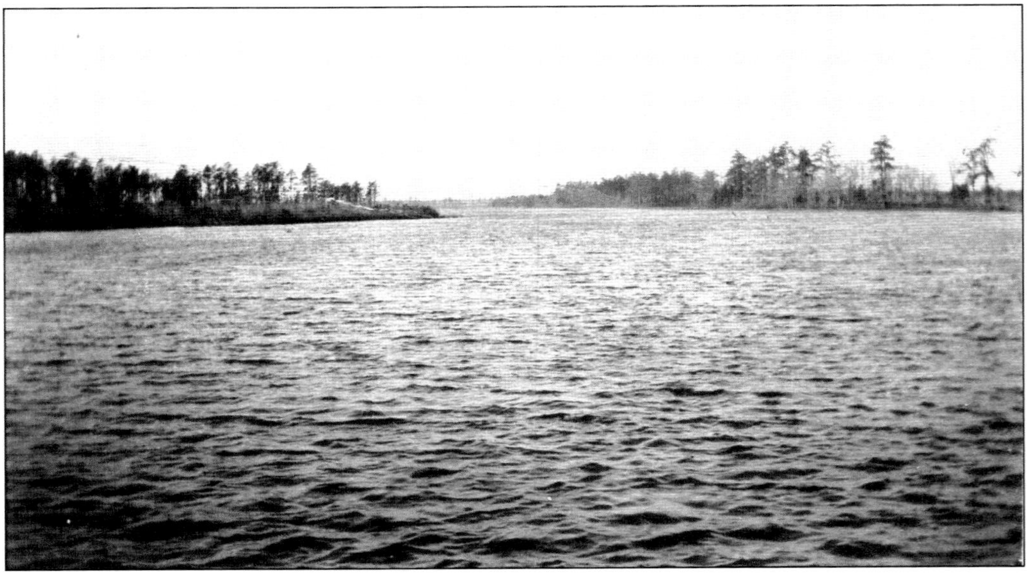

Here is Atsion Lake as it appeared in 1916. There were no log cabins for campers on the north shoreline and no bathing beach on the south shore. In those days, the lake was pristine.

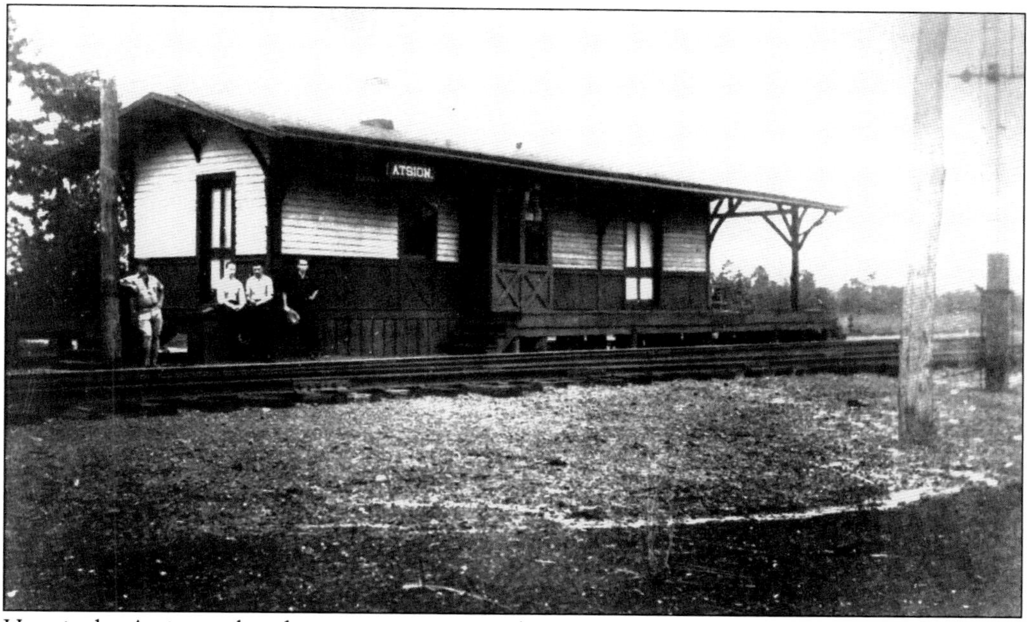

Here is the Atsion railroad station as it appeared in 1920. It was erected about 1870 and used as a passenger and freight station for the New Jersey Southern Railroad. Due to declining traffic, the station was then abandoned and closed in 1949.

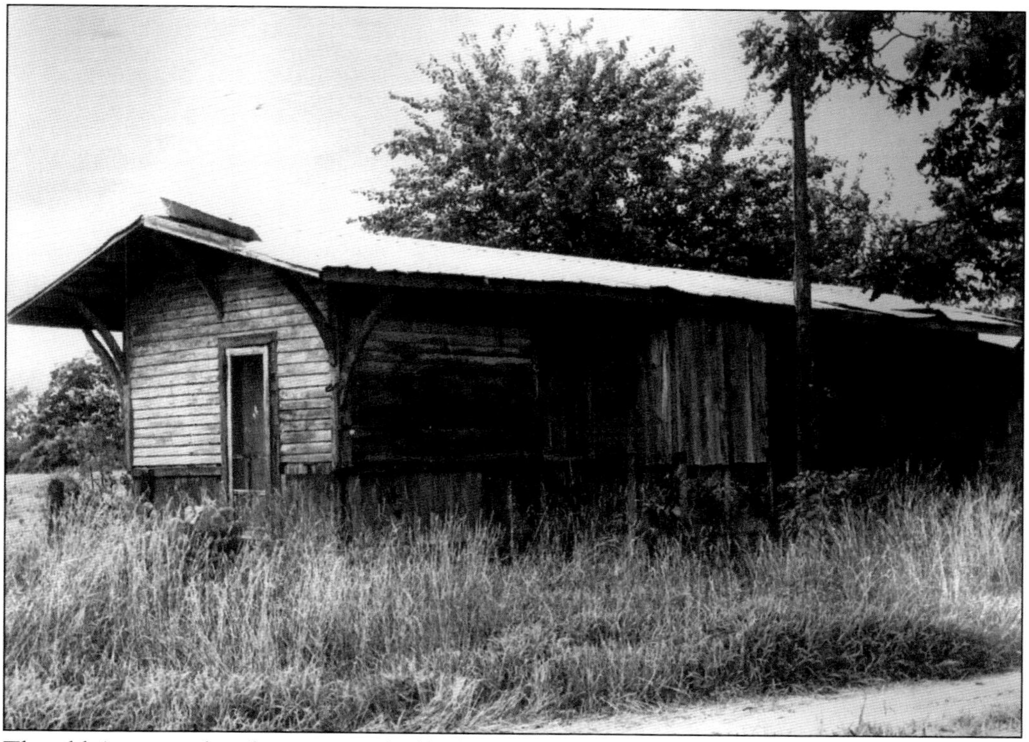

The old Atsion railroad station gradually deteriorated, as most everything has in Atsion. It was finally moved to the farm of Hobart Gardner in nearby Indian Mills and used as a home for migrant workers. For a brief time, it appeared at the Philadelphia Flower Show in 1976 and was then dismantled.

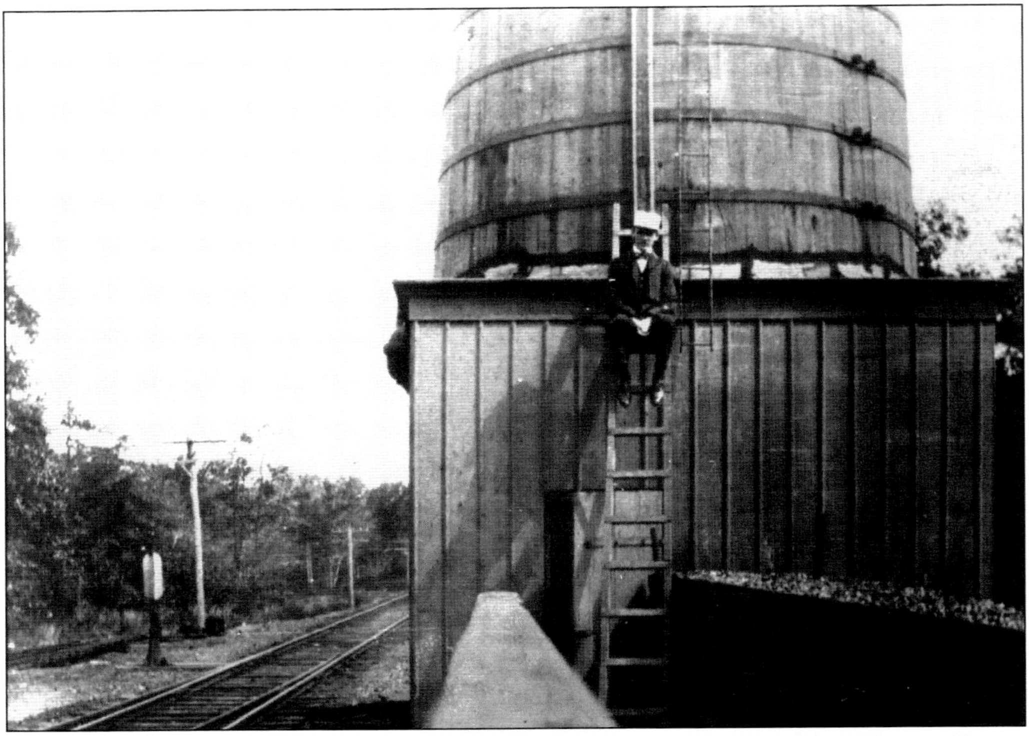

John Etheridge was the son of Andrew Etheridge, who was the manager of the Wharton Estate. John became the stationmaster at the Atsion railroad station. He held this position for 46 years. He is seen here sitting on the ladder of the Atsion water tower in 1920.

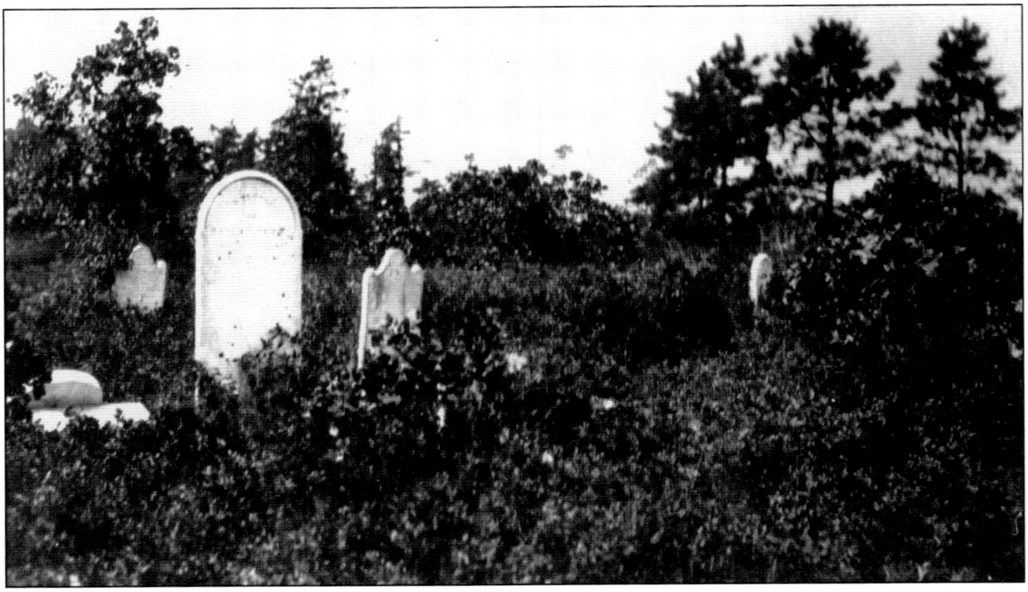

The oldest cemetery at Atsion is the one that lay partially hidden in the woods on the west side of Route 206. The graveyard at one time contained more than 60 individual burials. The scene above is as it appeared in 1916. No one seemed to care. The place was overgrown and eventually forgotten, except by the vandals, who seemed to delight in toppling headstones or stealing them to use as stepping stones.

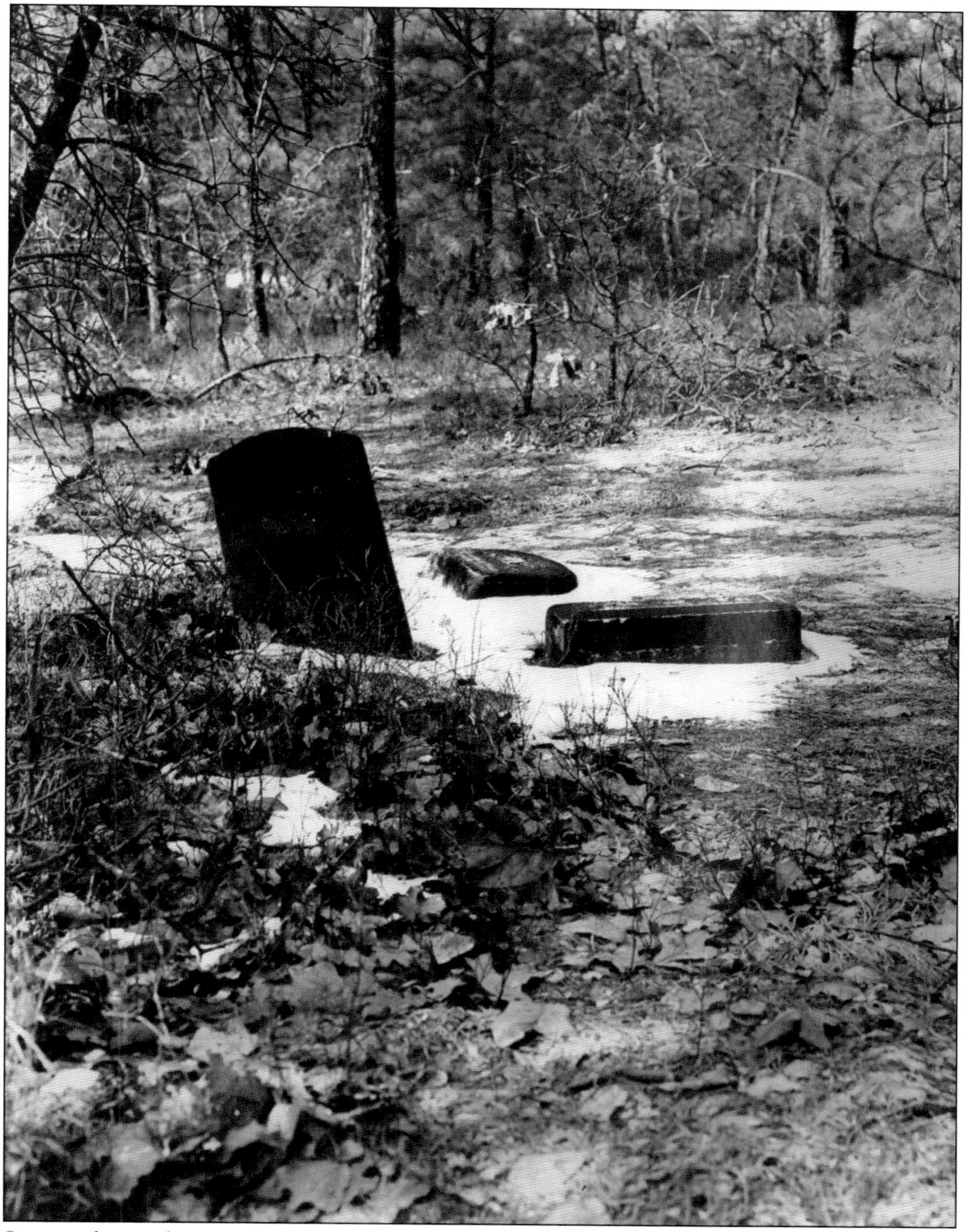

Some refer to the graveyard as the "Catholic Cemetery" because of the many Irish names buried here. A man named John Ross was buried here. He died on February 22, 1804, at the age of 20. He was the son of John and Dolly Ross, who came from the parish of Magilligan in County Derry, Ireland. There are two parishes in Northern Ireland by this same name. One is Catholic, and the other is Presbyterian. Without further proof, it would be difficult to determine whether the burials here are one religion or the other. It should be known that there were many Presbyterian followers in the area due to the presence of Rev. John Brainerd preaching at Brotherton Reservation to whites and Native Americans alike.

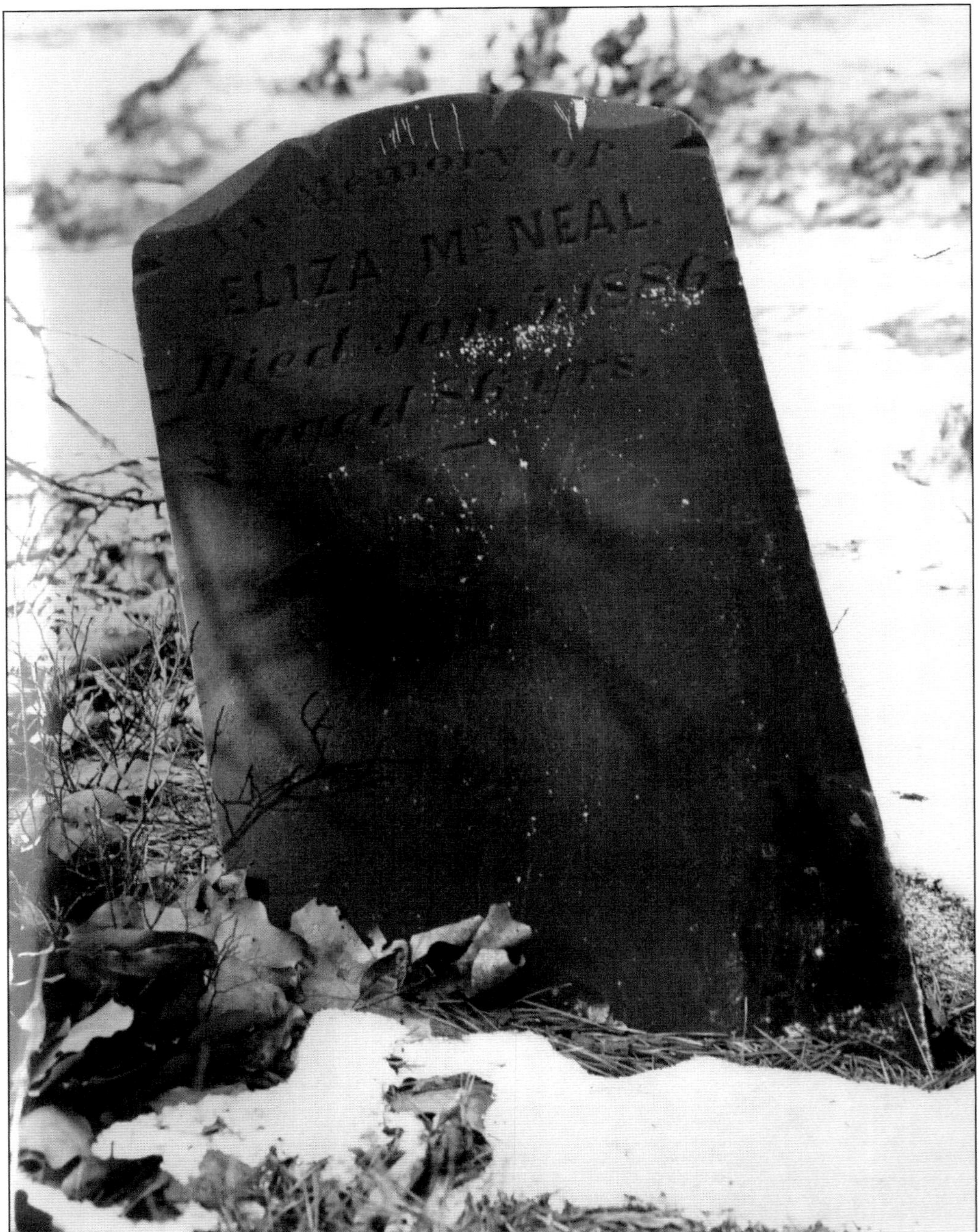

The only complete headstone surviving today is that of Eliza McNeal, who died on January 5, 1886, at 86 years of age. There is also a Daniel McNeal, "A Native of Ireland." Shamong Township records reveal a Michael McNeal, son of Daniel and Eliza McNeal, died on January 28, 1900. He was 66, single, and a day laborer. He was born around 1834 and may also be buried here. These headstones are enclosed by a 10-foot-square fence at one end of a bathing beach complex. Many graves lie buried under the asphalt parking lot.

This sand trail once led back to the ancient Atsion cemetery where many of the workers from the early 1800s lie buried. With the renovations that occurred to the bathing beach nearby, traces of this trail are gone.

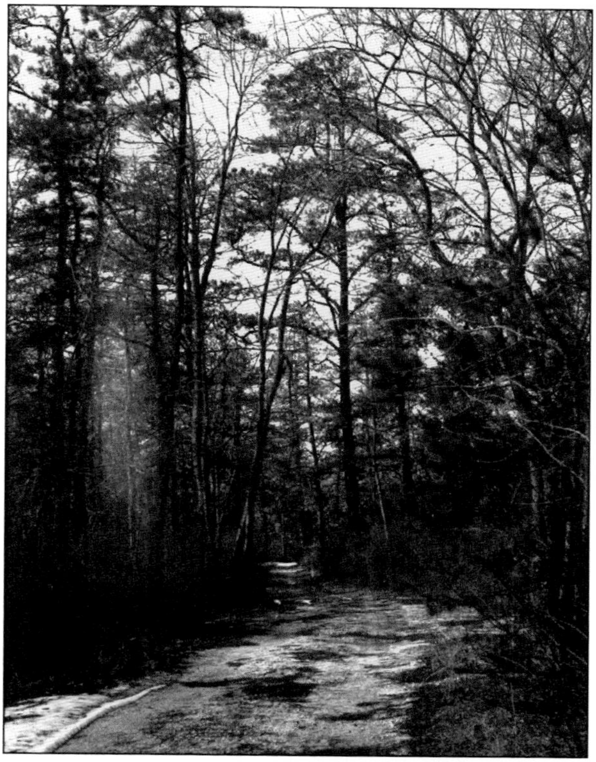

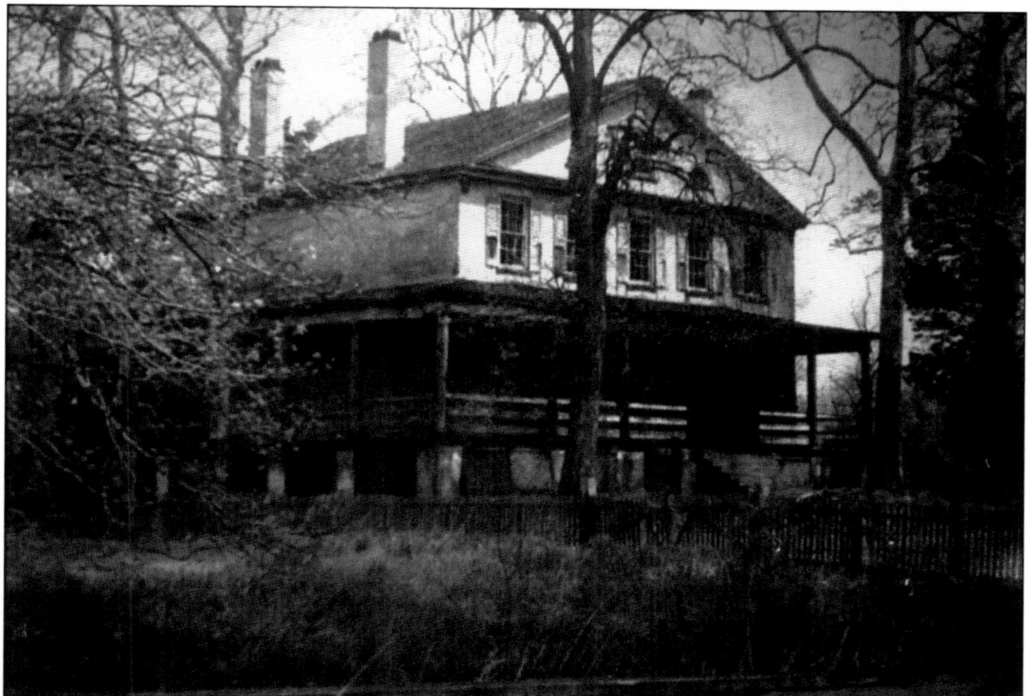

Here is the Richards Mansion as it appeared in the early 1930s. It lies vacant and neglected awaiting an unknown fate. The once classic Greek Revival–style building was deteriorating rapidly prior to its purchase by the State of New Jersey in 1954 and subsequent restoration.

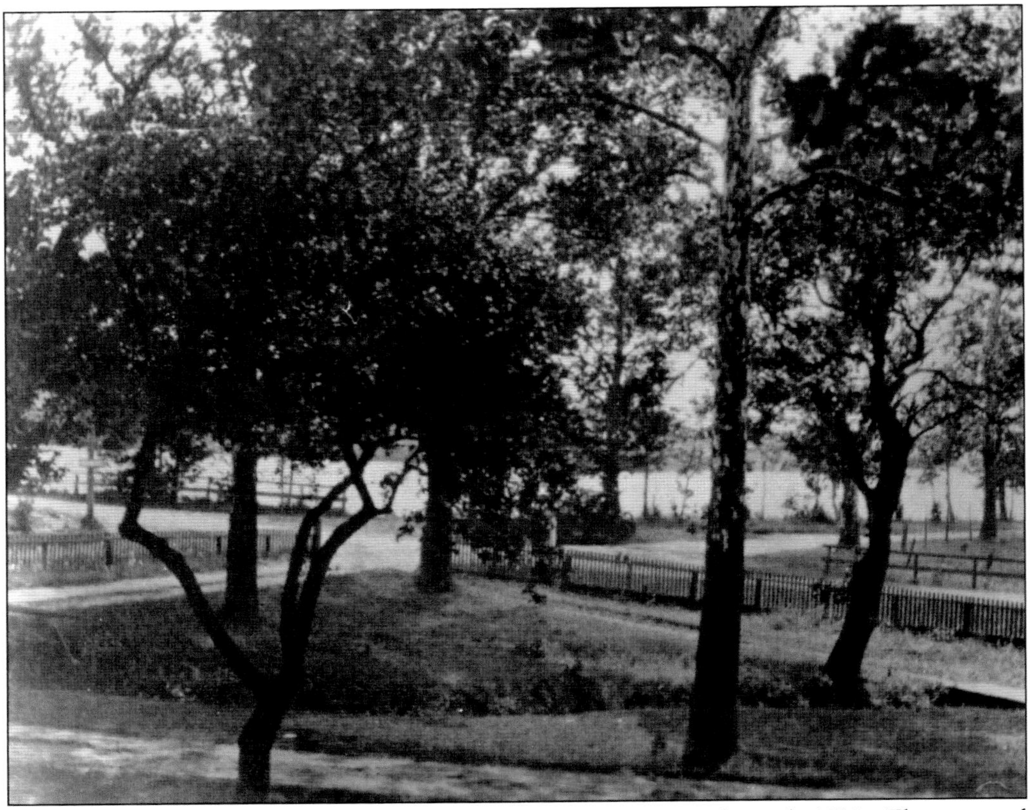

This scene was taken from the porch of the Richards Mansion in the early 1930s. The unpaved road in front of the split-rail fence is now Route 206. The road to the right along Atsion Lake is the unpaved Atsion Road.

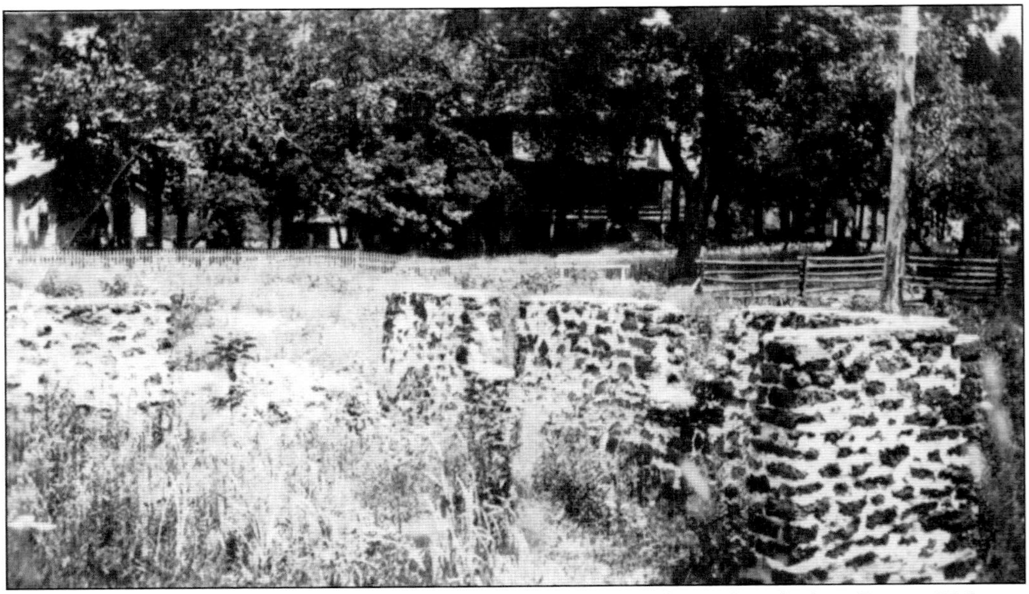

The ruins of the once multistoried gristmill are seen in the 1930s, before Route 206 was constructed in 1939. The Richards Mansion can be seen in the background.

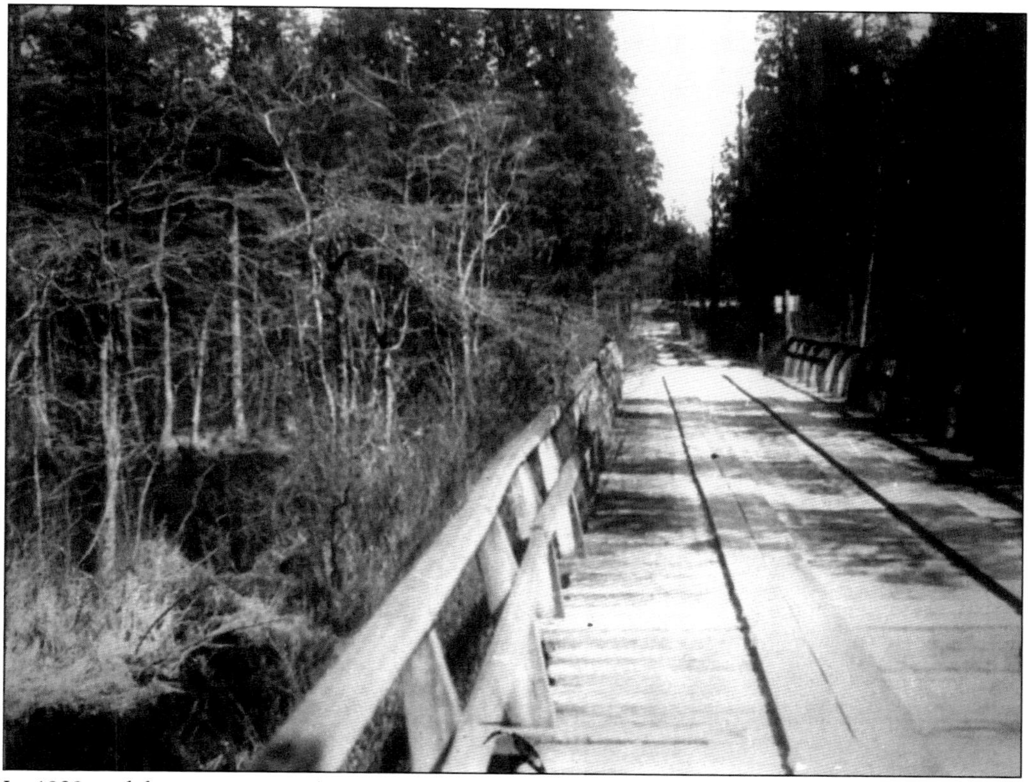

In 1939 and for many years thereafter, this bridge carried travelers over the Batsto River. The Tuckerton Stage Road continues through the woods to Quaker Bridge, which lies a short distance ahead.

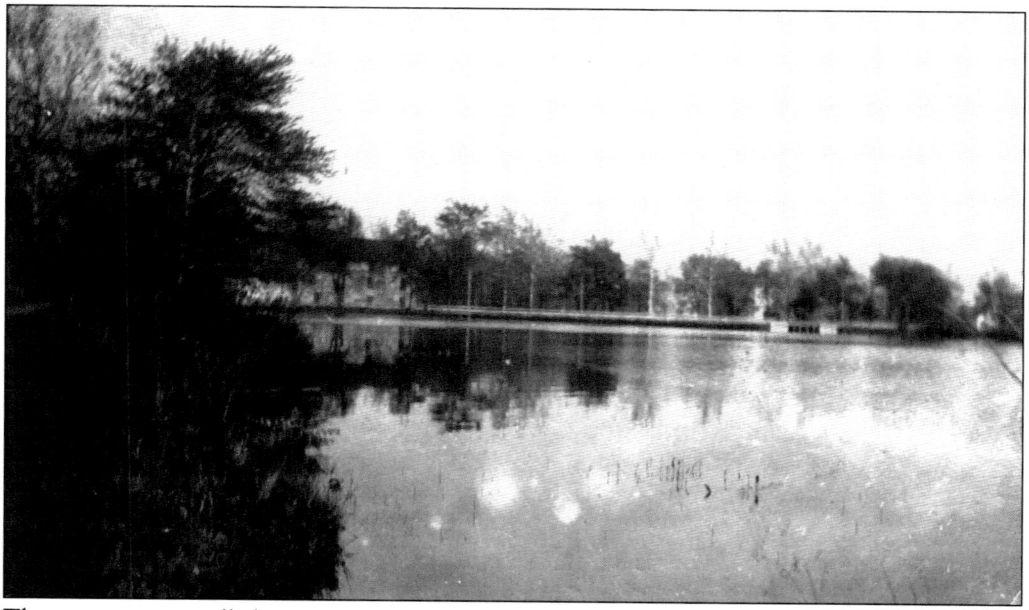

The ancient gristmill that once stood at the head of the lake can be seen in this early 1900s photograph to the far left.

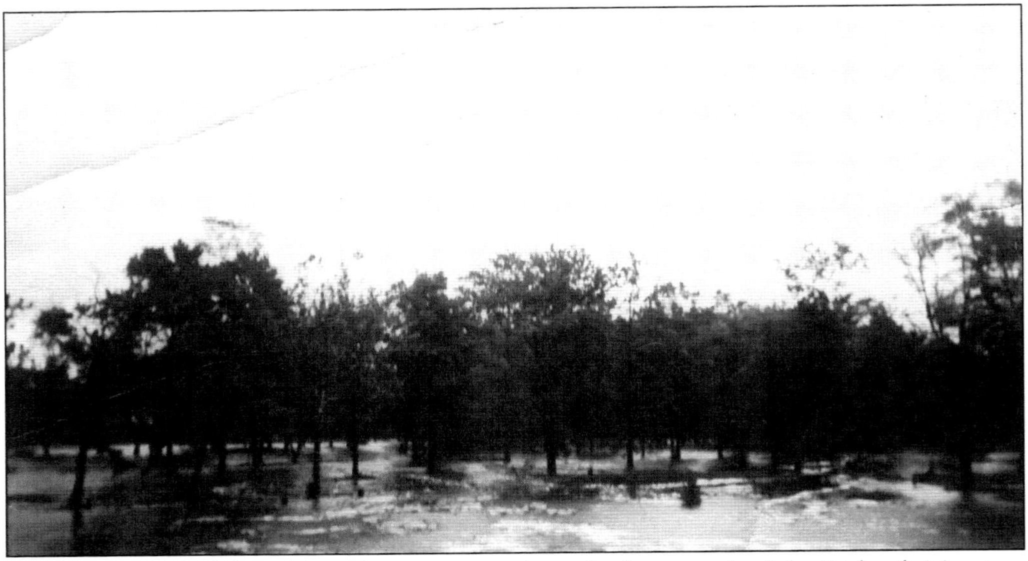

The flood of 1938 did not spare Atsion, as seen from the front porch of the Richards Mansion. Quaker Bridge Road lies entirely underwater.

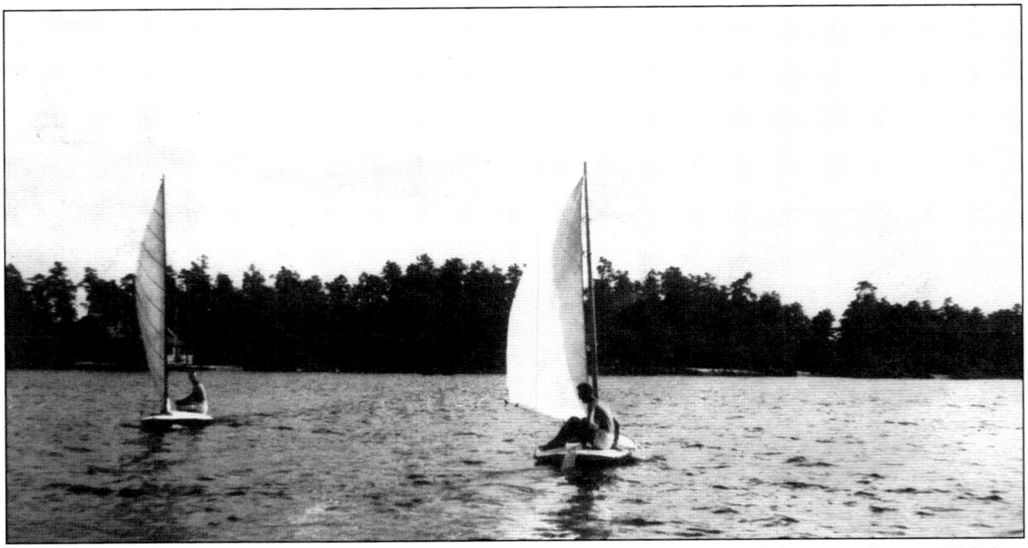

Sailing was very popular on Atsion Lake in the 1930s. It remains one of the most beautiful lakes in the Pinelands.

Six

RURAL LIFE

For many years, the Native Americans at the Brotherton Reservation had failed to exhibit much in the way of being industrious. There age-old dislike for farming chores was evident in that the women did most of this work. The men spent their time fishing, hunting, and drinking. Numerous reports of alcohol abuse were found in Rev. John Brainerd's journal.

Following Brainerd's departure in 1777, the Native Americans gradually became disheartened with their lifestyle. The women and men continued to make baskets and brooms for sale at distant markets, but the tilled fields of crops were allowed to go dormant. Eventually most of the cleared land was leased to area farmers. The rights to cut timber were also leased to white settlers in the area.

As time passed, the Native Americans became increasingly depressed and despondent. When an invitation to join their cousins in New York State was received, they were only too happy to comply. The reservation lands were sold at auction in 1802. The 83 remaining Native Americans were then transported to New York State. Area farmers quickly took advantage of the opportunity to obtain the land. Lots were sold in 100-acre plots at $2 to $3 per acre. Many names familiar to the area such as Haines, Wilkins, Prickett, Peacock, Branin, Taylor, and Troth, from nearby Medford, were the purchasers. They resold the land at a profit, and the former reservation was transformed into farmland.

A second generation of landowners came into place such as Wright, McNeal, Dellett, Crain, Armstrong, Bozearth, and others. Large farm families were the norm, and the population quickly increased. A gristmill and sawmill complex began in 1806. The Native American sawmill was rebuilt and enlarged and again became productive.

Taverns were already in place just over the reservation borders, such as Clines and Sign of the Buck, both on Atsion Road, and Half Moon and Seven Stars, on Tuckerton Stage Road.

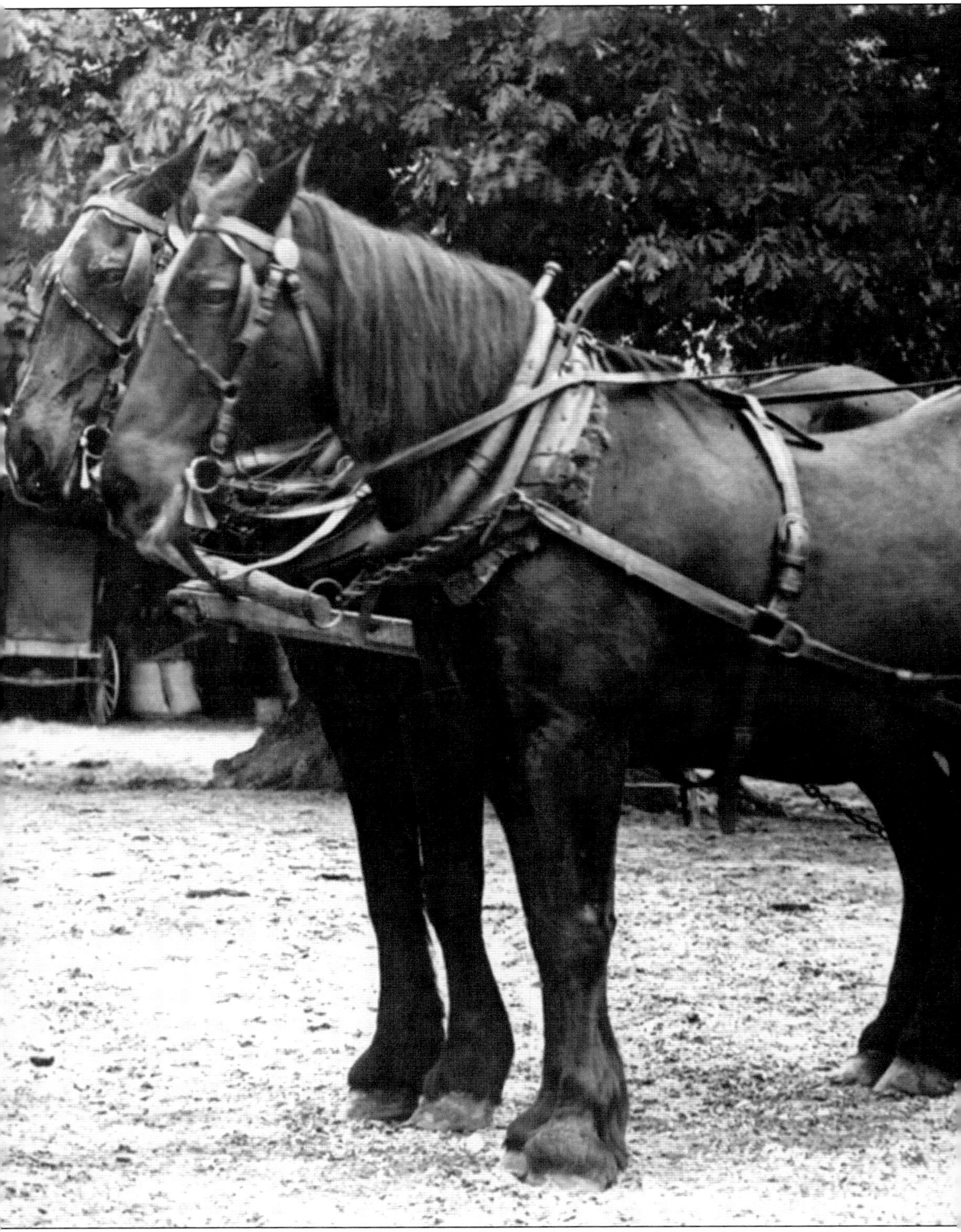

Seen here is a typical Shamong farm family during the 1890s. They are believed to be members of the Phillips family who had a farm on the Stokes Road for many years. The plowing of farm

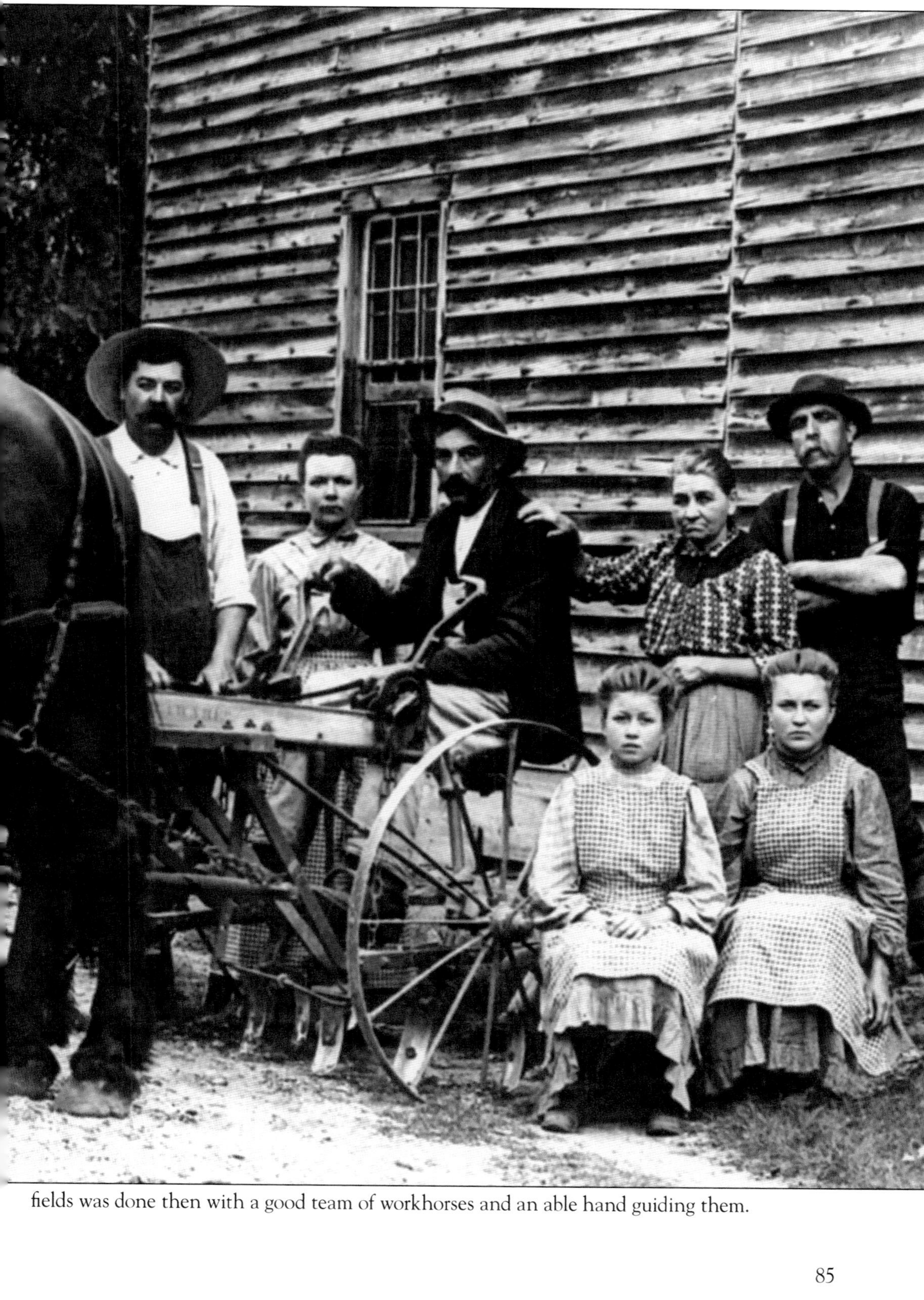

fields was done then with a good team of workhorses and an able hand guiding them.

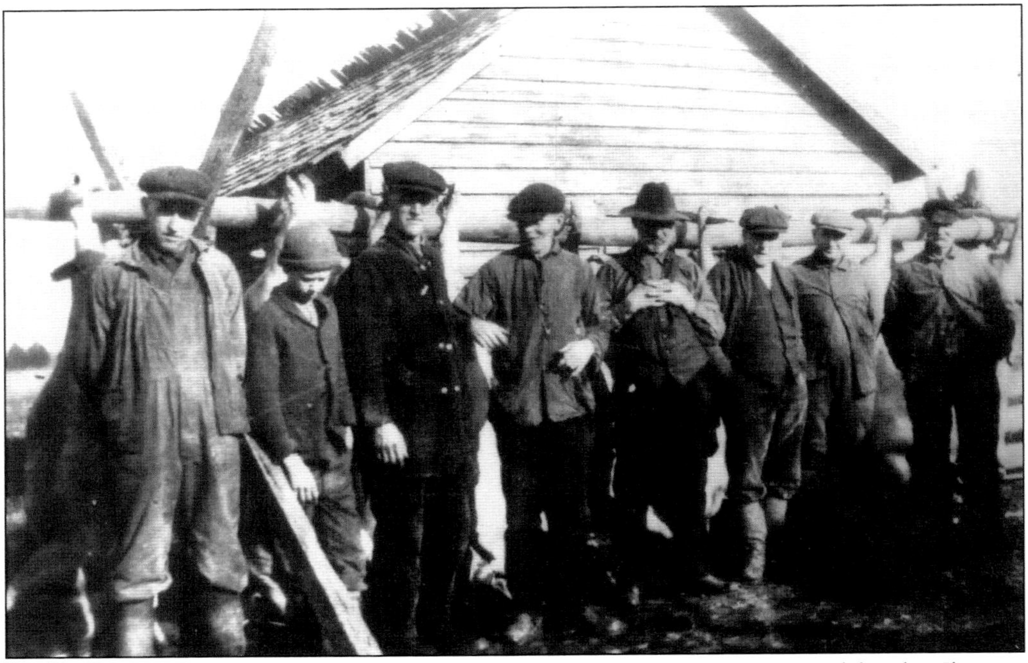

Hog killing was an annual chore that required plenty of help from friends and family. This is a scene taken in 1930. Seen standing are, from left to right, Harley Wright, William Lemmon, John Shinske, Bill Gaskill, Uncle Bill Gaskill, George Gaskill, Henry Wright, and Billy Misener.

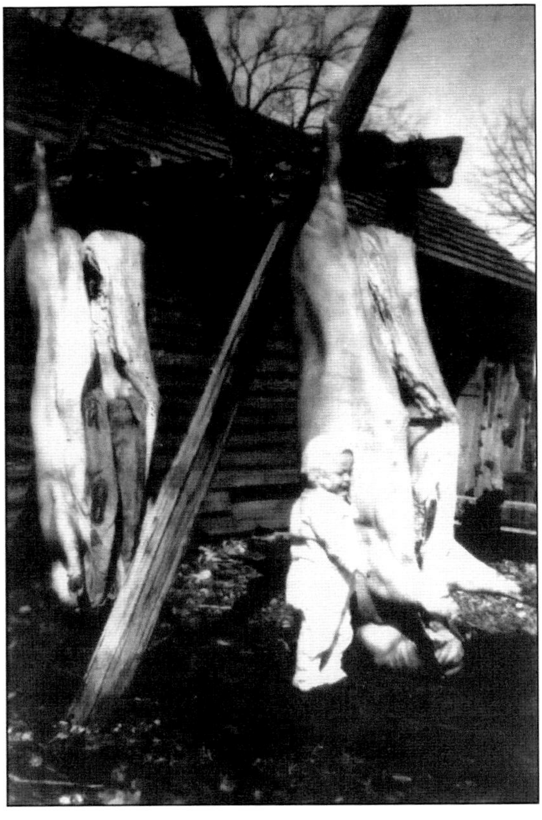

Little Bill Lemmon is seen standing next to a 910-pound pig after it was slaughtered. This scene is from the James Emmons farm.

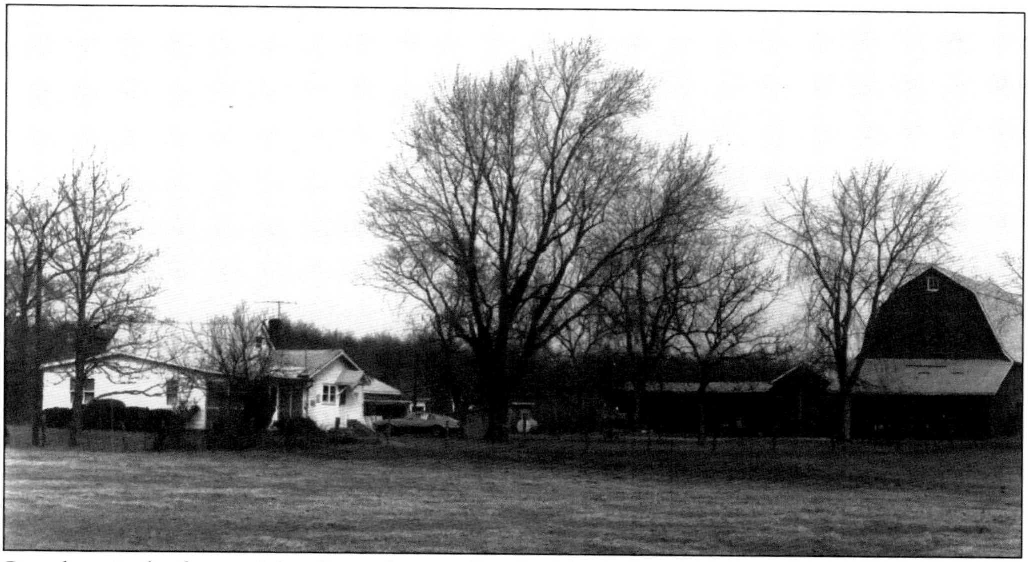

Seen here is the former John Crain farm and outbuildings. In later years, the farm was owned by John Jennings. It was originally lot No. 25, consisting of 100 acres, purchased by John Troth from the Indian Commissioners when the Brotherton Reservation was sold at auction.

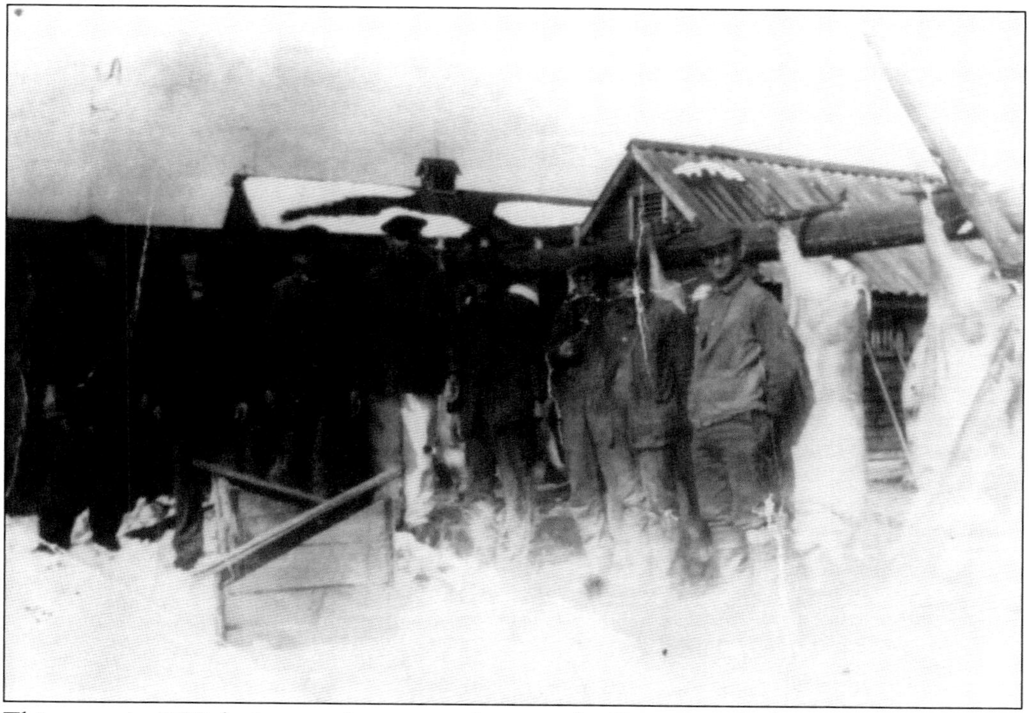

This scene in 1930 depicts another group of men at the Henry Wright farm during the annual hog killing.

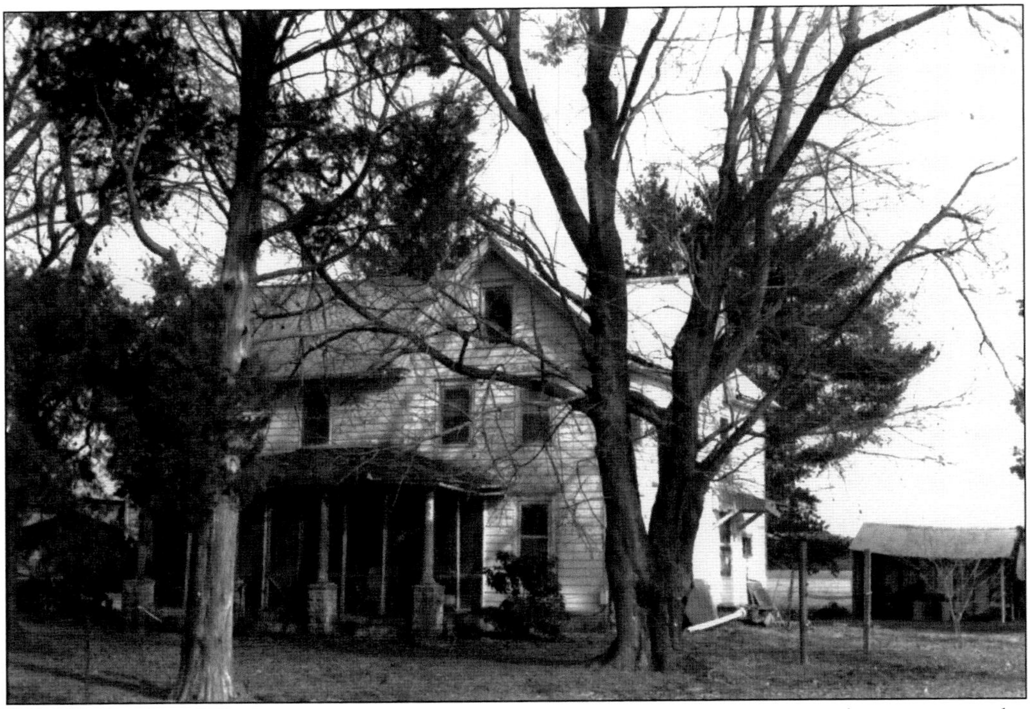

This property was purchased as lot No. 24 in 1802 by Arthur Thompson, who was once the proprietor of the Quaker Bridge Tavern some distance away. He did not live on this property, and his widow later sold it to Robert McNeal in 1832. The home was built at this time. It then passed to his nephew John McNeal. A murder occurred at this home on January 19, 1889, when John accidentally shot a neighbor, James Dellett Jr. McNeal was charged with murder and remained in jail for three months. He was eventually found not guilty, and the shooting was considered accidental. Also pictured are the ancient outbuildings that have been here for well over a century. The farm was located on what was then known as the Murphy Road but is now Indian Mills Road. It has been owned by the Gatley family since 1925.

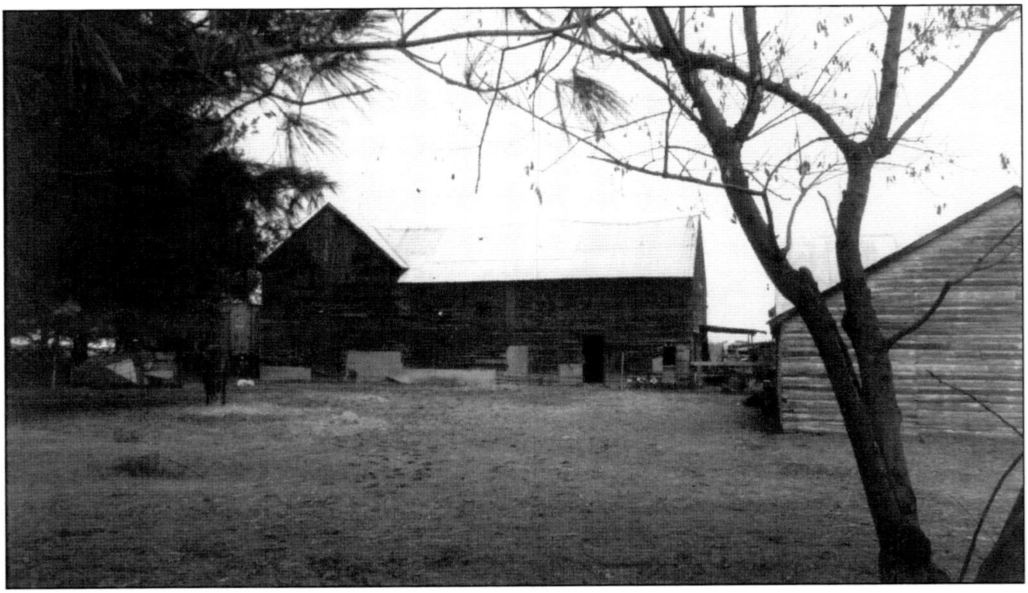

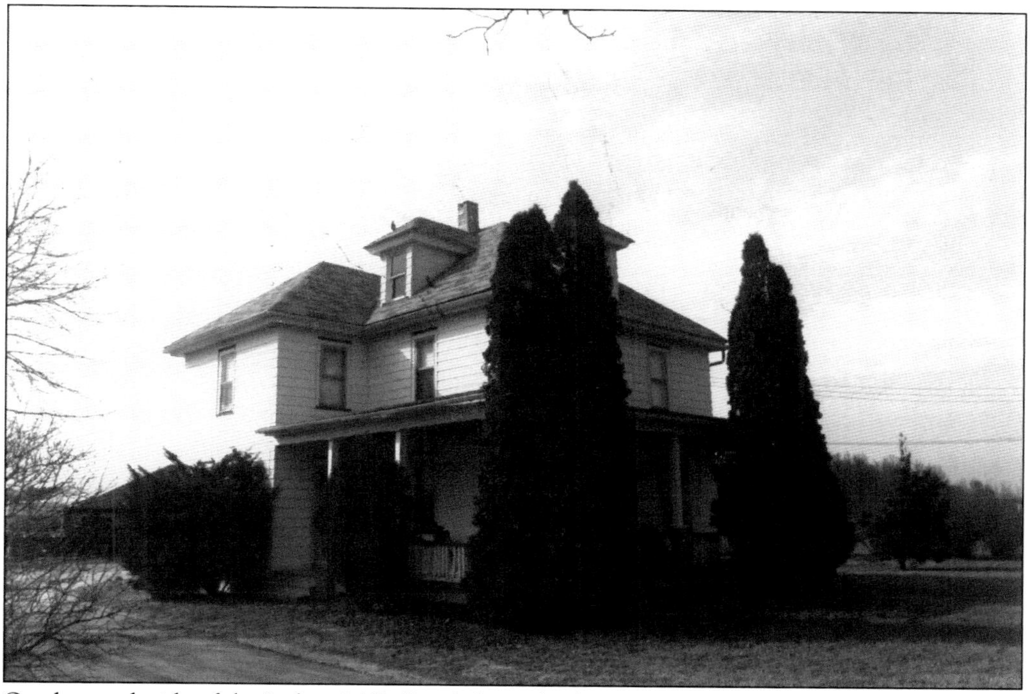

On the south side of the Indian Mills Road, formerly the Murphy Road, stands a farmhouse built about 1905 on the foundations of a still older home that had belonged to the Powell family in the 1800s. The home is in a dilapidated condition and has not been occupied for quite some time. It had last been known as the Morris Abrams farm. Abrams had lived here and worked the farm. The Abrams barns had formerly stood to the rear and side of the main house.

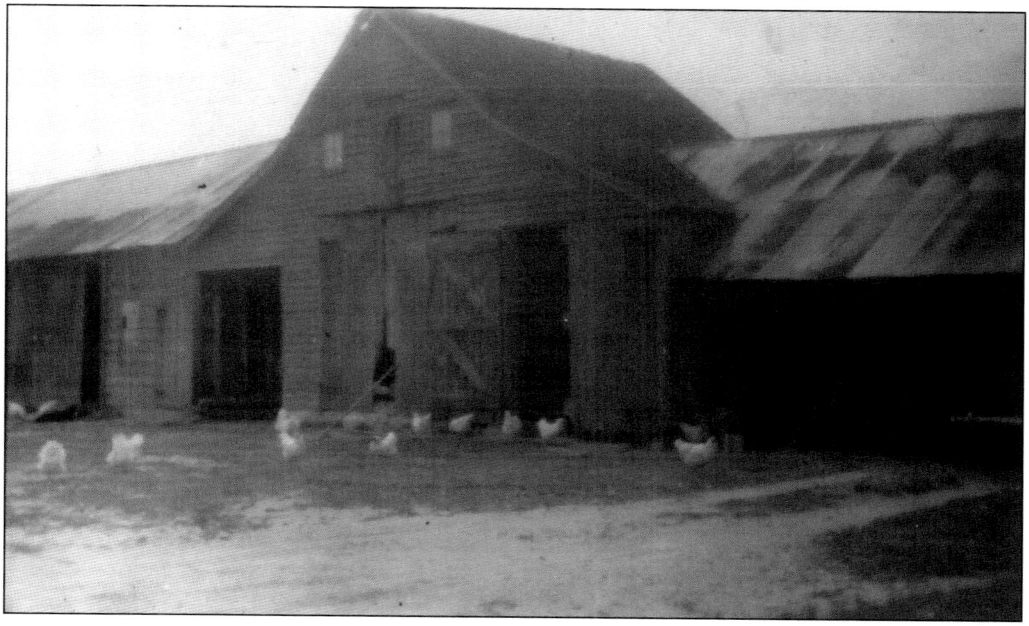

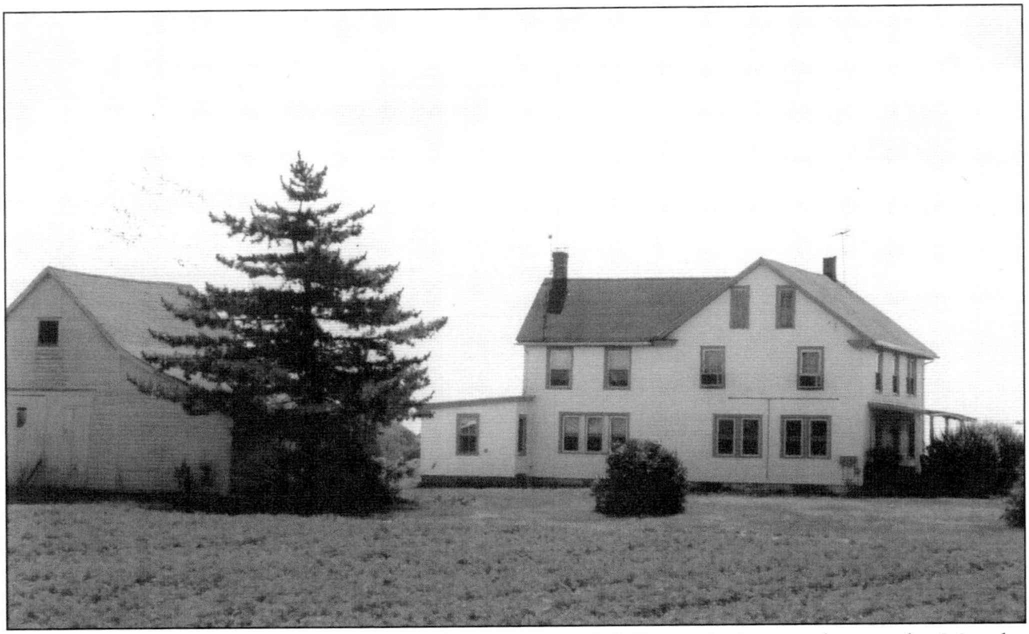

This was originally sold as lot No. 23 of 100 acres to Job Peacock. It was also on the Murphy Road. Nathan Wright lived in this farmhouse in the mid-1800s as did his son Henry and next his grandson Henry Jr. The family was well known in the area. Henry Jr. was the welfare director in Shamong Township for many years. As a young man, he and his wife, Josephine, had lived in one of the old double-frame houses at Atsion.

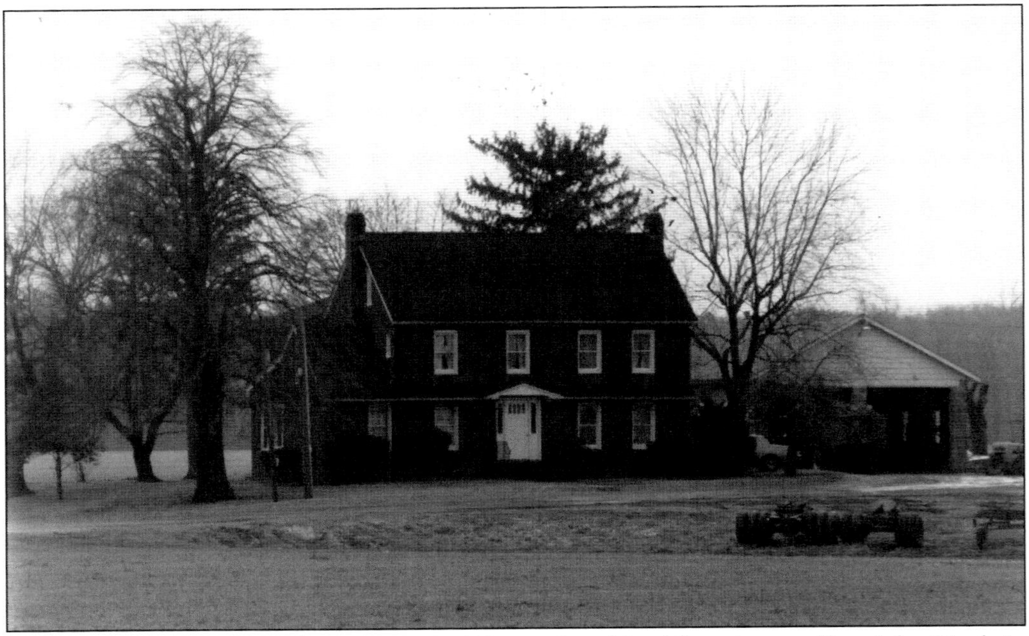

This farm was another of the reservation 100-acre lots (No. 19) and was sold to John Troth in 1802. It also became the homestead farm of Raymond and Mary Abrams in the early 1900s, where they raised a large family. At one time, each of the Abrams sons had their own farm, and nearly all farms in Shamong Township were owned by a member of this family. Several farms are still owned by the Abrams clan.

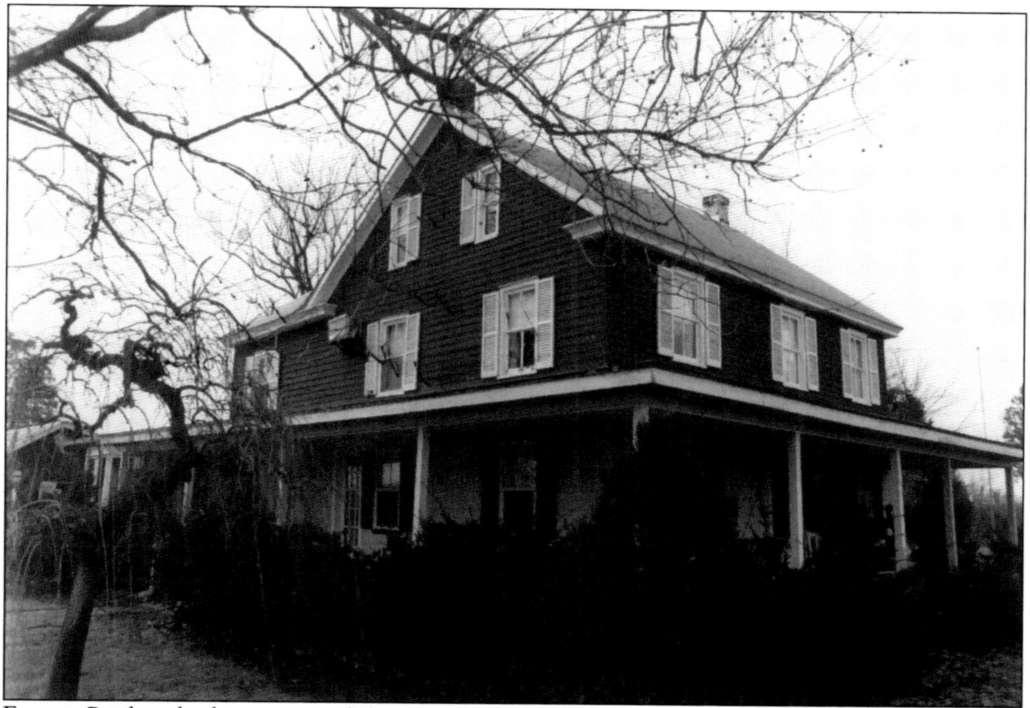

Francis Prickett had once owned this land known as lot No. 18 of the reservation lands. In later years and in the latter 1800s, it was owned by Wilber Hagerthy, who operated a grocery store in the front portion of the farmhouse. A natural spring is in the home's rear.

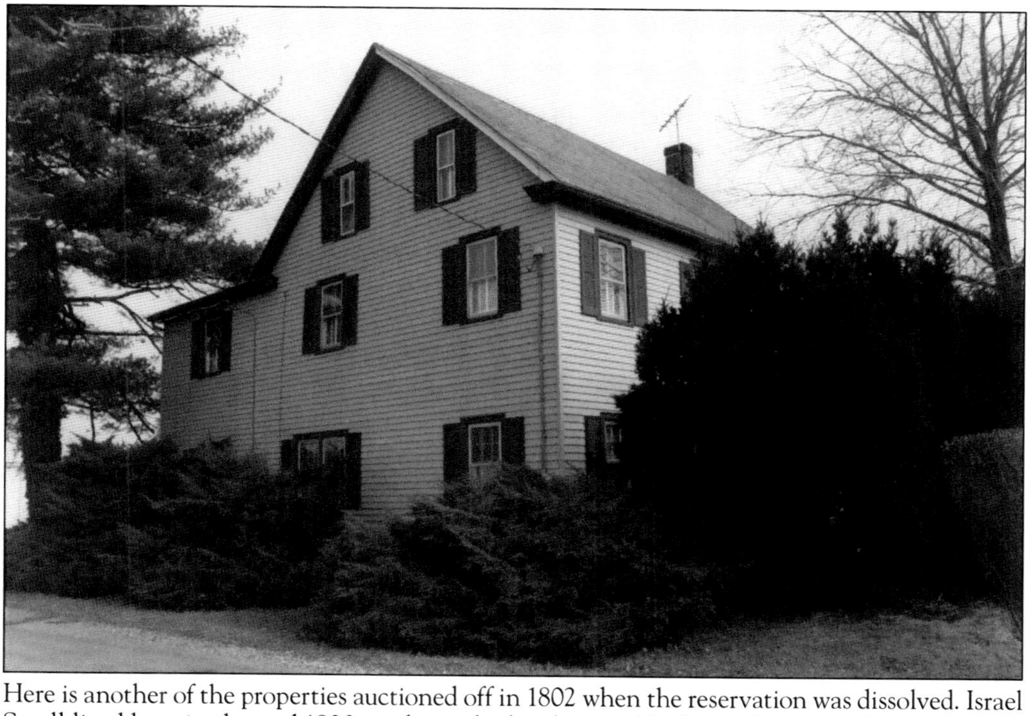

Here is another of the properties auctioned off in 1802 when the reservation was dissolved. Israel Small lived here in the mid-1800s and was the local constable. It was later owned by R. Everett Abrams and his wife, Elva. It is still in the Abrams family and a productive farm.

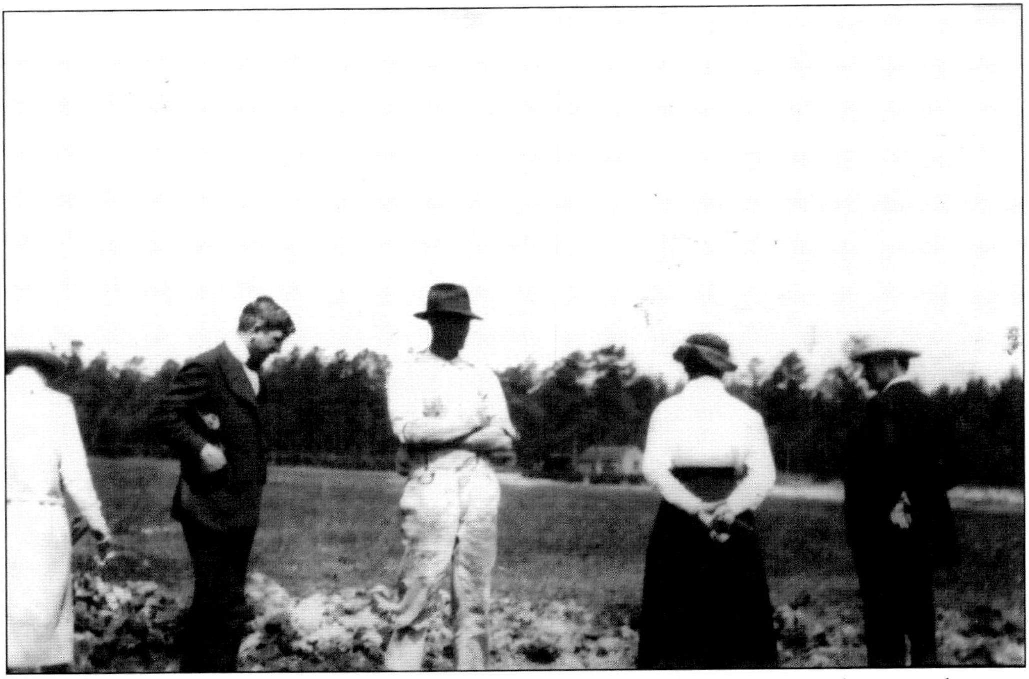

Proceeding out the Hampton Furnace Road from Route 206 for approximately two miles, one will come to an area of deserted cranberry bogs. This was once known as Deep Run Bogs, and there were several workers cottages here during the early 1900s. This scene was taken around 1910, and the bog owners are inspecting the crop.

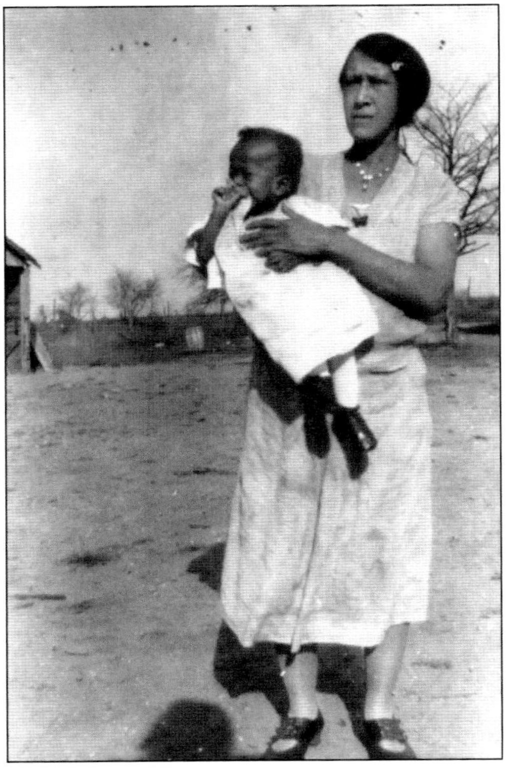

The Still farm was once located on Stokes Road, just outside the Brotherton Reservation boundaries. Cora F. Still is shown here in 1933 holding her son William.

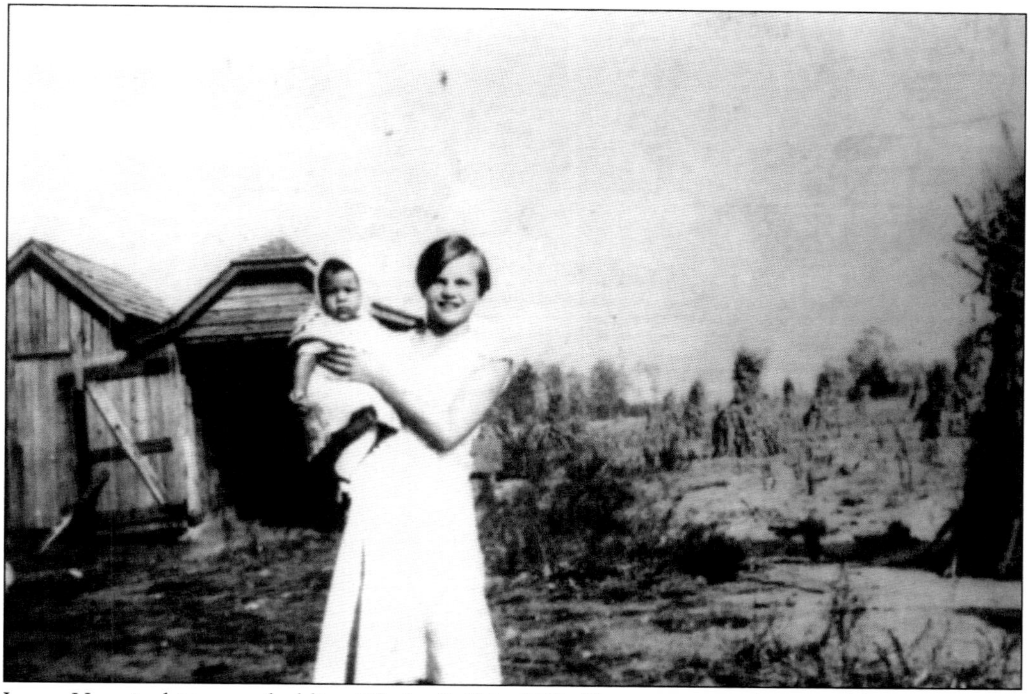

Laura Hartzinski is seen holding Gladys Still in 1933. She was a next-door neighbor to the Still family, who had a small farm on Stokes Road. The family had lived there for several generations and was descended from Levin and Charity Still.

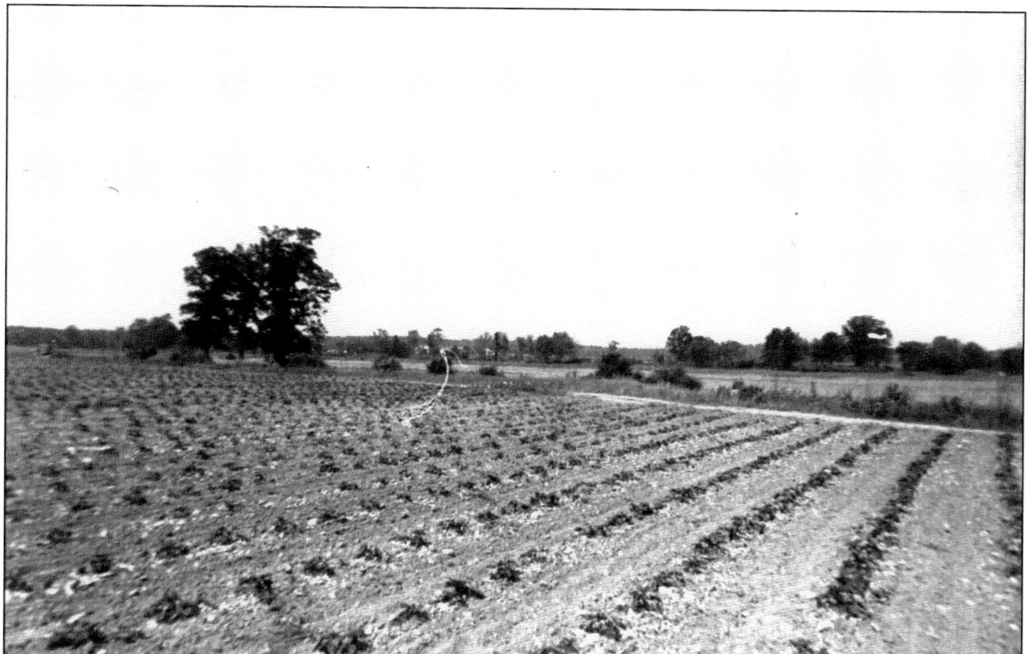

Cultivated fields once bordered the old gristmill pond that is now known as Indian Mills Lake. This scene was taken near the dam, before any houses were built along the lakefront.

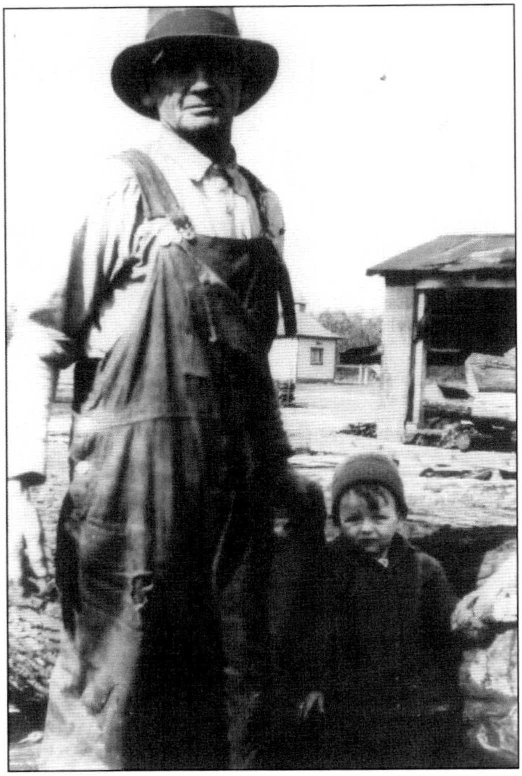

In 1930, Samuel Giberson is seen working on his farm along Tuckerton Road. He is accompanied by young Bill Lemmon.

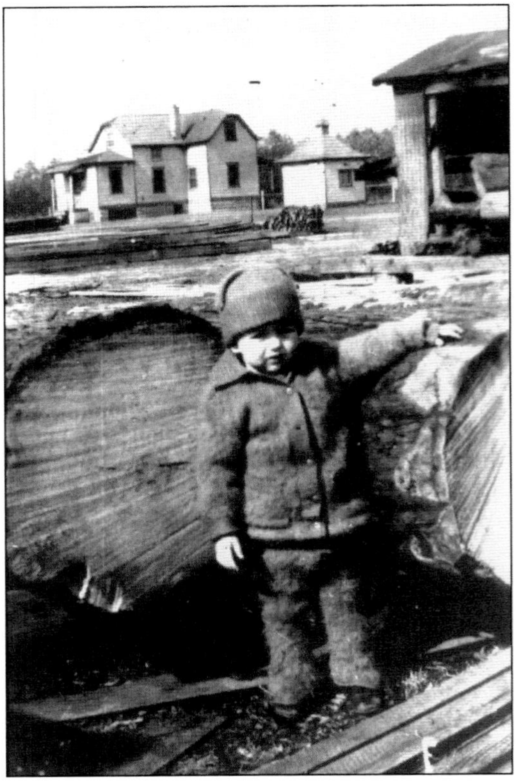

Little Bill Lemmon in the 1930s is seen playing near the Giberson Sawmill. The Giberson farmhouse is in the background. The house still stands, but the rest of the farm is a housing development known as Fox Sparrow Rise along Tuckerton Road.

Samuel Giberson is standing on his farm property in 1930. He appears to be dressed for a special occasion. He usually wore an old hat and coveralls on his farm and sawmill.

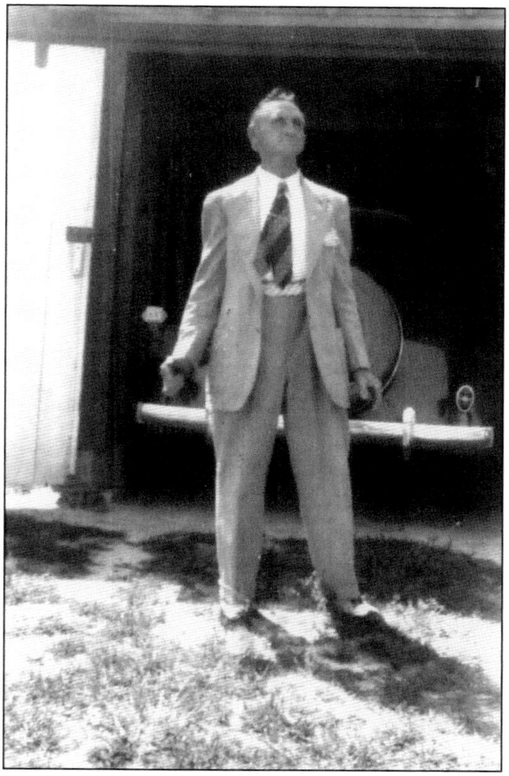

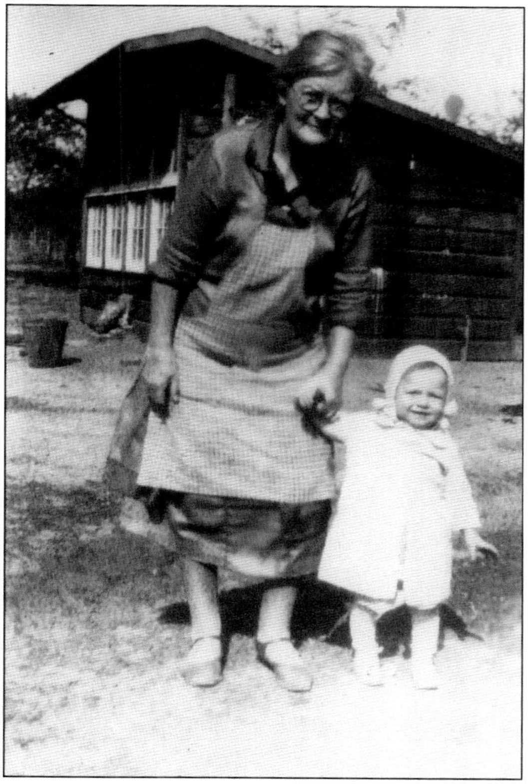

Minnie Gaskill is taking a walk with young Bill Lemmon on the Giberson farm.

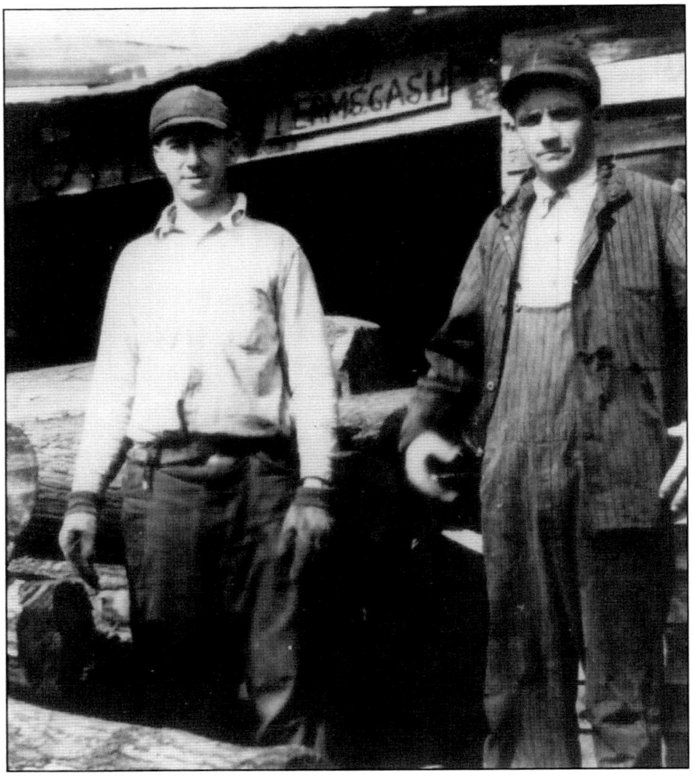

Lewis Giberson and Bill Lemmon work on the Giberson farm along Tuckerton Road. The photograph was taken in the 1930s.

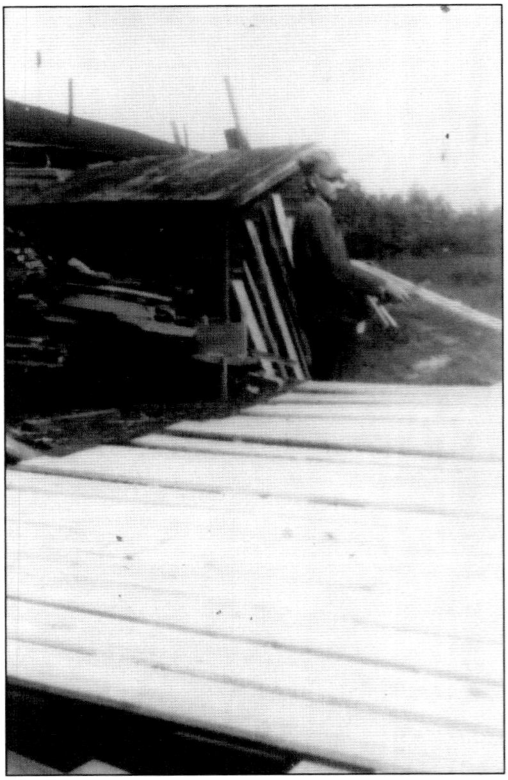

Lewis Giberson is seen working at the sawmill on the Giberson farm. It was once located along Tuckerton Road. Only the farmhouse has survived. The rest of the farm is now a housing development.

Seven

Education in Days Gone By

The era of the one-room schoolhouse began very early in what was to become Shamong Township. In 1805, a schoolhouse was erected by Upper Evesham Preparative Meeting (Quakers) on three acres of ground. It was located near the old sawmill of the reservation Native Americans. In those days, schools were not graded. There was only one teacher for upwards of 40 pupils ranging in age from 5 to 16. Most, if not all, of these one-room schoolhouses were heated by a potbellied stove using wood or coal for fuel. They were placed in the center of the room with smoke being vented outside by a chimney. The children got to school by either walking or by horse-drawn buggy or wagon. There was no indoor plumbing. Outhouses were the norm for students as well as the homes of their parents. The students, boys and girls alike, were required to carry drinking water, by bucket, from the nearest stream, or the nearest farmer's well. A single cup, dipped into the bucket, was used by all. The school day was from 9:00 a.m. to 4:00 p.m. with an hour off for lunch. The basics of reading, writing, and arithmetic were taught. The majority of the school population consisted of farm children. They rarely attended school beyond the elementary grades, as farm chores were the priority.

In the area of the original Shamong Township there were five one-room schoolhouses. Tabernacle No. 90 was in the center of the village by that name and was built in 1856. Free Soil School No. 91 was built in 1858. Hartford School No. 92 was built around 1805 and faced Wright's Lane (now known as Schoolhouse Lane). Union School No. 93 was located on Old Indian Mills Road and was built in 1859. Old Atsion School was built in 1872 in the village of Atsion. It was replaced in 1916. The Old Indian School was built in 1907 and replaced the Hartford School nearby. By 1922, all the one-room schoolhouses were closed and replaced by a centrally located school. Children were then bussed to school.

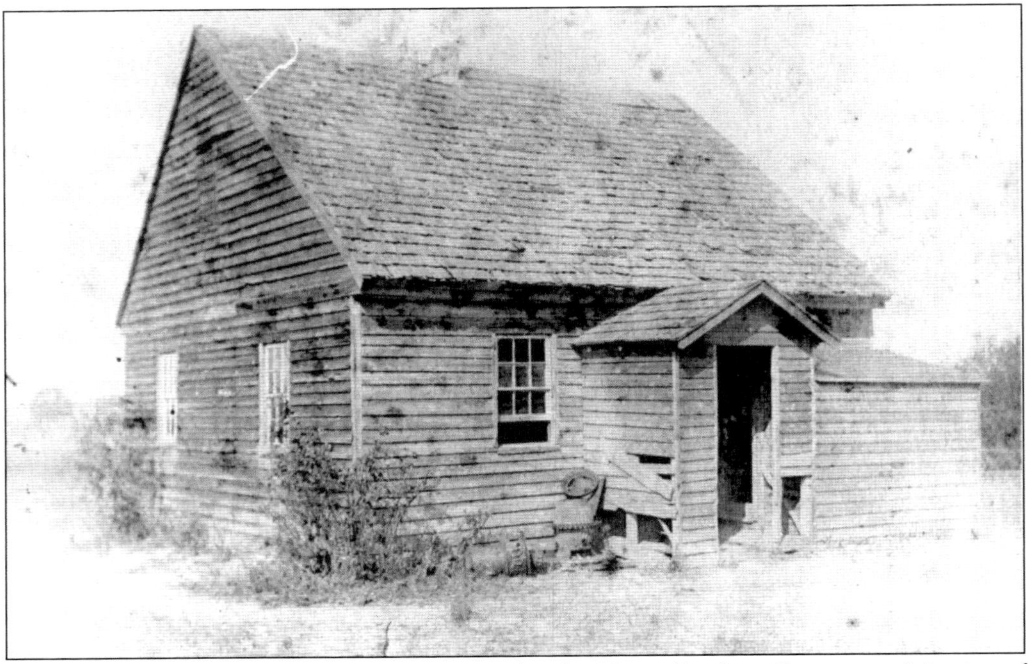

The Hartford School was erected around 1805 by the Upper Evesham Preparative Meeting of Medford. Three acres of land were provided. This may have served as a Quaker meetinghouse as well. A graveyard was adjoining the meeting/schoolhouse. This photograph was taken in the early 1900s, when the school was in the process of being replaced.

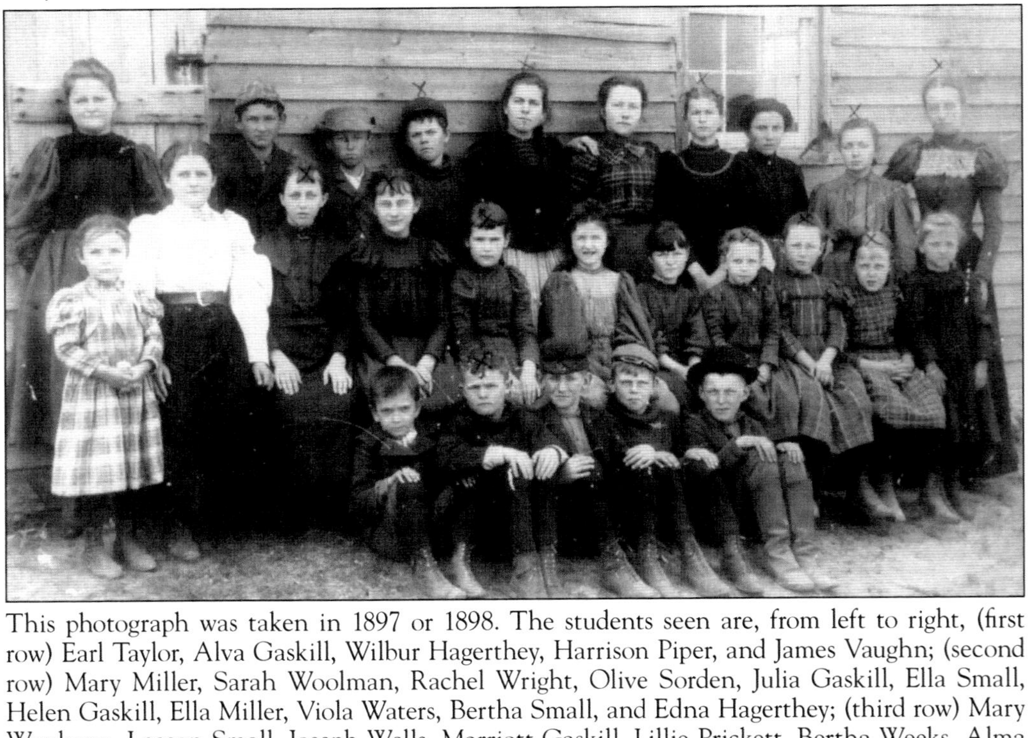

This photograph was taken in 1897 or 1898. The students seen are, from left to right, (first row) Earl Taylor, Alva Gaskill, Wilbur Hagerthey, Harrison Piper, and James Vaughn; (second row) Mary Miller, Sarah Woolman, Rachel Wright, Olive Sorden, Julia Gaskill, Ella Small, Helen Gaskill, Ella Miller, Viola Waters, Bertha Small, and Edna Hagerthey; (third row) Mary Woolman, Leeson Small, Joseph Wells, Marriott Gaskill, Lillie Prickett, Bertha Weeks, Alma Prickett, Laura Sorden, Emma Bozearth, and Sally Taylor (the teacher).

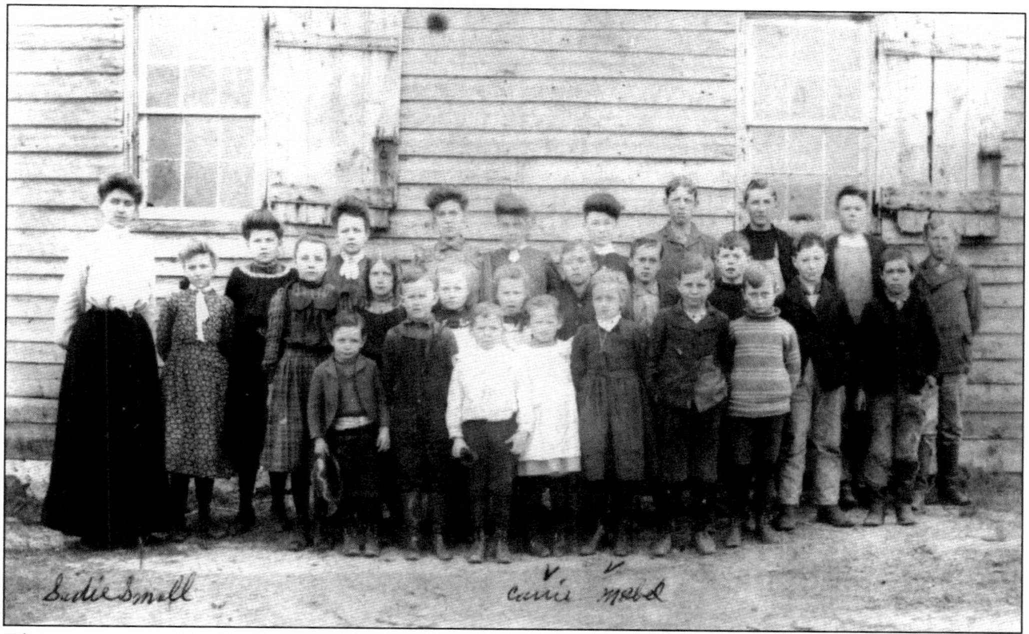

This scene outside the Hartford School building was taken in 1904. In no particular order are the teacher Sadie Small (far left), Edna Hagerthey, Lizzie Crain, Mary Miller, Nettie Miller, Clement Miller, Leah Prickett, Willie Miller, Eva Dellett, Laura Bozearth, Merle Prickett, Ruth Waters, Bertha Small, Carrie Patterson, Raymond Crain, Mabel Mingin, Viola Waters, Carlton Bozearth, Eddie Cline, Harry Miller, Fremont Gaskill, Harold Bozearth, Wilbur Hagerthey, Samuel Waters, Alva Gaskill, Norman Bozearth, and Asbury Cline.

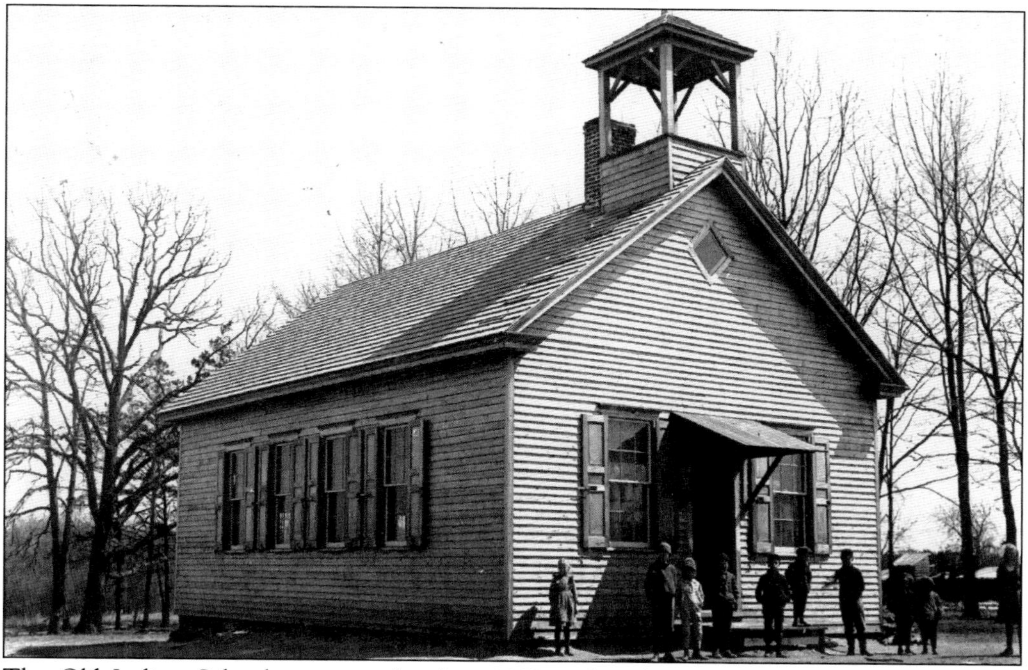

The Old Indian School was completed in 1907 and replaced the Hartford School, which was nearby. The Old Indian School faced Stokes Road, Route 541. It was later used as a cranberry packinghouse.

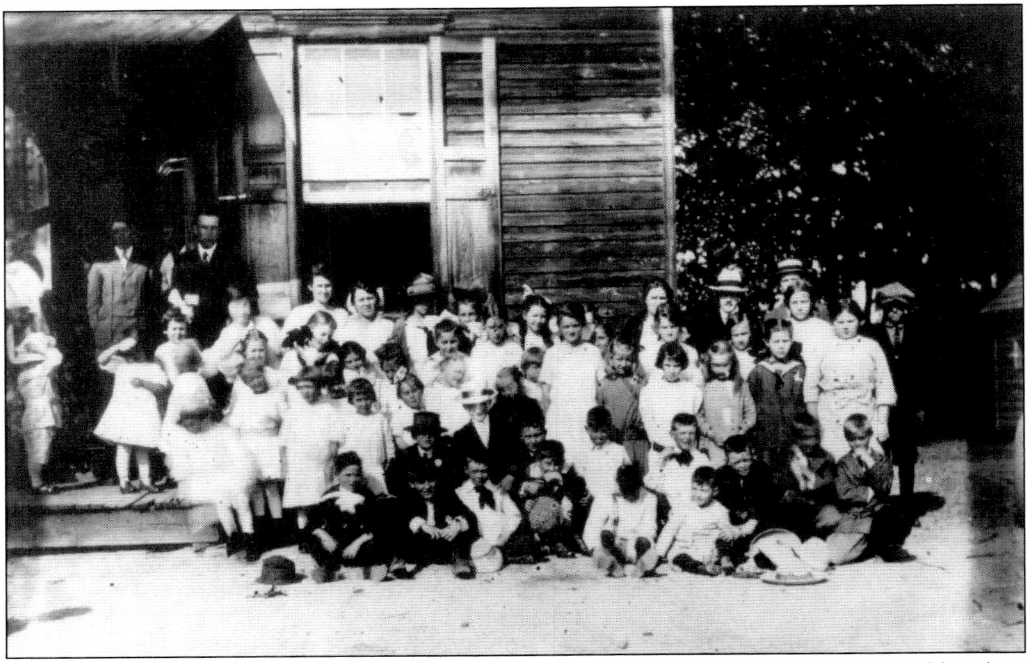

This photograph, taken about 1907, shows a group of students and parents at the Old Indian School. When the Indian Mills Elementary School opened in 1922, this school closed. It was sold to Lewis Shrider Sr. at an auction for $555. During Prohibition, it was rumored that the building was being used as a still and burned to the ground at that time.

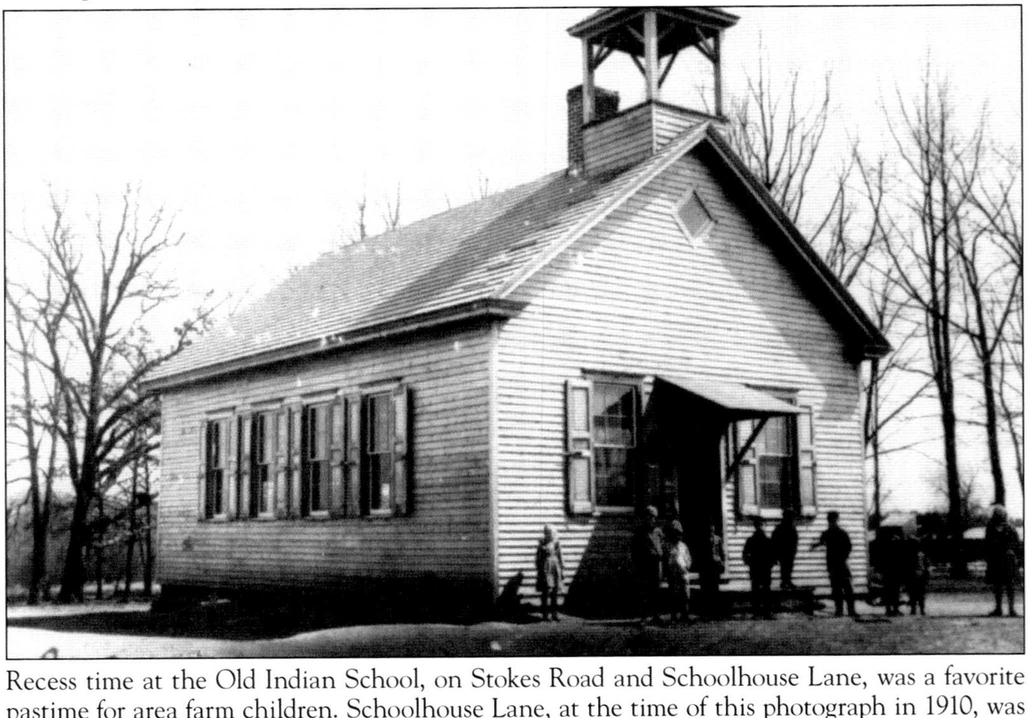

Recess time at the Old Indian School, on Stokes Road and Schoolhouse Lane, was a favorite pastime for area farm children. Schoolhouse Lane, at the time of this photograph in 1910, was known as Wright's Lane. Children from ages 5 to 14 attended here. In those days, most children did not attend school beyond this point.

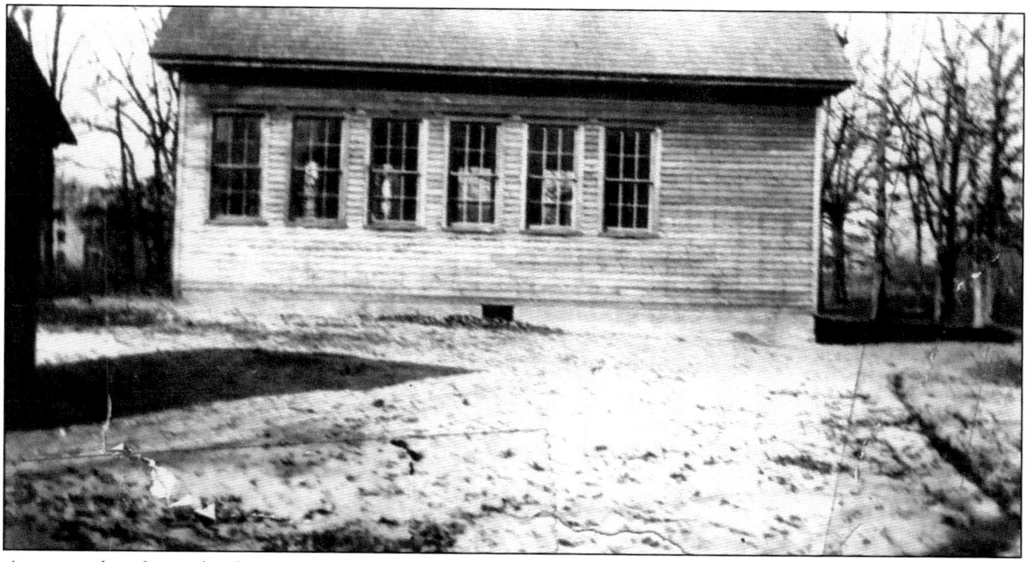

A new school was built at Atsion in 1916 at a cost of $1,000. This photograph was taken shortly after the new schoolhouse was completed. The first school built at Atsion in 1872 stood about 30 feet east of this school and can be seen on the far left of this picture. The new building has six windows on each side.

Free Soil School, sometimes known as the Baker School, was erected in 1858 on land donated by John Crain. He would later become the district school superintendant. In 1900, Hannah Taylor was the teacher at a salary of $35 per month. In 1922, the school was closed and then sold to Vernon Drayton for $633. He converted the old school into a private dwelling. In the 1970s, the Indian Mills Fire Company burned the home to the ground as part of a fire drill.

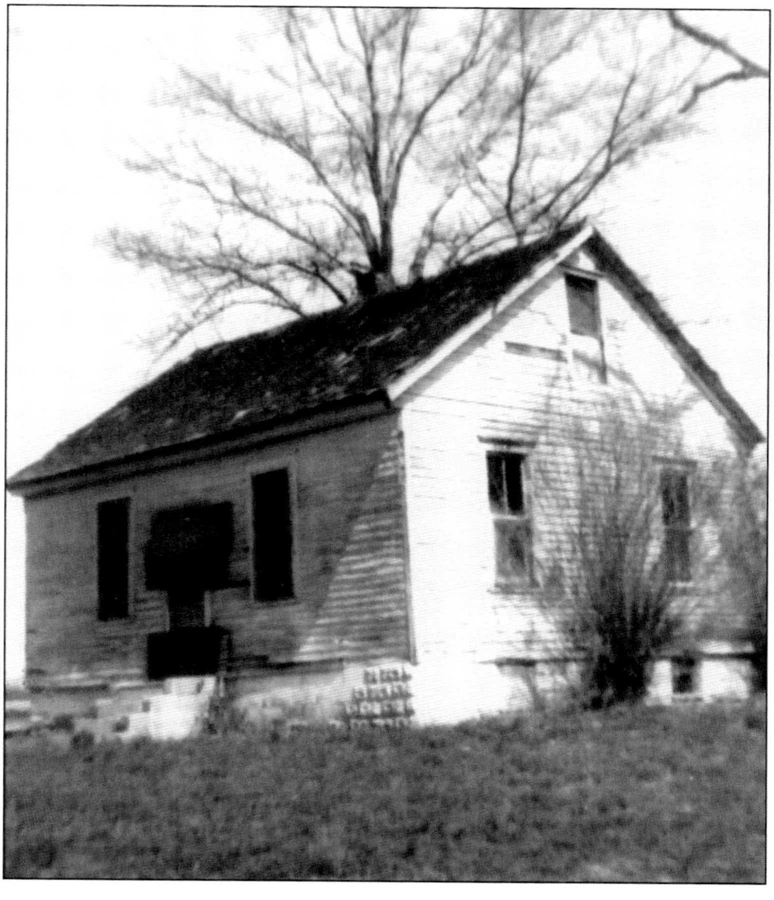

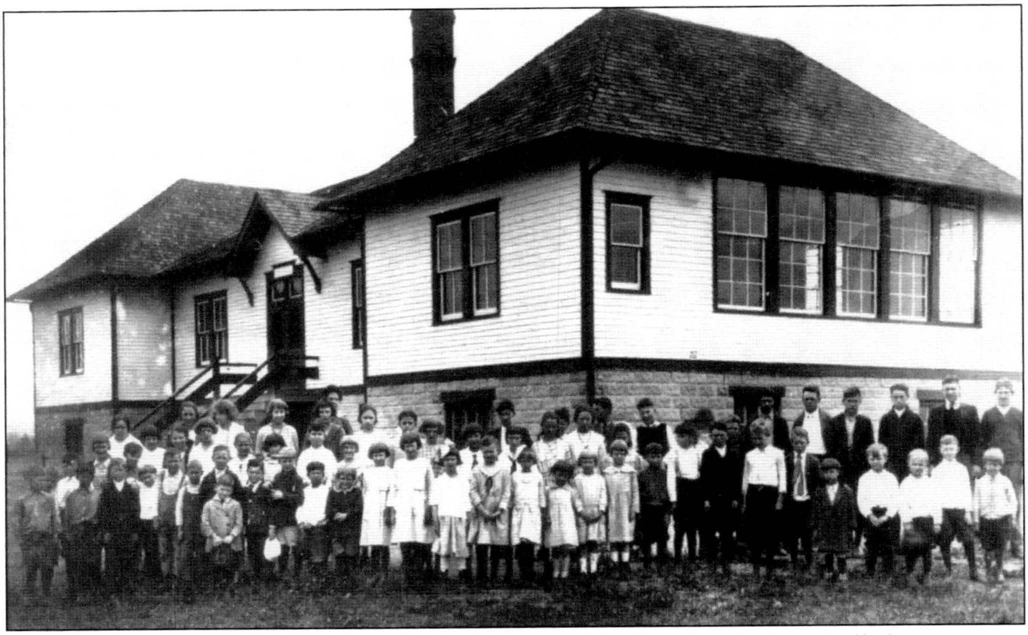

The Indian Mills Elementary School was built in 1922 after the closing of all the one-room schoolhouses in Shamong Township. It was of frame construction and contained three separate rooms. The school still stands today but has had brick veneer applied as well as numerous alterations and additions over the years. The author's three sons, Scott, Shawn, and Shane, attended here in the 1970s, from kindergarten through eighth grade.

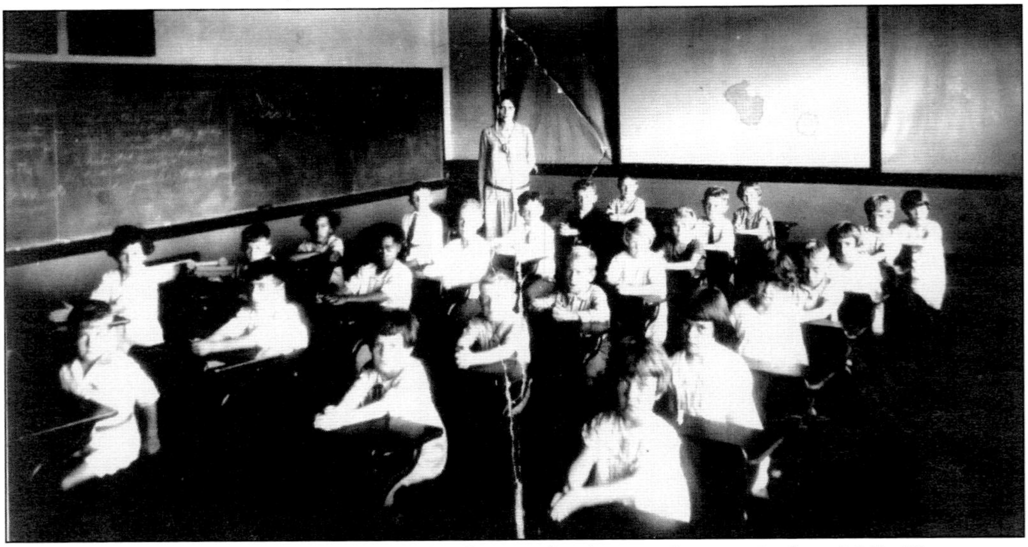

This scene is from 1926 and pictures the first-grade class at the new Indian Mills Elementary School, located on Indian Mills–Medford Road. Seen here, from front to back, are (first row, near blackboard) Hulda Patterson, Tom Drayton, Leona Still, and Arnold Mall; (second row) Milton Zimmerman, John Chappine, Evelyn Still, Tommy Gardner, Bernard Milley, Tony Tassone, and Sonny Crain; (third row) Helen Drayton, Elvin Wright, John Abrams, Vision Jennings, Nellie Vaughn, John Gatley, and Nola Adams; (fourth row) Helen Crain, Ruth Etheridge, Libby Abrams, Benjamin Toner, Anna Weeks, Lewis Vaughn, and Gladys Crain. Standing in the rear is the teacher, Verna Colton.

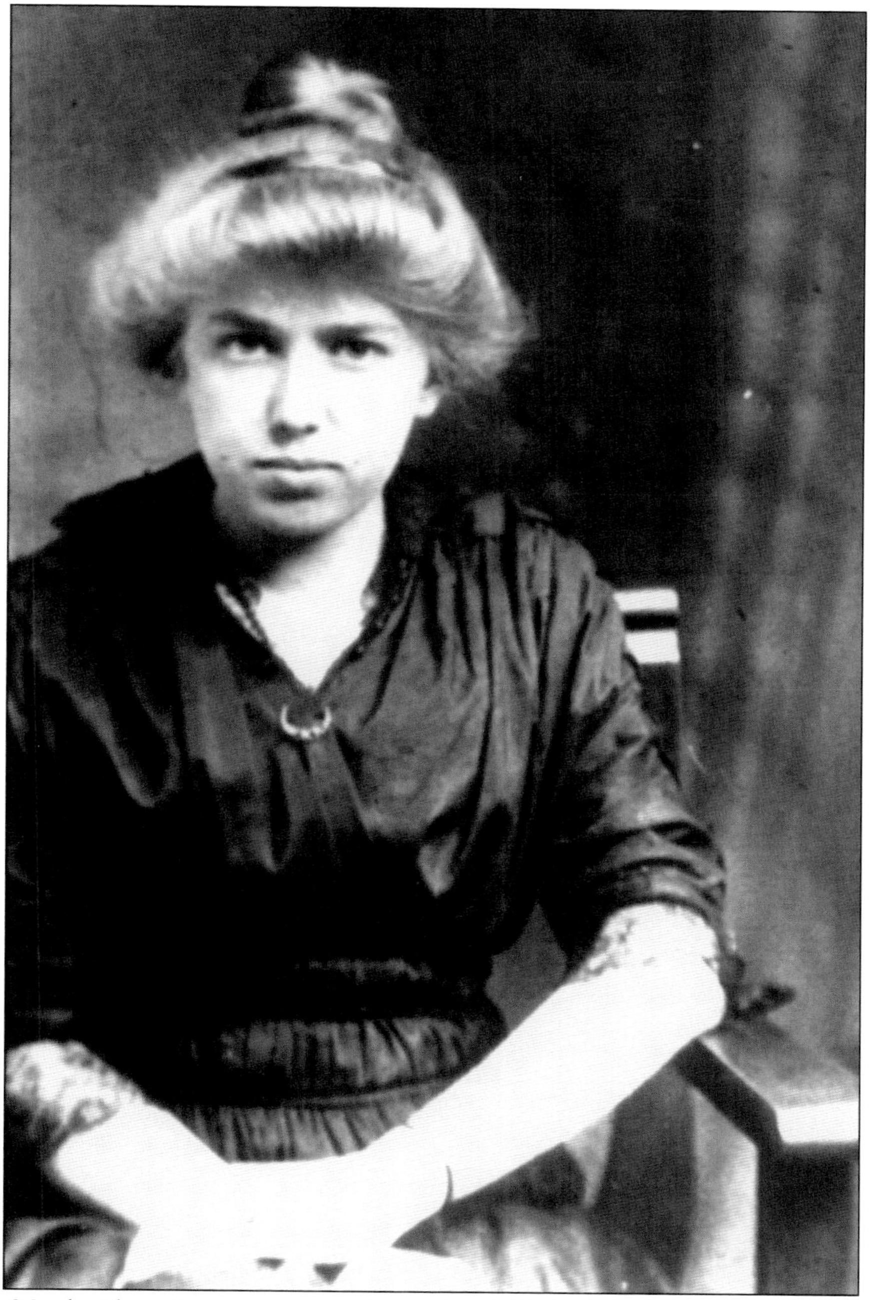

In 1915, Martha Sharp Paxson was a teacher at the Old Indian School. It was the first year that the Indian Mills schools were graded. During the week, she boarded with John and Sarah Crain, since she lived some 35 miles from the home of her parents in Yardville. She had come right out of high school to teach. When the weekend came, John would pick her up at school at 2:00 p.m. with a horse and wagon and take her on unpaved sand and gravel roads to get the train from Medford to Mount Holly. She would then taken a trolley from Mount Holly to Burlington and then go by train to Yardville, where her parents would meet her at the station to take her home by automobile. She finally arrived home at 7:00 p.m. A long journey to say the least, when today the entire trip can be made in 45 minutes.

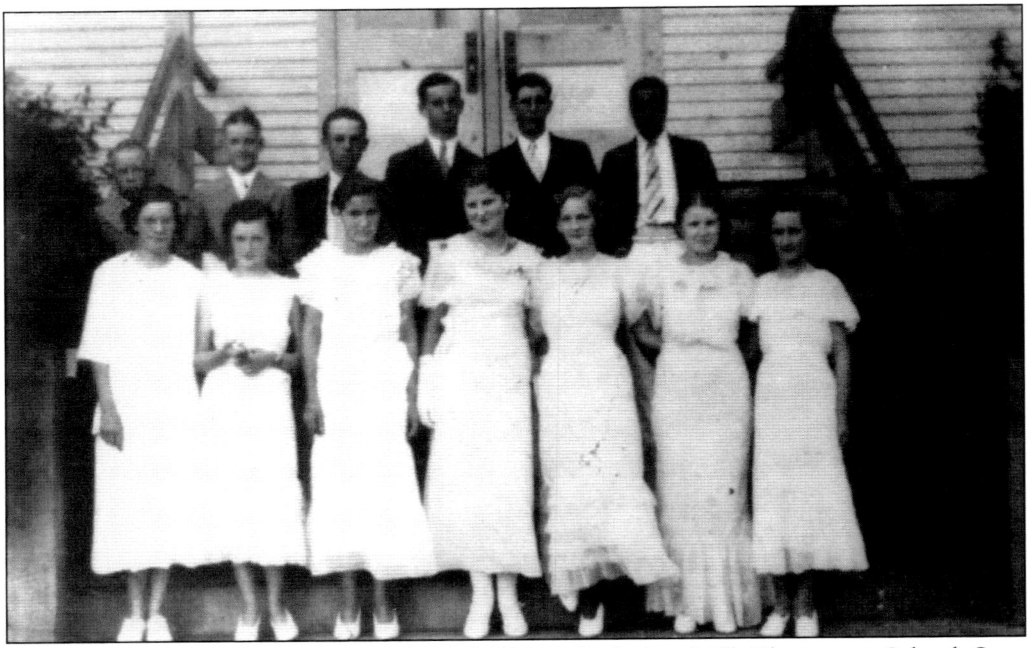

This is the eighth grade graduating class of 1934 at the Indian Mills Elementary School. Seen here, from left to right, are (first row) Gladys Crain, Ruth Etheridge, Elizabeth Abrams, Hulda Patterson, Ethel Roeder, Louise Wells, and Martha Mathis; (second row) Elmer Cowperthwaite, Milton Zimmerman, John Gatley, Frisco Abrams, Tom Russell, and Edward Still.

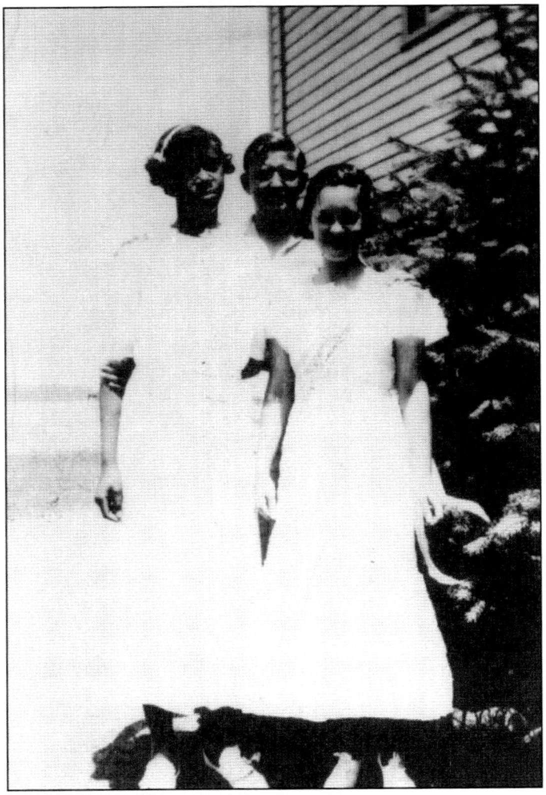

This photograph of three classmates at the graduation in 1936 shows Evelyn Still to the left, next Pickett Russell and Maud Russell.

Eight

The Deer-Hunting Clubs

In the early days, the practice of hunting deer was much different than it is today. The Native Americans hunted with a bow and arrow by stalking their prey. When they had sufficient hunters they would also set brush fires to flush out the deer. The Native Americans were conservative in hunting and only killed enough deer to satisfy their immediate needs. After the colonists came, the Native Americans aggressively hunted the deer in exchange for various goods traded by the colonists.

In modern times and prior to much in the way of regulation, deer were at the mercy of the hunter. In addition to firearms, they were also hunted with dogs and by the use of traps. By 1874, the native red wapiti deer of New Jersey had become so decimated that they neared extinction. Deer season was closed in Burlington and Ocean Counties for five years. In 1881, the season closed throughout the entire state for three years. It closed again in 1899 and did not reopen until 1909.

Restocking had begun in 1904 by importing the now familiar Virginia white-tailed deer. Regulations were put in place that only 12-gauge shotguns and buckshot were permitted to be used. The normal firearm deer season would begin the first full week of every December and run from Monday through Saturday. Only antlered deer with horns at least three inches in length could be taken. With positive and controlled hunting the deer herd in New Jersey has flourished.

Most organized deer-hunting clubs maintain their own clubhouses. Members can number anywhere from 20 to 60. To harvest deer, the clubs employ what is known as the deer drive. It consists of two teams. The members of one group are the "drivers" and the others are "standers." Every drive usually begins with the drivers yelling, "Yo Buck," and driving the deer ahead of them. Other drivers make noise with whatever is available, including pots, pans, and whistles. They literally create a wall of noise to drive the deer toward the standers. Then shots are fired.

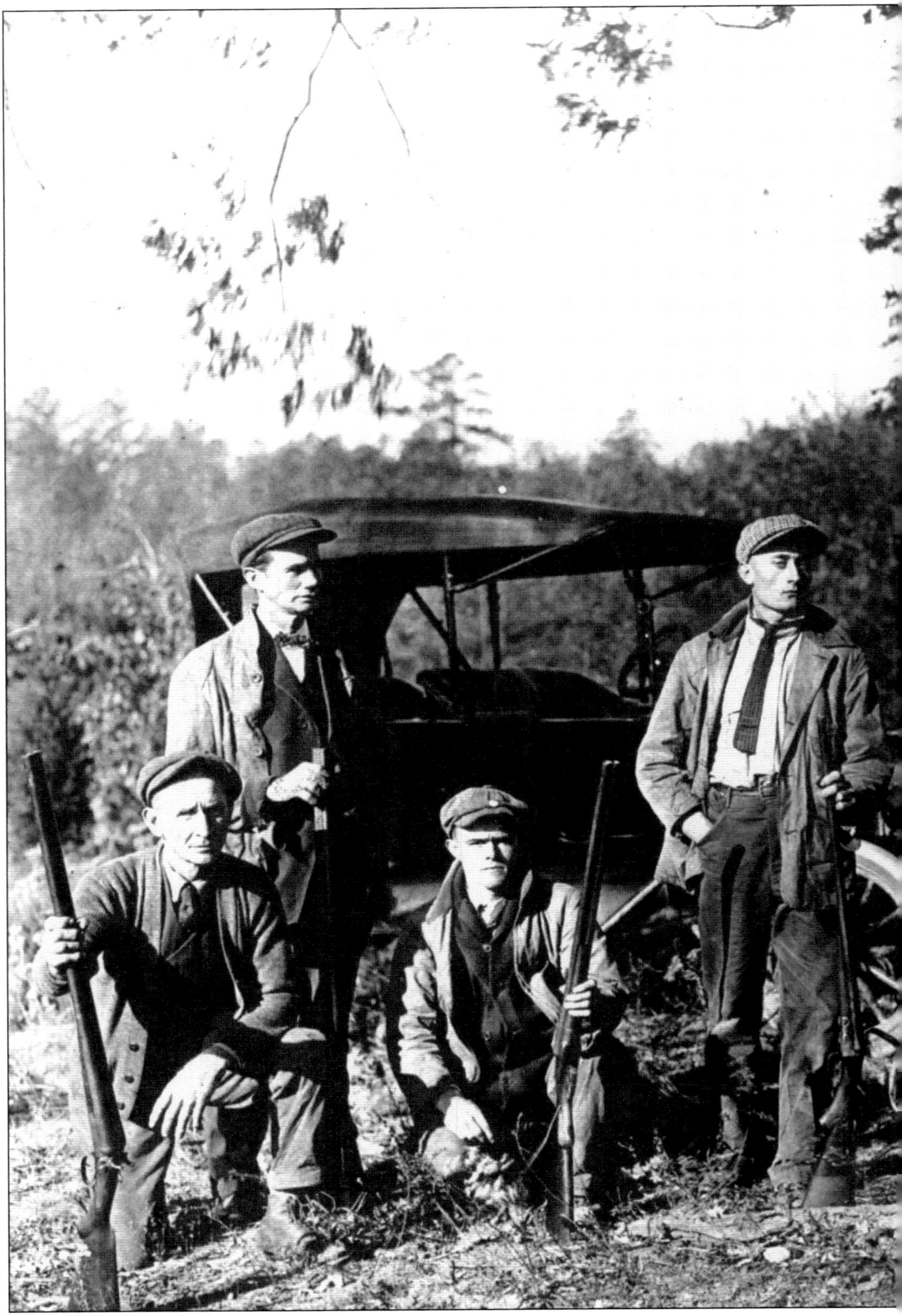

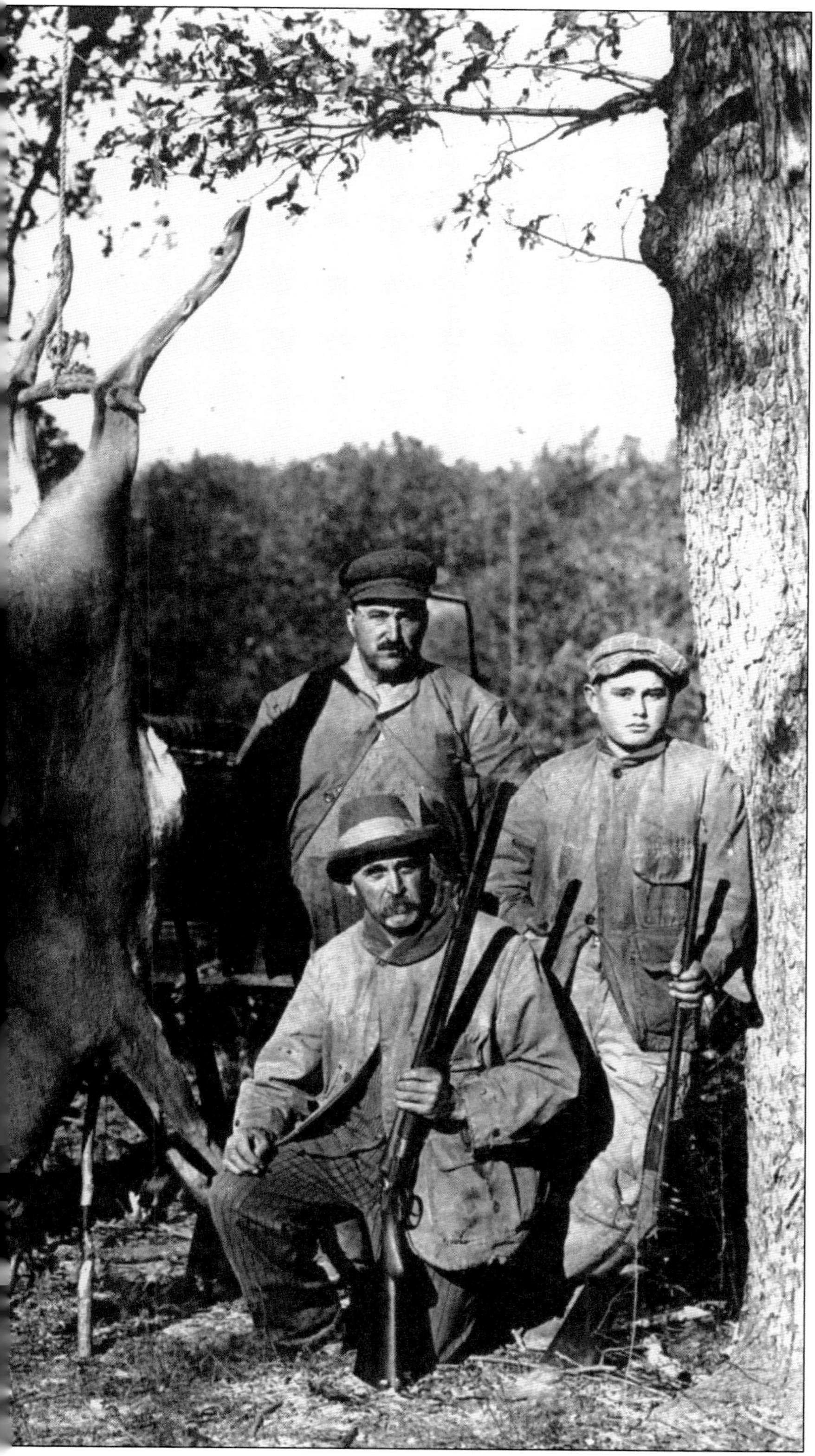

Shown here is a group of family and friends in about 1920. From left to right are John "Bull" Miller, John Brown, Alva "Duff" Gaskill, Harold Bozearth (who killed the eight-point deer), Alfred Bozearth (kneeling and father of Harold), Charles Bozearth (brother to Alfred), and Walter Bozearth (son of Charles). Harold was a lifelong resident of Shamong Township. He was born in January 1897 and died in January 1978 at age 81. He was the Shamong Township clerk for 50 years. He lies buried in the Baptist cemetery in Marlton.

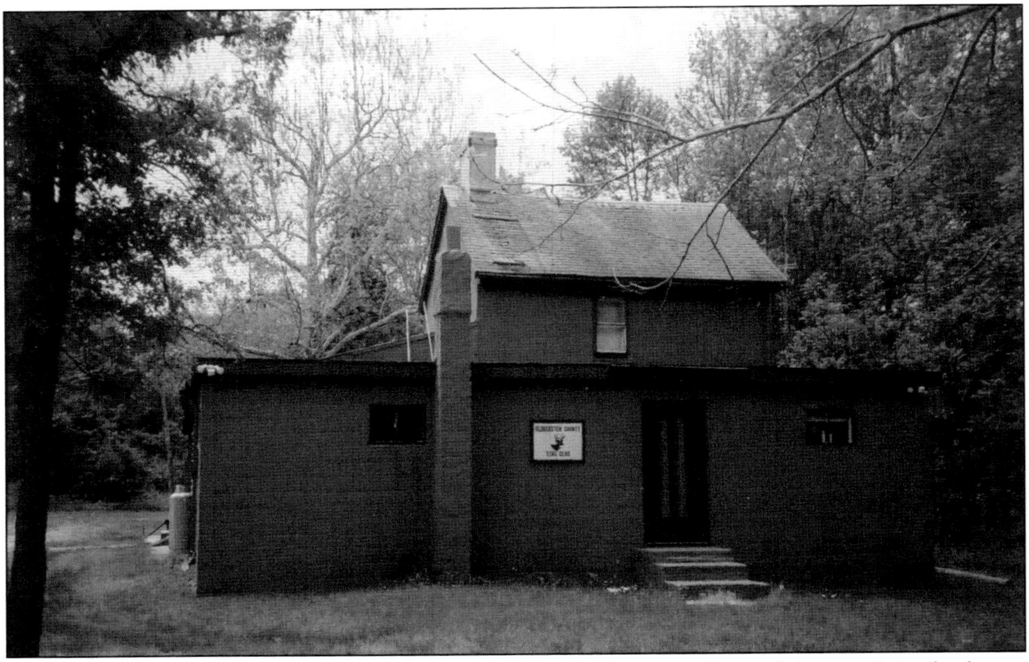

This building is located on Quaker Bridge Road in the former village of Atsion. It is the home of the Gloucester County Stag Club. It was once the home of George and Irene Hyland. Both had worked in the cotton mill owned by Maurice Raleigh. Their daughter Anna Hyland later married George Cavileer, and they had a luncheonette at Dutchtown just south on Route 206.

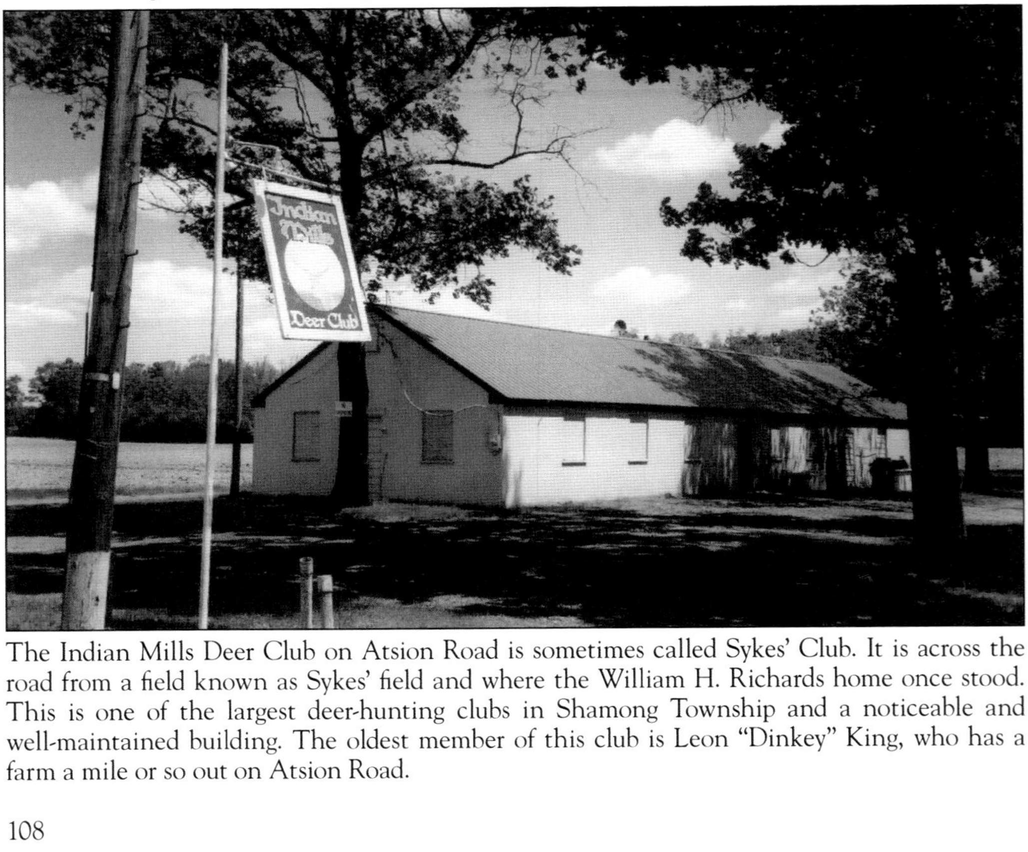

The Indian Mills Deer Club on Atsion Road is sometimes called Sykes' Club. It is across the road from a field known as Sykes' field and where the William H. Richards home once stood. This is one of the largest deer-hunting clubs in Shamong Township and a noticeable and well-maintained building. The oldest member of this club is Leon "Dinkey" King, who has a farm a mile or so out on Atsion Road.

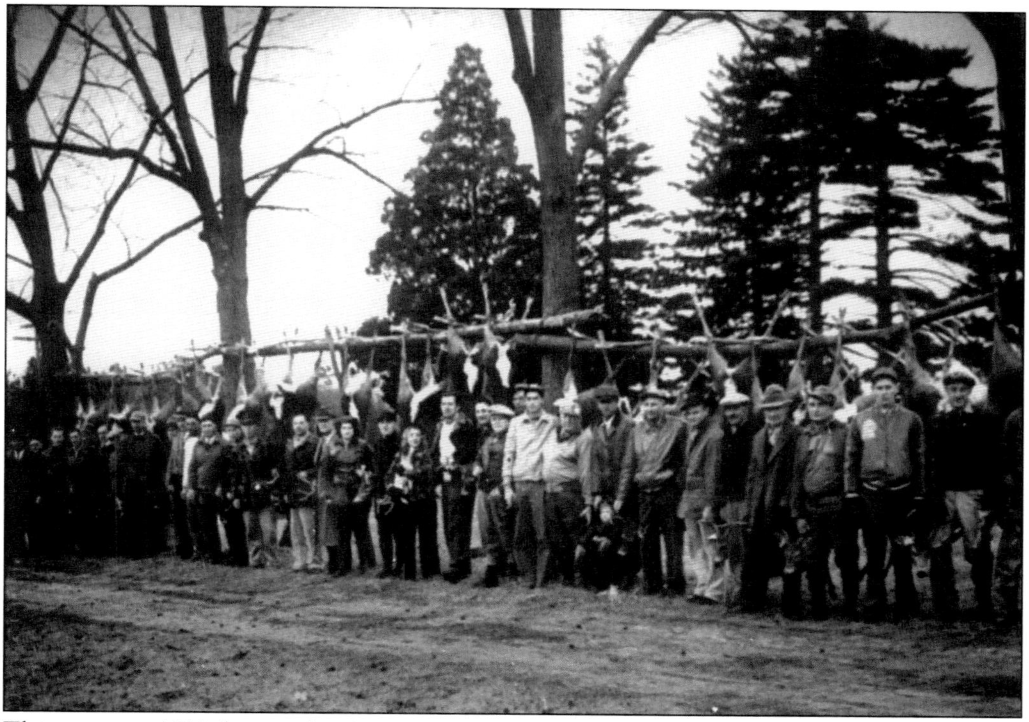

This scene in 1939 depicts the Atsion Deer Club. Displayed are 27 antlered deer taken by the club. This is certainly a record that has probably never been broken. This club is no longer in existence, but many of the members may have been absorbed by other clubs in the area.

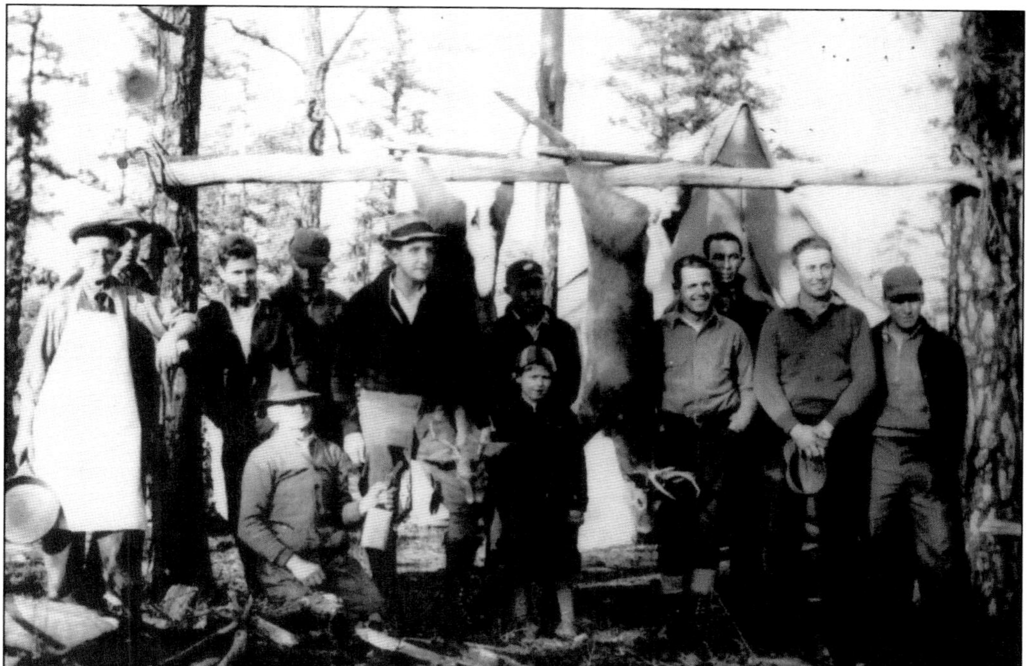

This group of Indian Mills hunters includes Pemberton Griscom, Sam Giberson, Joe Redrowe, and Elton Flickner in the 1930s. This scene is in Mount Laurel at a friend's property.

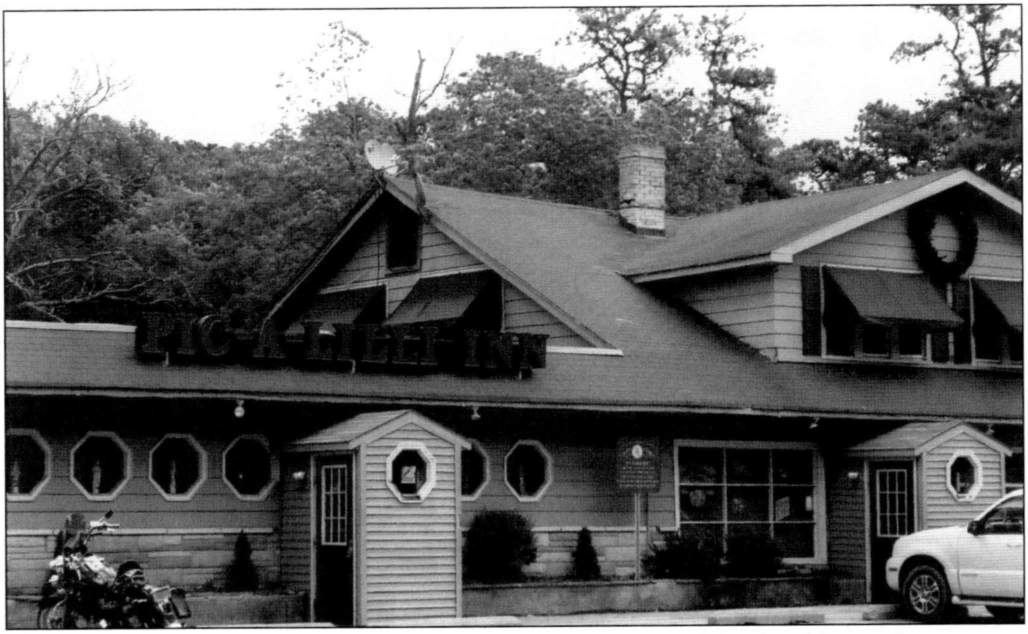

Four generations of the Russell Family have owned and operated this local bar and restaurant. It was so named, Pic-a-Lilli Inn, for the original founders, Pickett and Lillian Russell. It is a busy establishment all during the year but especially during deer season, when many of the hunters come by at night to check to see how the other clubs are doing in the area. A tote board has been kept in years past to record how many deer have been killed by each club.

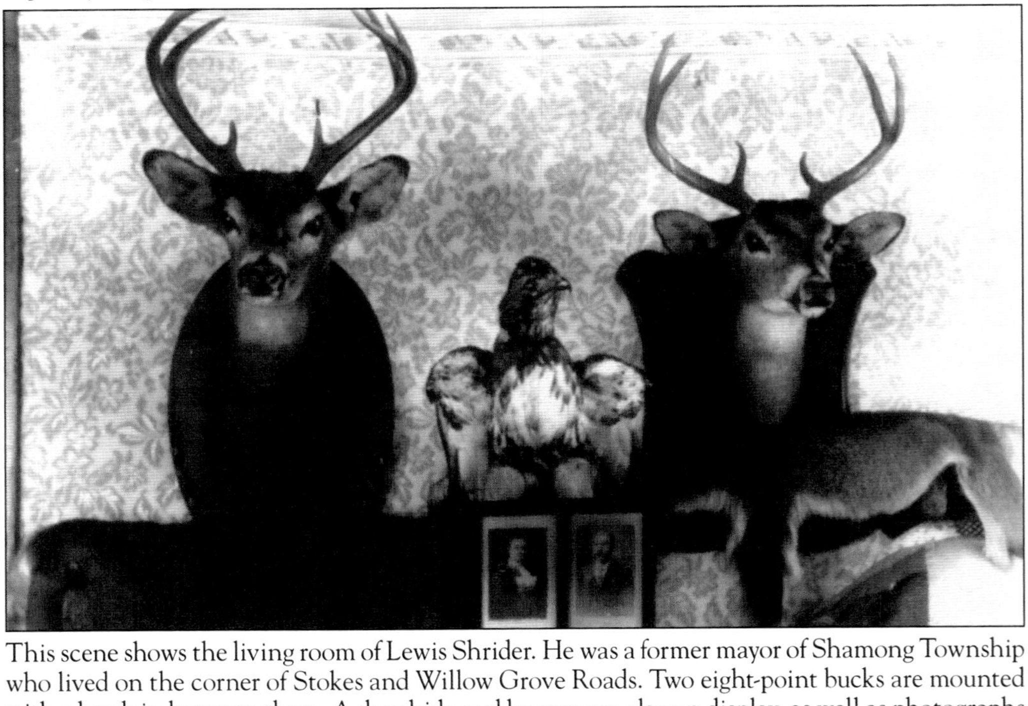

This scene shows the living room of Lewis Shrider. He was a former mayor of Shamong Township who lived on the corner of Stokes and Willow Grove Roads. Two eight-point bucks are mounted with a hawk in between them. A deer hide and hooves are also on display, as well as photographs of his parents. Deer hunting is in the blood of many Shamong residents. It is a way of life in the Pinelands.

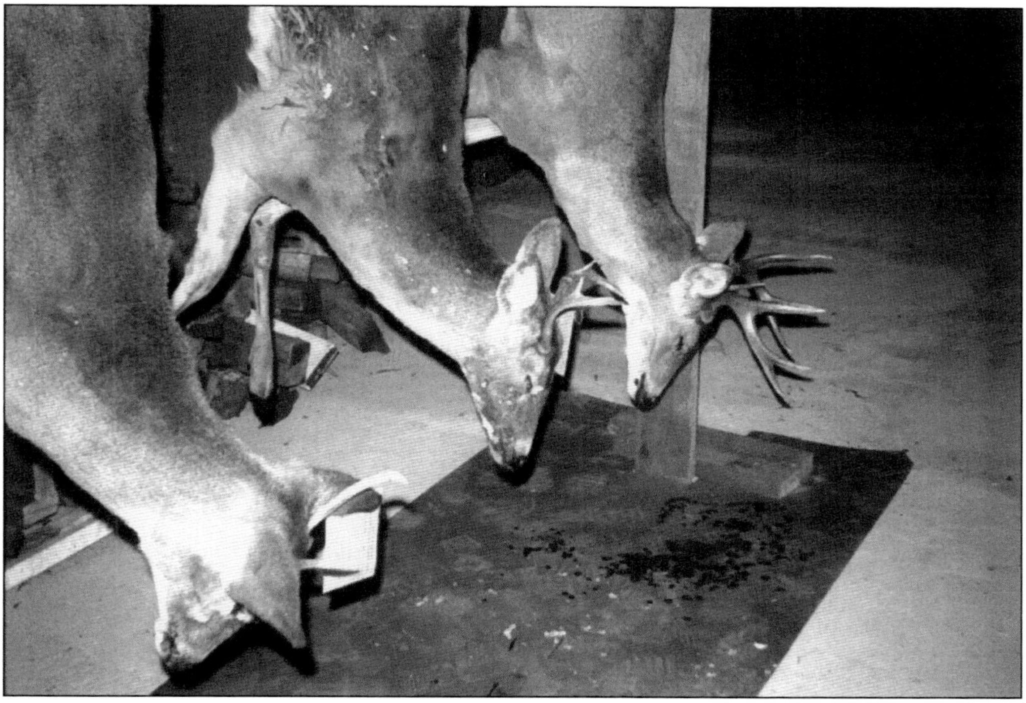

It is common practice for the many clubs in the area to hang the day's kill. The photograph above shows a spike buck, next a Y buck, and last an eight pointer. The photograph below depicts two spike bucks, a Y buck, and an eight pointer. A Y buck is determined by each antler having two tines. A spike buck is one that has just a single tine or point on each side, usually only three or four inches in length. An eight pointer is one that has four tines on each side.

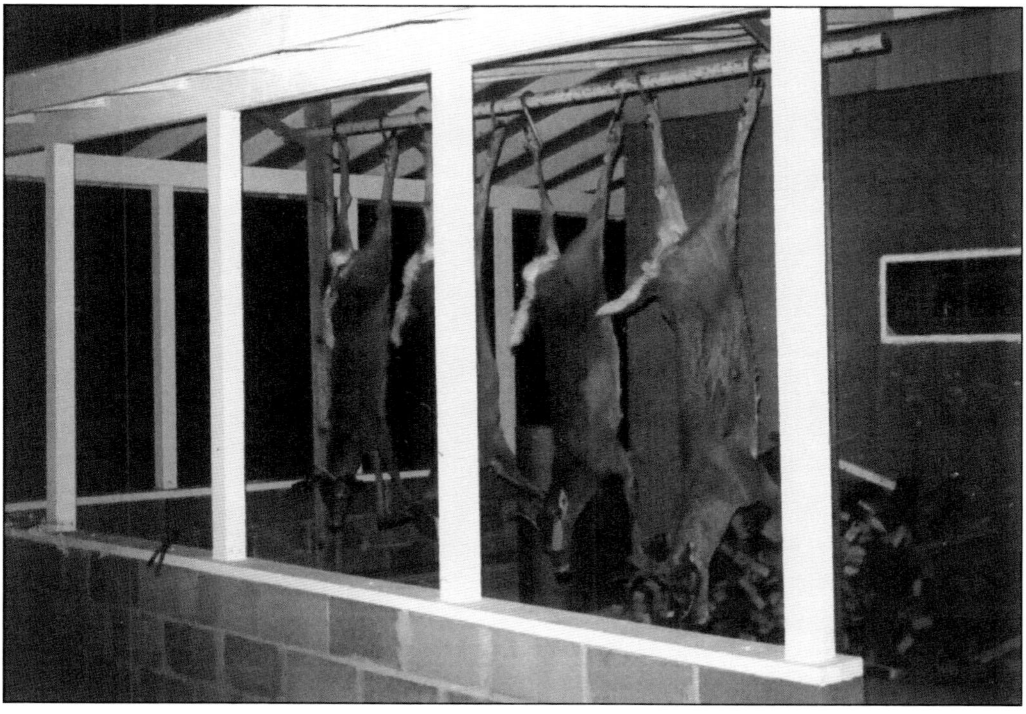

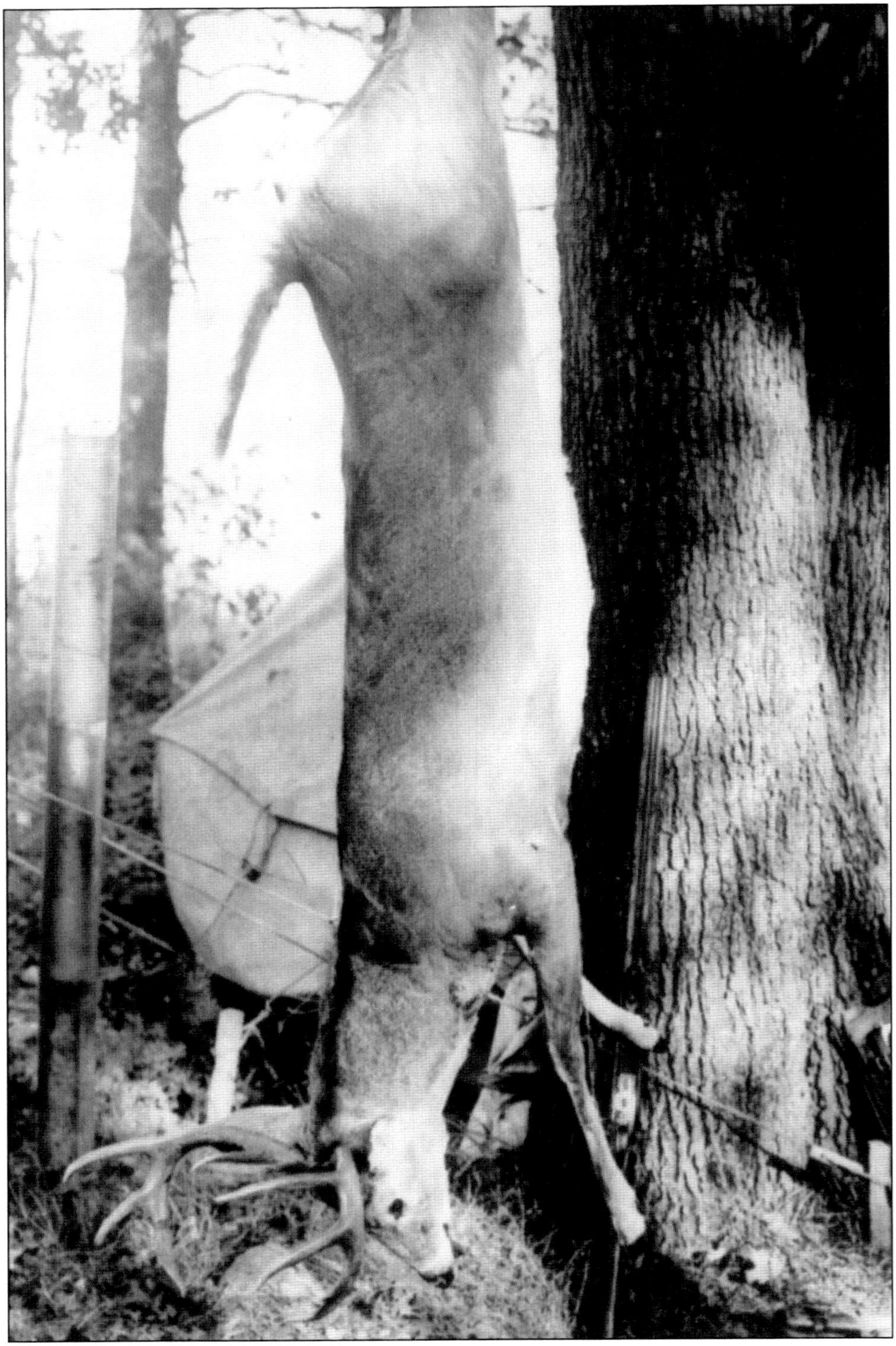

This is the first legal deer killed in Shamong Township in 1909. Hunting deer in New Jersey was prohibited in 1899 due to a drastic reduction in the deer herd throughout the state. It was finally reopened in 1909, as the herd had been replenished to once again allow the hunting of antlered deer.

Nine

Early Taverns

In the latter half of the 18th century, taverns were in record numbers throughout Burlington County. The area of Shamong Township was no exception. Several major stagecoach routes traversed the area. The Great Road to Little Egg Harbor (Tuckerton), which is now partly called Carranza Road, had several taverns along its route through the wilderness. The Fox Chase Tavern opened in 1800. It was operated by William Fox and later by Hosea Moore. It was located at the current entrance to Seneca High School. Next came Kemble's Inn, located in the village of Tabernacle. It was built in 1850, toward the end of the stagecoach era. The inn at Hampton Gate was established in 1812 by David Cavileer. It was near the Hampton Ironworks and frequented by the workers there. The Turckerton Stage Road had the Half Moon and Seven Stars Tavern established by John King in 1800. It was located at a small settlement known as Flyatt. Today it is just a lonely intersection. A short distance away stood Small's Tavern and Hotel, erected in 1830. On Atsion Road once stood John Piper's Sign of the Buck, erected in 1791. This later was sold and became Josiah Smith's Tavern. The Indian King Tavern of Ephraim Cline opened in 1798. It was very near the Atsion Ironworks and a favorite of the workers there. Atsion Road was the main stage road from Mount Holly, through Medford, Atsion, and then on through the Pinelands to Tuckerton. Just a short distance west of Clines was where the Philadelphia Stage Road joined Atsion Road.

There was no doubt there were many other so-called "jug taverns" along the major stage routes, where lodging, refreshments, and water for the horses could be obtained. A botanist named John Torrey wrote a letter to a friend, Zachariah Collins, in 1818. William Cooper was his traveling companion. He describes what a harrowing experience he had in traveling through the Pine Barrens. He writes, "some places we put up at were not fit for an Arab. With difficulty we persuaded them to take us in."

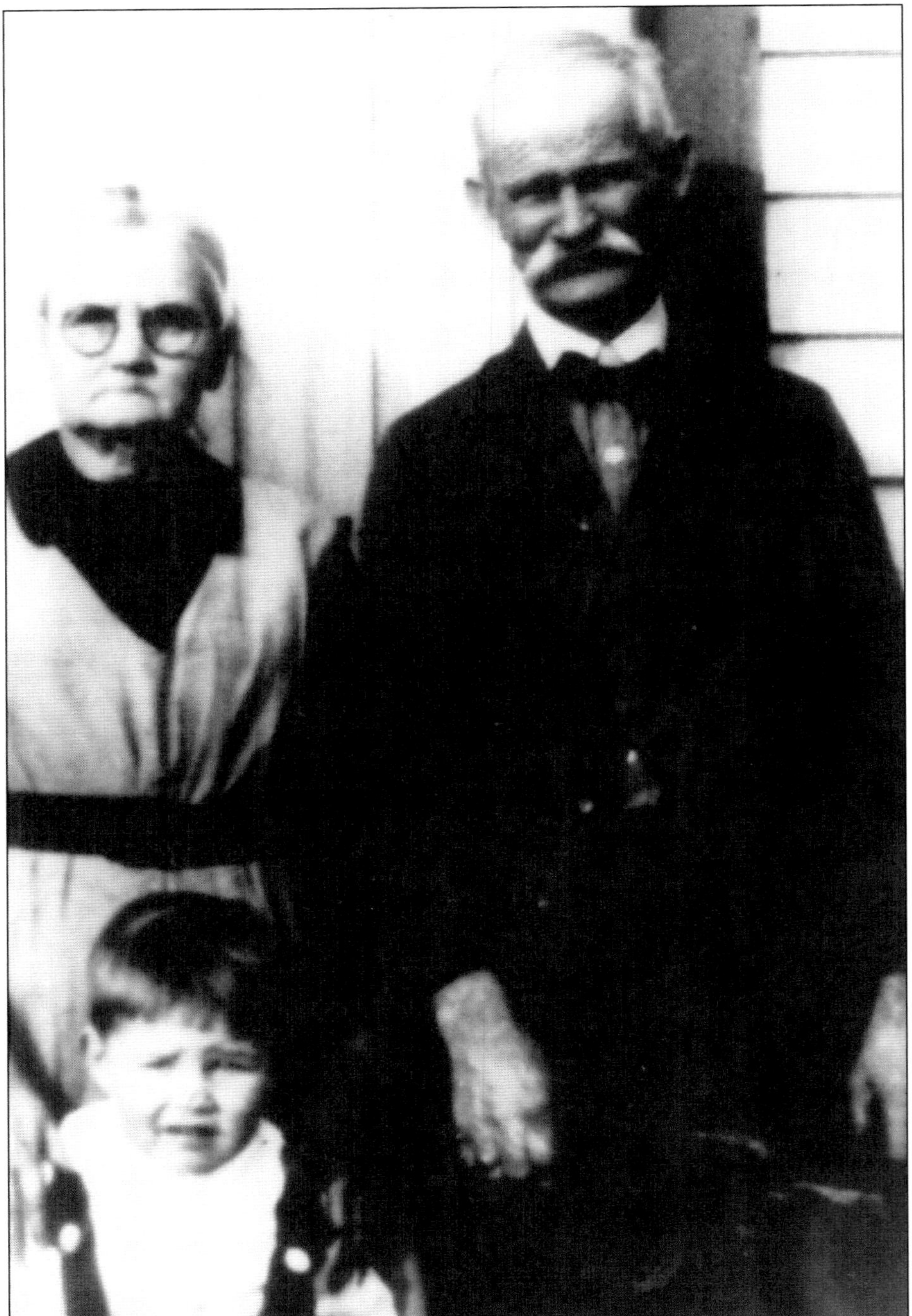

What had been known as Small's Tavern and Hotel for the better part of a century became known as Baker's Hotel. It was purchased by a Medford couple, George and Hannah Baker, shown above. Their grandson Fred also appears in the photograph, taken in 1920. They were the proprietors of the old hotel from 1904 until 1922. During that time they raised a family of five children, named Herbert, Edward, Rose, Fred, and Bertha. The Bakers were very active in their church, and as such, church activities were also held at the old hotel. At that time, the bar remained closed.

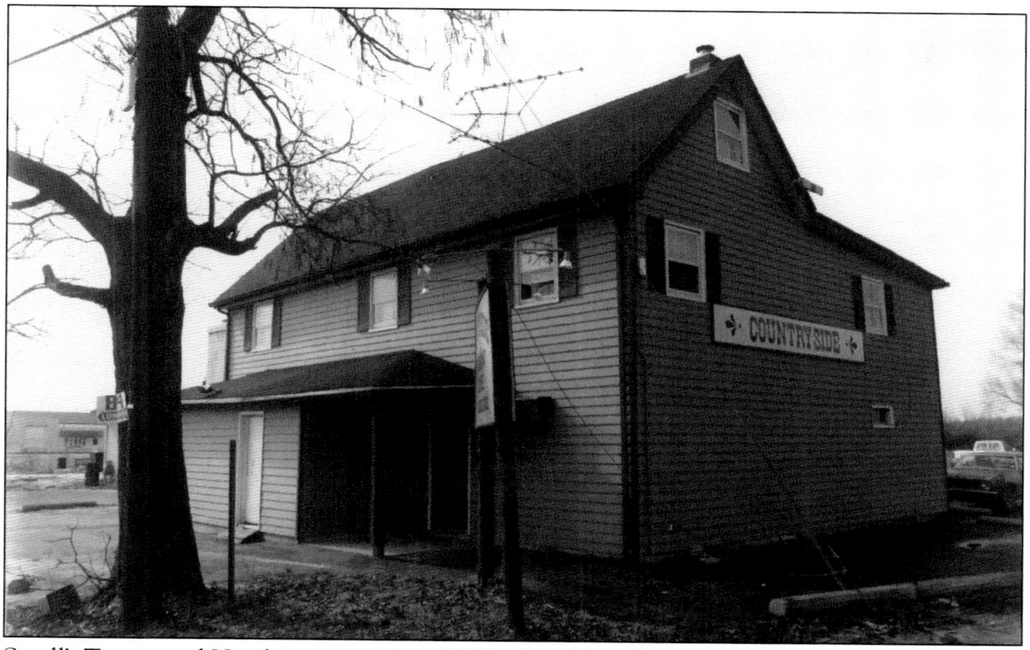

Small's Tavern and Hotel was erected in 1830 by Israel Small. It was simply referred to as Smalls. It was located just west of what had been the boundary of the Brotherton Reservation. It stood at the intersection of the old road from Red Lion to Josiah Smith's, now known as Oak Shade Road. It intersected with the Road to the Indian Town, also known as the Murphy Road, or Road to Bedford Mills. Now it is known as Medford–Indian Mills Road. The old hotel and tavern had once had local township meetings held there, as well as various church activities. It was an active gathering place for township residents. For many years, it was also known as the Tumble Inn, when owned by Charles and Mamie Jennings from 1930 until the 1960s. Recent owners decided to remodel the old tavern and discovered irreparable termite damage. A new restaurant and tavern has taken the place of this venerable spot so dear to many in Shamong Township.

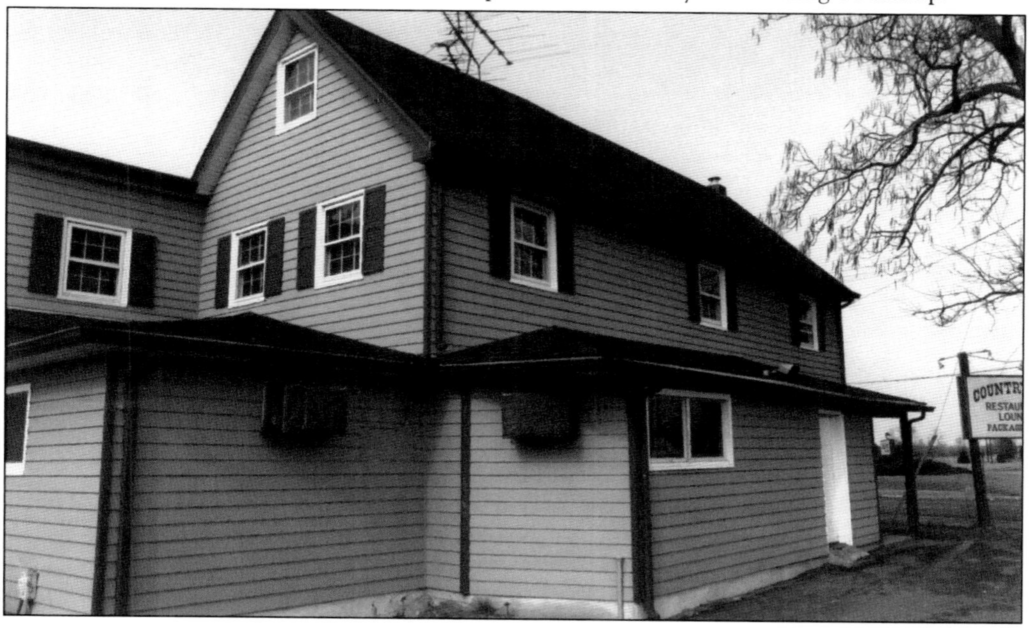

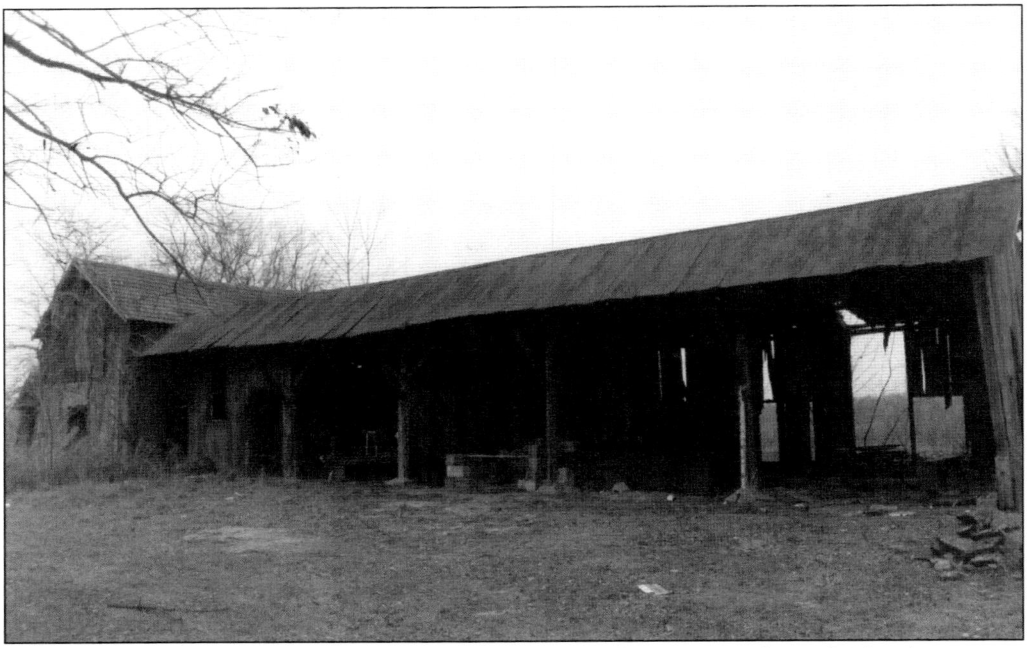

These are the carriage sheds that once stood behind Small's Tavern and Hotel. They have given way to modern times and were torn down many years ago. The photograph was taken in 1960. The area is now part of the restaurant parking lot.

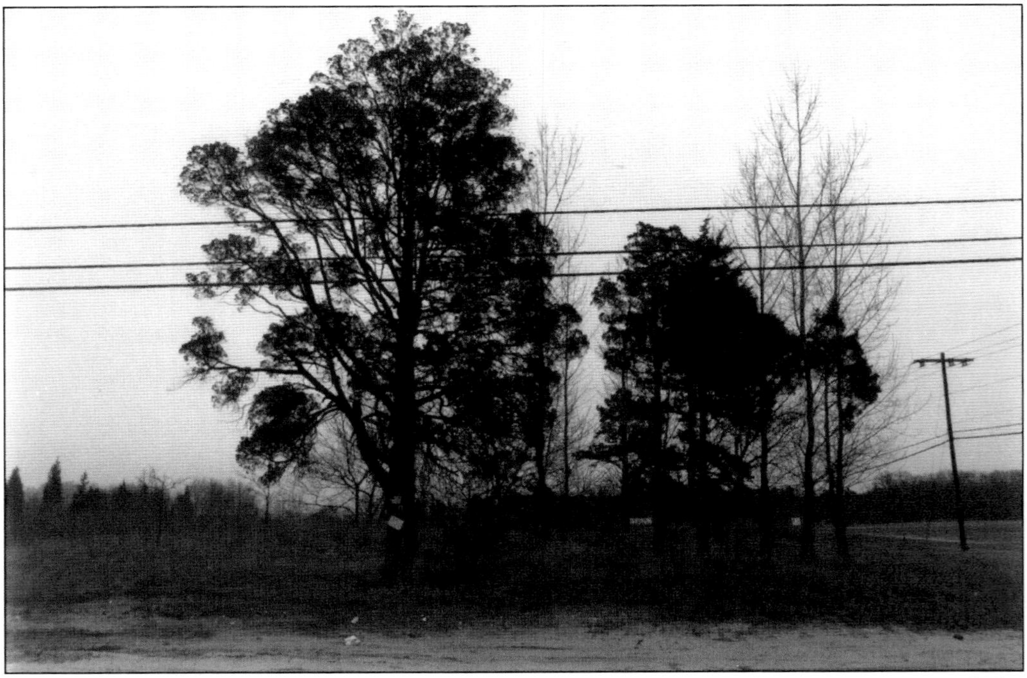

At the intersection of this lonely spot, which is marked by red cedar trees, once stood the Half Moon and Seven Stars Tavern. It was erected by John King in 1800. The property once contained a large frame tavern house, barn, stable, wagon house, and horse sheds on 70 acres of land. Some 12 acres of land had an apple orchard and meadow all under cedar fencing. The immediate area has always been known as Flyatt, Fliatum, or Fly-at.

An excavation of this once-important tavern site was conducted by Indian Mills Historical Society members Don Catts, Bob Jones (now deceased), and the author. Although permission had been granted by the owner, Jerome Jennings, it was later rescinded due to fear of injuries at this busy intersection. During the limited excavation, remains of part of the original *c.* 1800 foundation were uncovered. It was made of native Jersey sandstone. It lay on a hard-packed clay floor of the cellar. Due to the limited time of this excavation, the exact extent of the foundation could not be determined. Future exploration of this site may provide additional important information. There is no doubt that the destruction of this tavern site was due to a severe fire in 1863.

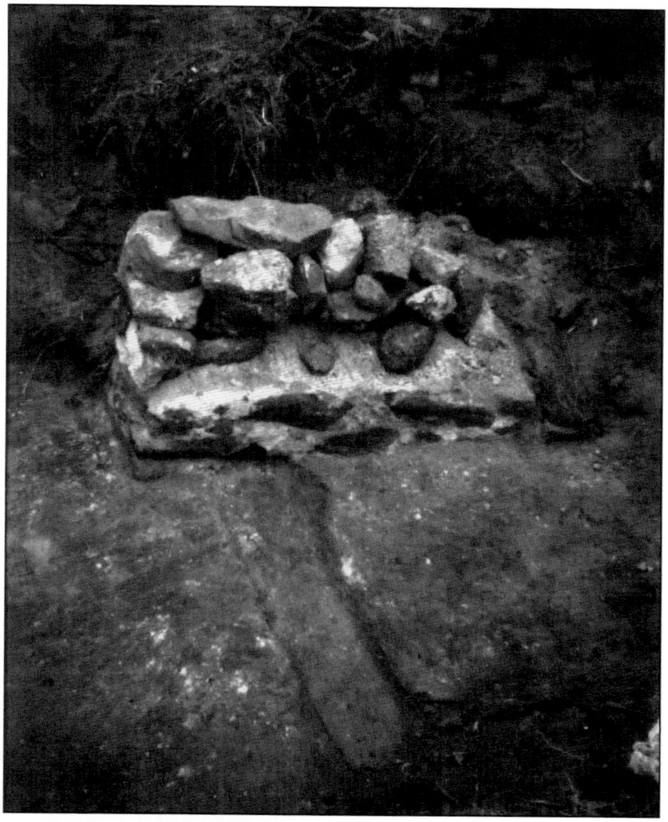

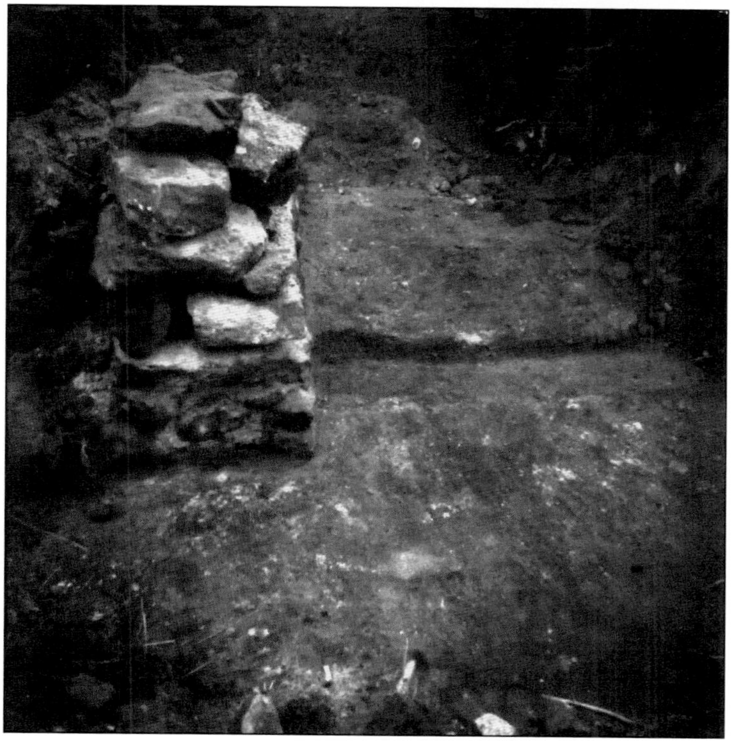

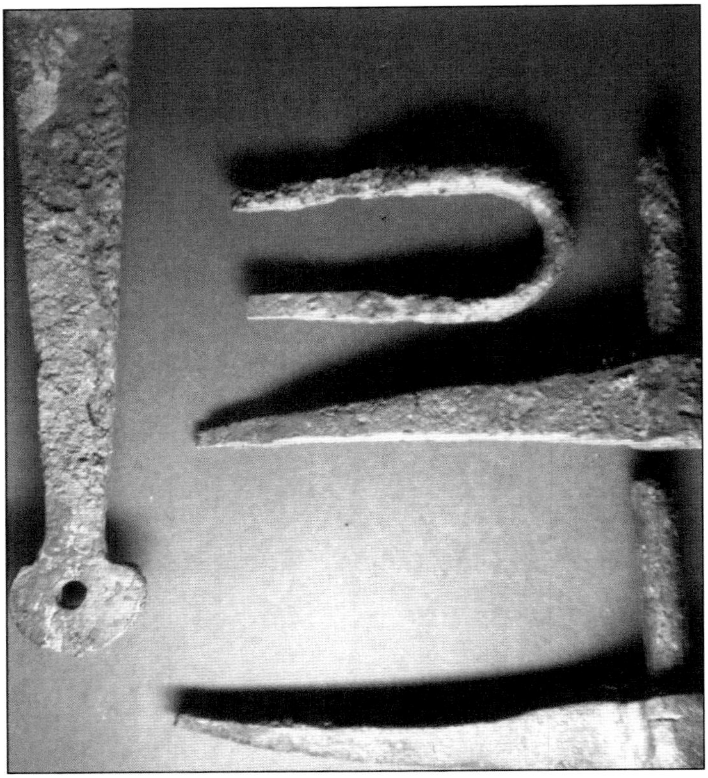

During the September 1975 excavations there were numerous artifacts uncovered that included hand-forged strap hinges, slipware fragments, buttons, an 1803 one-cent piece, 1862 and 1863 Indian-head pennies, many nails and bottle fragments, and other items. These artifacts are on display in showcases owned by the Indian Mills Historical Society inside the courtroom of the Shamong Township municipal building.

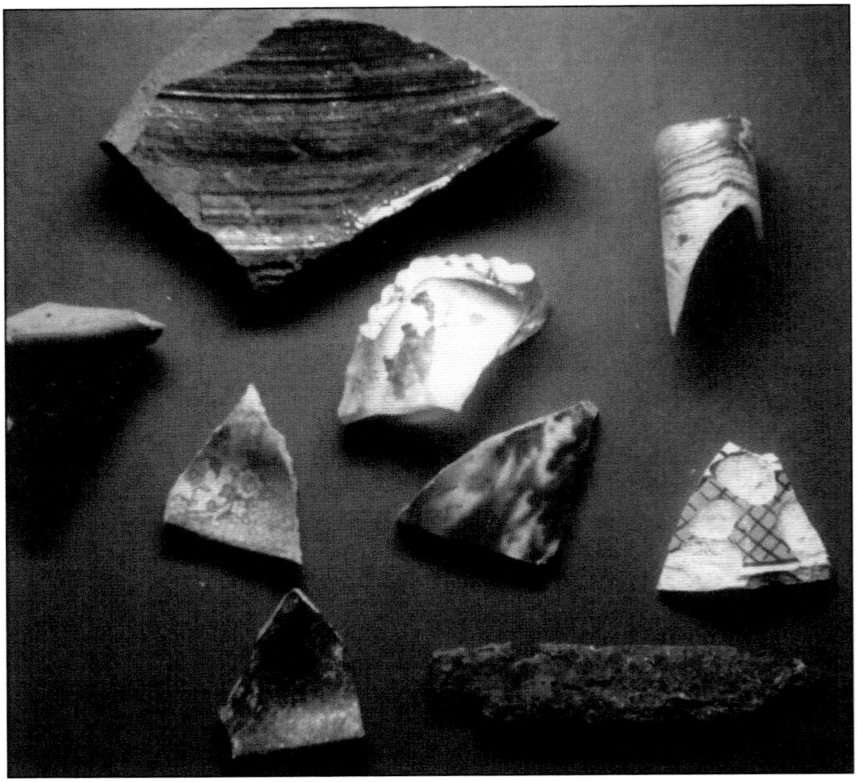

Ten

The People of Old Shamong

They came from all walks of life, the rich, the poor, and everywhere in between. From the earliest days of settlement to the present, the people of Shamong have contributed to their fellow citizens. The township has always been considered a rural community. Due to building restrictions of the Pinelands Comprehensive Management Plan, as well as local ordinances, it will probably always remain so. Approximately half of the township is contained within the Wharton State Forest. It is wilderness by any stretch of the imagination and is treasured by those who live here to enjoy it. The people of Shamong live close to nature, and most, if not all, prefer it that way. There are paved roads throughout the settled areas but no sidewalks, which befits a rural area. Traveling in the forested sections is primarily on unpaved sandy trails. In many places, a four-wheel-drive vehicle is heartily recommended. Cultivated fields are a prominent part of the landscape, and descendants of early settlers comprise most of the farm people. There are some residential developments in small clusters throughout the township. Many are wooded, and the people have moved here to enjoy the rural life, far away from the congestion that has plagued more developed areas. The people of yesteryear came from all types of backgrounds. The saga of James Still, the son of former slaves, is one example. In spite of a humble beginning, his determination to succeed, in spite of adversity, led to his just reward. He was born in a log cabin near the mill where his father worked. He practiced medicine by making home remedies from roots and herbs. He became known as Dr. James Still, in spite of the fact that he was not a licensed physician. His fame spread far and wide. He went to patient's homes by horse and carriage, throughout the area, as well as maintaining an office in nearby Cross Roads. In time, he became one of the wealthiest landowners in Medford. Others who came from various backgrounds, with stories of their own, will be told on the following pages.

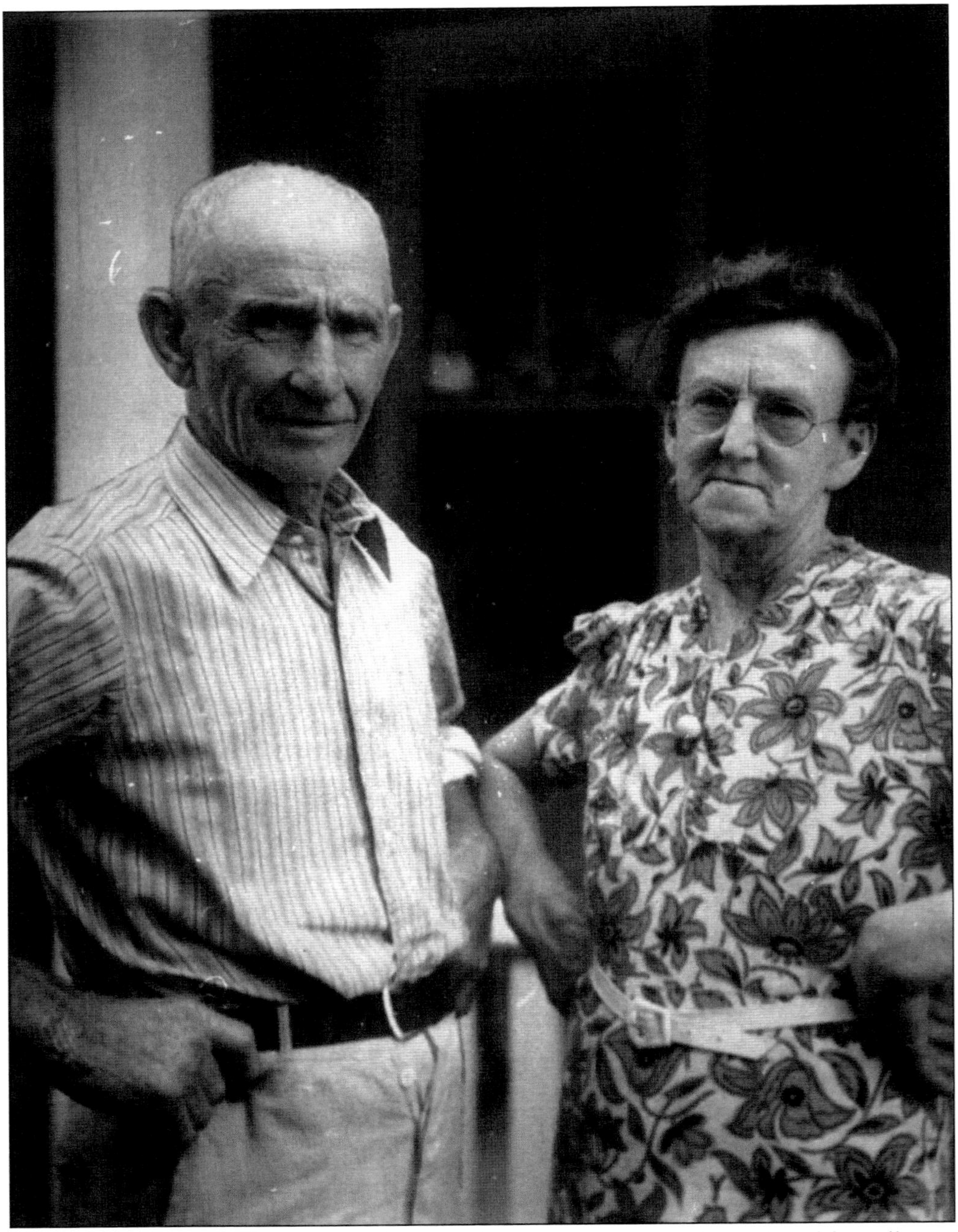

Many generations of the Miller family have lived at the same area on Atsion Road for well over a century. John "Bull" Miller is shown here in 1939. He was a local farmer who also had blueberry and cranberry crops on his property. He was also a skilled carpenter who passed his skills onto his son Frederick "Fritz" Miller. The Millers are still prominent in the township today. His father, Theodore, was the local constable in the late 1800s. His wife, Ella, was also descended from early settlers in Shamong. Her maiden name was Doughty. She was the daughter of Samuel and Selena Doughty who lived on Dingletown Road (now known as Forked Neck Road). Her father was the builder of "Indian Ann" Robert's home in 1884. Ella was known throughout the township for her green-tomato pie.

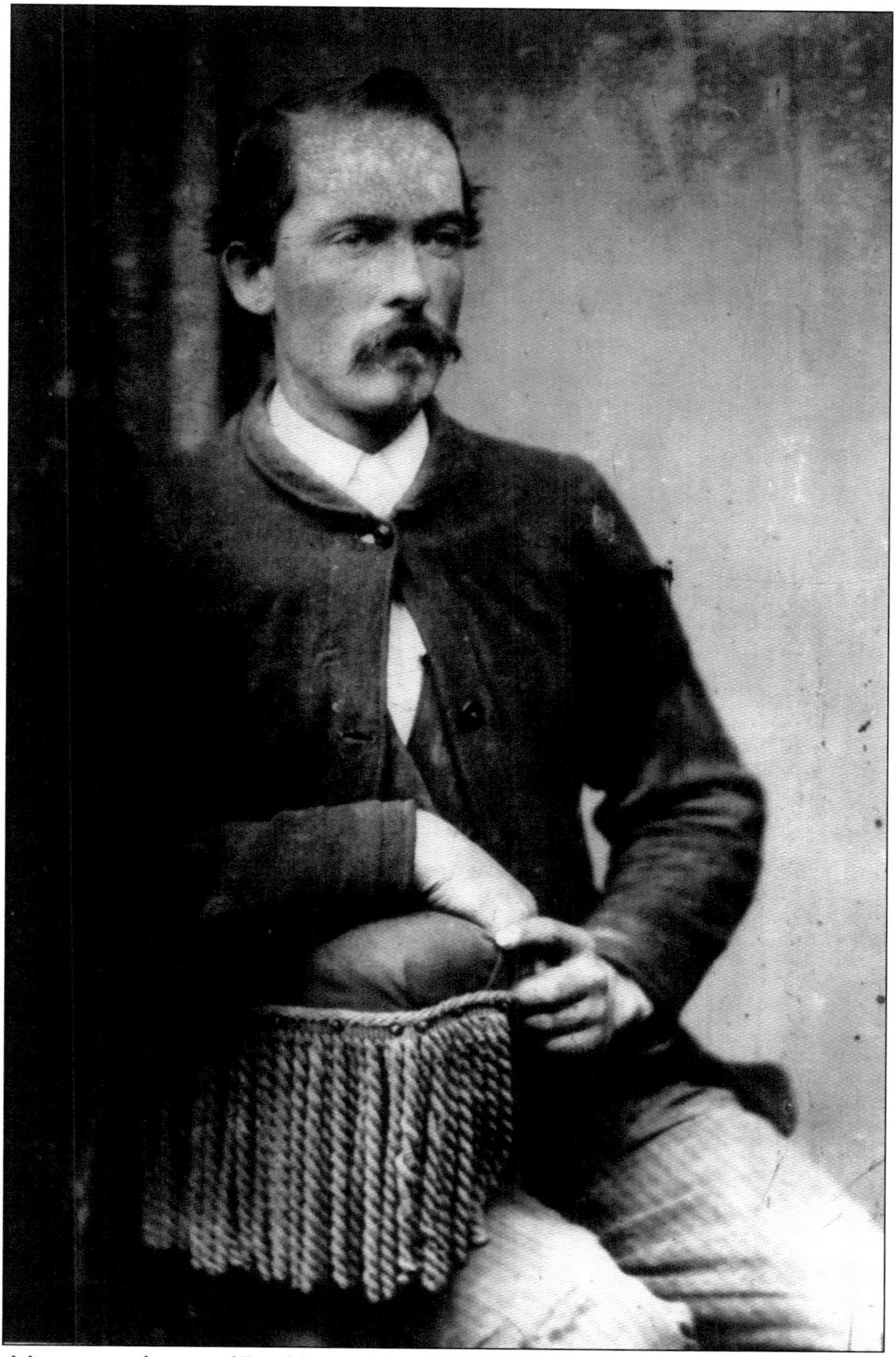

John Mingin was the son of Franklin Mingin and Sarah Cline. He was born at Batsto on April 3, 1846. He worked part of his life as a mason. He married Elizabeth Miller, who once worked at the Atsion cotton mill. They later owned a farm close by the Miller farm where they raised all types of crops as well as having cranberry bogs. John was also a talented violinist and played at many affairs in the community. He died at the age of 78, on December 26, 1924.

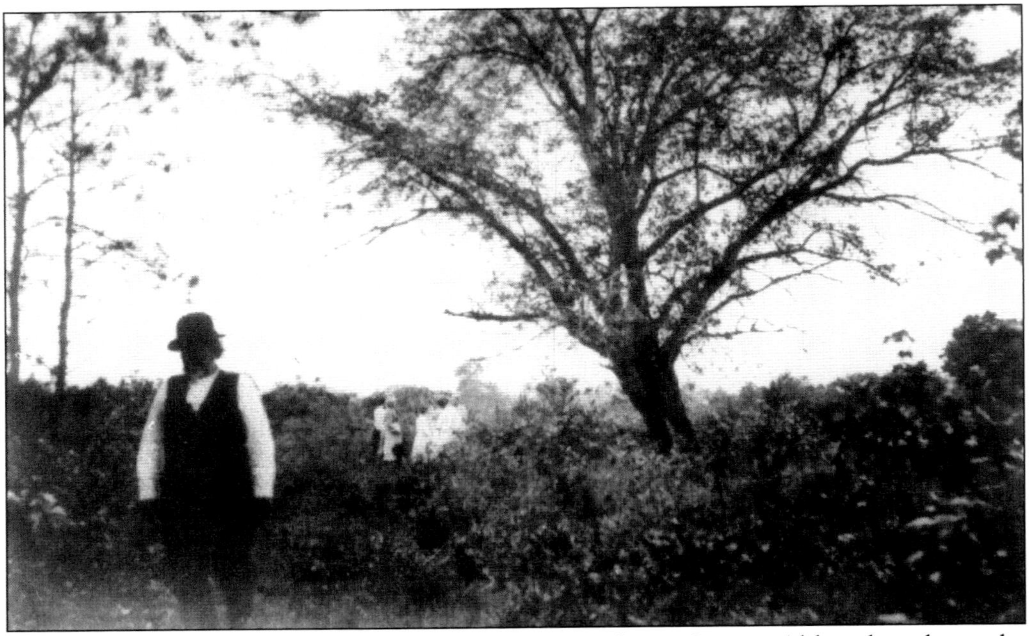

John James Gardner was born on October 17, 1845, in Atlantic County. Although underage, he enlisted as a private in the Civil War on August 9, 1861. He was only 15 years old at the time. He served for three years in Company G, 6th Regiment, New Jersey Volunteers. He graduated from the University of Michigan in 1867 and then went into politics in his native Atlantic County, serving as alderman and also as coroner. He became mayor of Atlantic City in 1868 and served there for four years. He was a United States congressman from 1893 until 1913. His later years were spent on an extensive farm in Shamong, where he died in 1921.

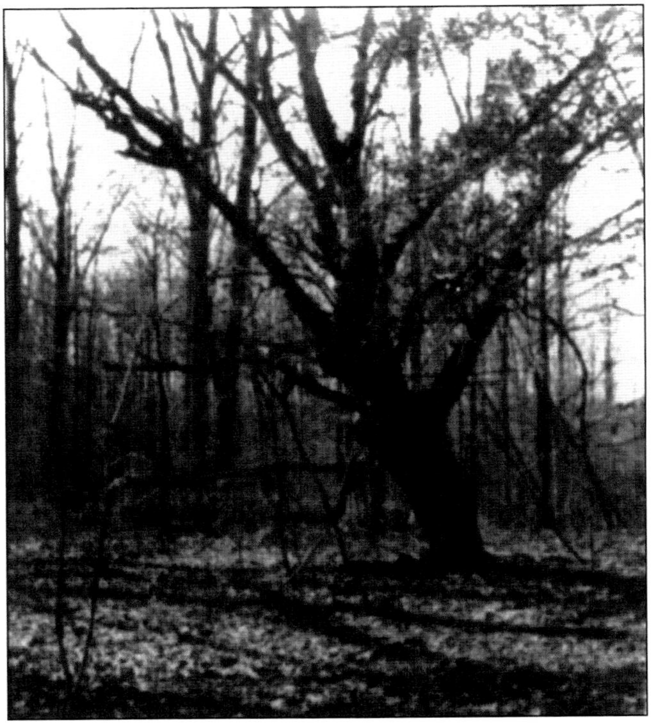

This photograph from the 1950s shows the "Treaty Tree" in its final years. Age-old traditions relate that this was once the gathering place of the Brotherton Reservation natives.

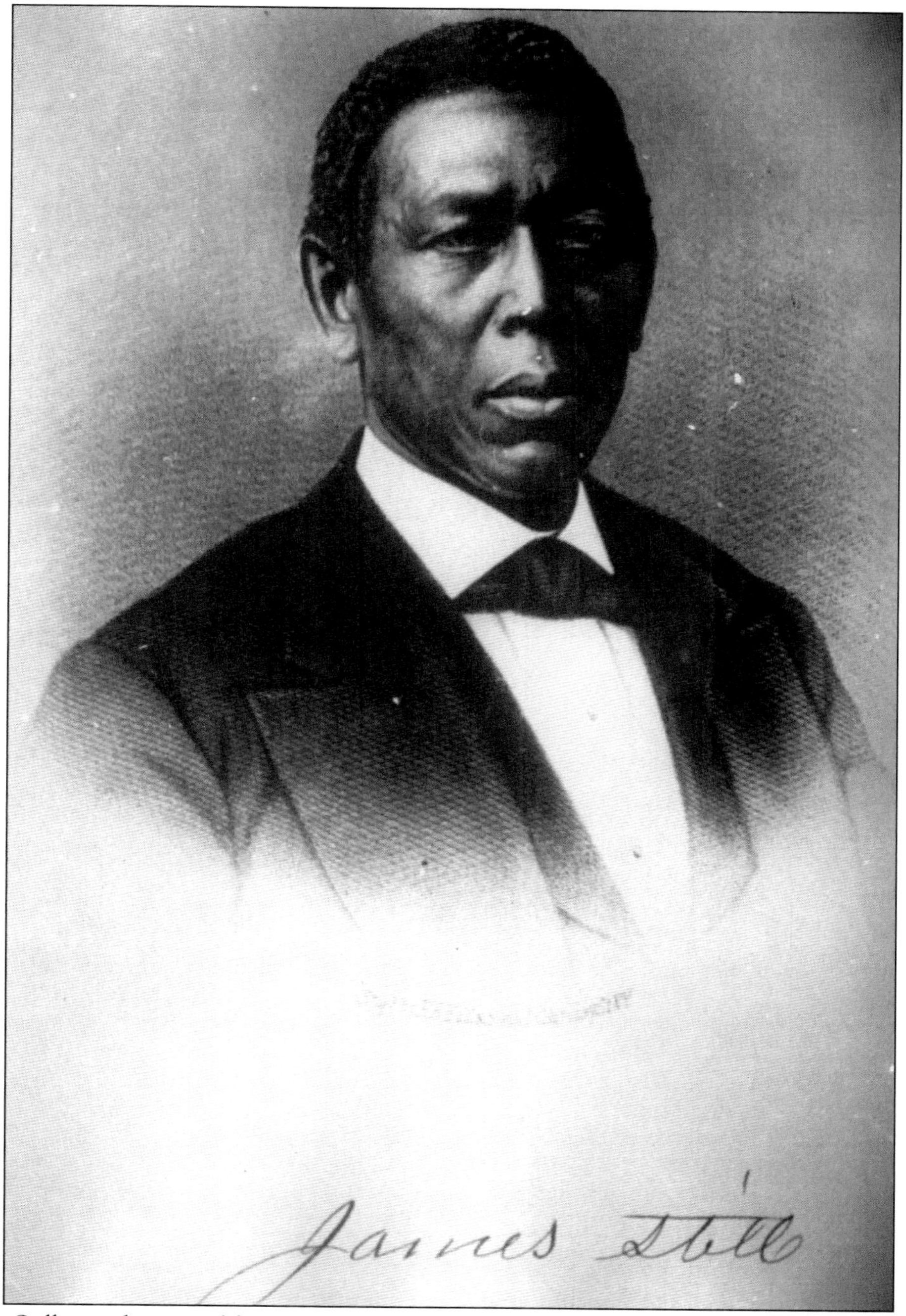

James Still was the son of former slaves named Levin and Charity Still. He lived in the most humble of circumstances with his brothers and sisters. The family lived in a log cabin on the old Shamong Indian Trail now known as Stokes Road. He only had three months of formal schooling and was essentially self-taught. He became a practitioner of home remedies that he made from roots and herbs. His remarkable cures became well known. He soon became the wealthiest landowner in the Medford area. He maintained an office next to his home. His autobiography is now a collector's item. He became a legend in the area, known as the "Black Doctor of the Pines."

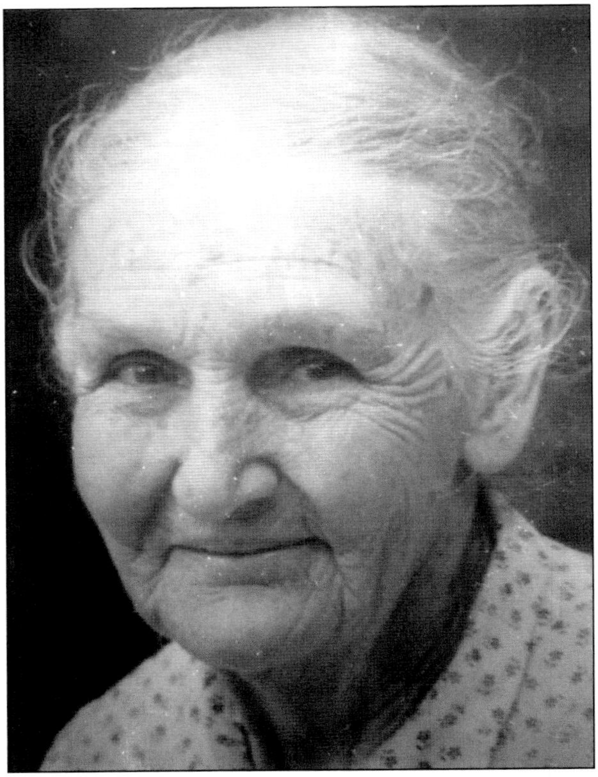

In 1939, at the age of 85, "Aunty" Mary Wills was known as a champion berry picker. She was born at Mount Tavern deep in the Pinelands and later lived in Atsion.

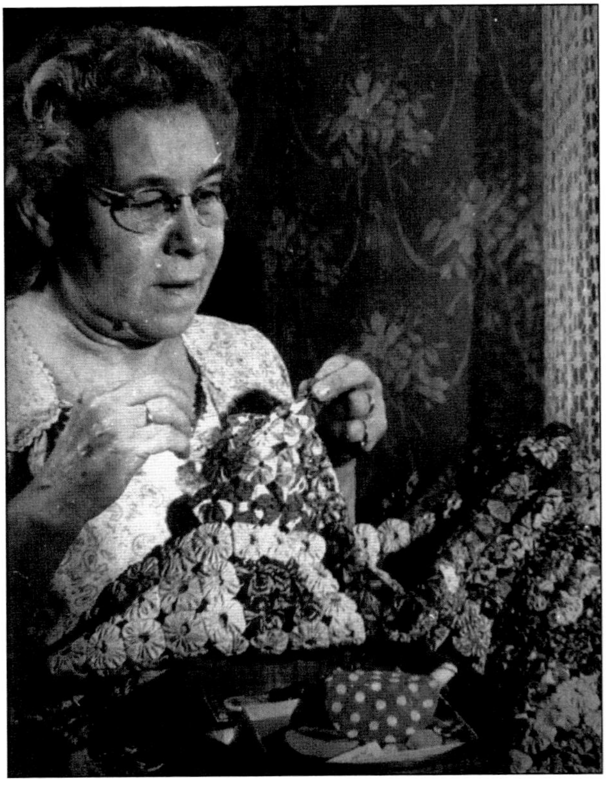

This photograph of Maude Kell was taken in 1939. She lived along the shores of Atsion Lake on Atsion Road. She is most remembered for her skills in making cranberry potpie. Her family was active in the cranberry growing industry nearby, at Hampton Bogs.

Samuel Still was a descendant of former slaves Levin and Charity Still. He lived for many years on the farm of his father along the Stokes Road. This is where most of the early Still family members trace their roots in South Jersey. The farmhouse is no longer there, but the land is still being farmed. The unmarked graves of many Still family members lie in a nearby graveyard.

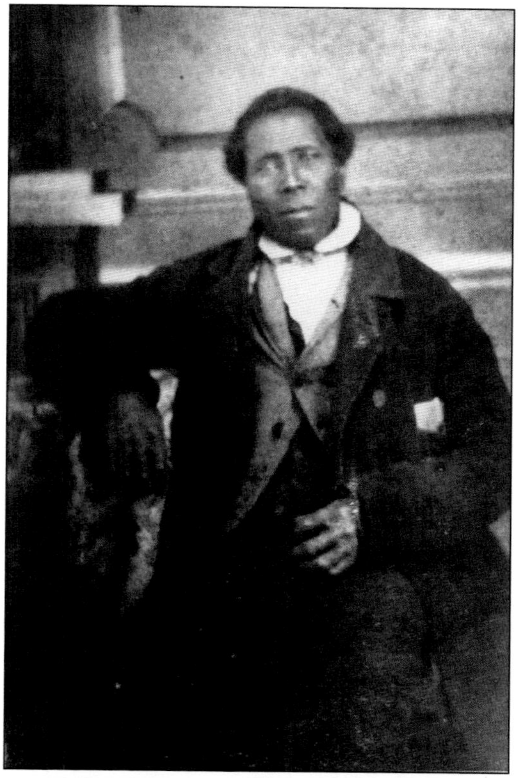

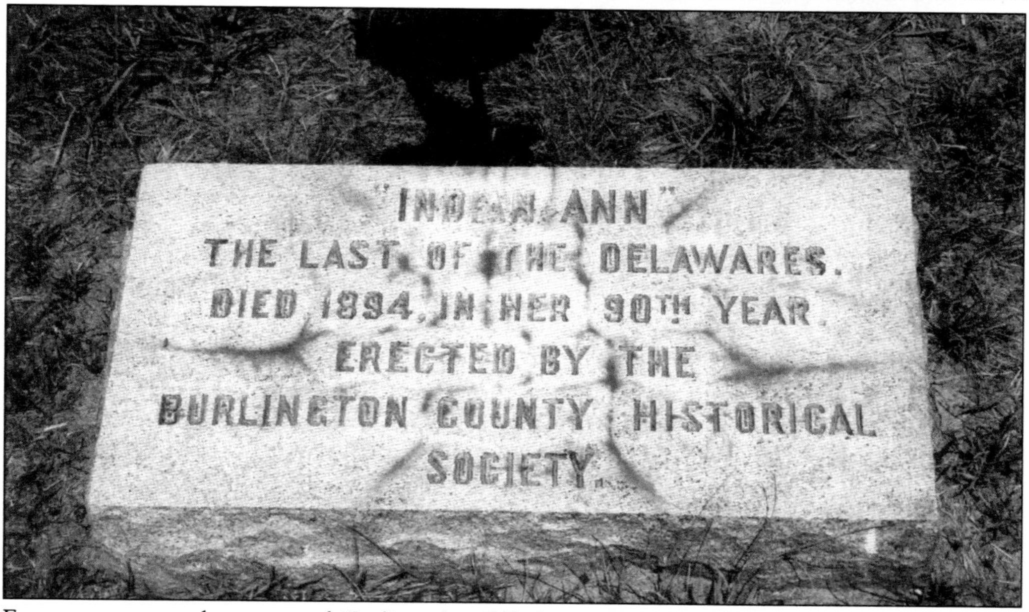

For many years, the grave of "Indian Ann" Roberts was unmarked until the location was identified by Nathaniel Ewan, the sage of Burlington County historians. Ann was the daughter of Elisha Ashatama, one of the elders of the Brotherton Reservation. She later married a man named John Roberts and lived on the Dingletown Road in Shamong till her death. She was the last of the full-blooded Delawares in New Jersey. No photographs of this venerable woman have ever been discovered.

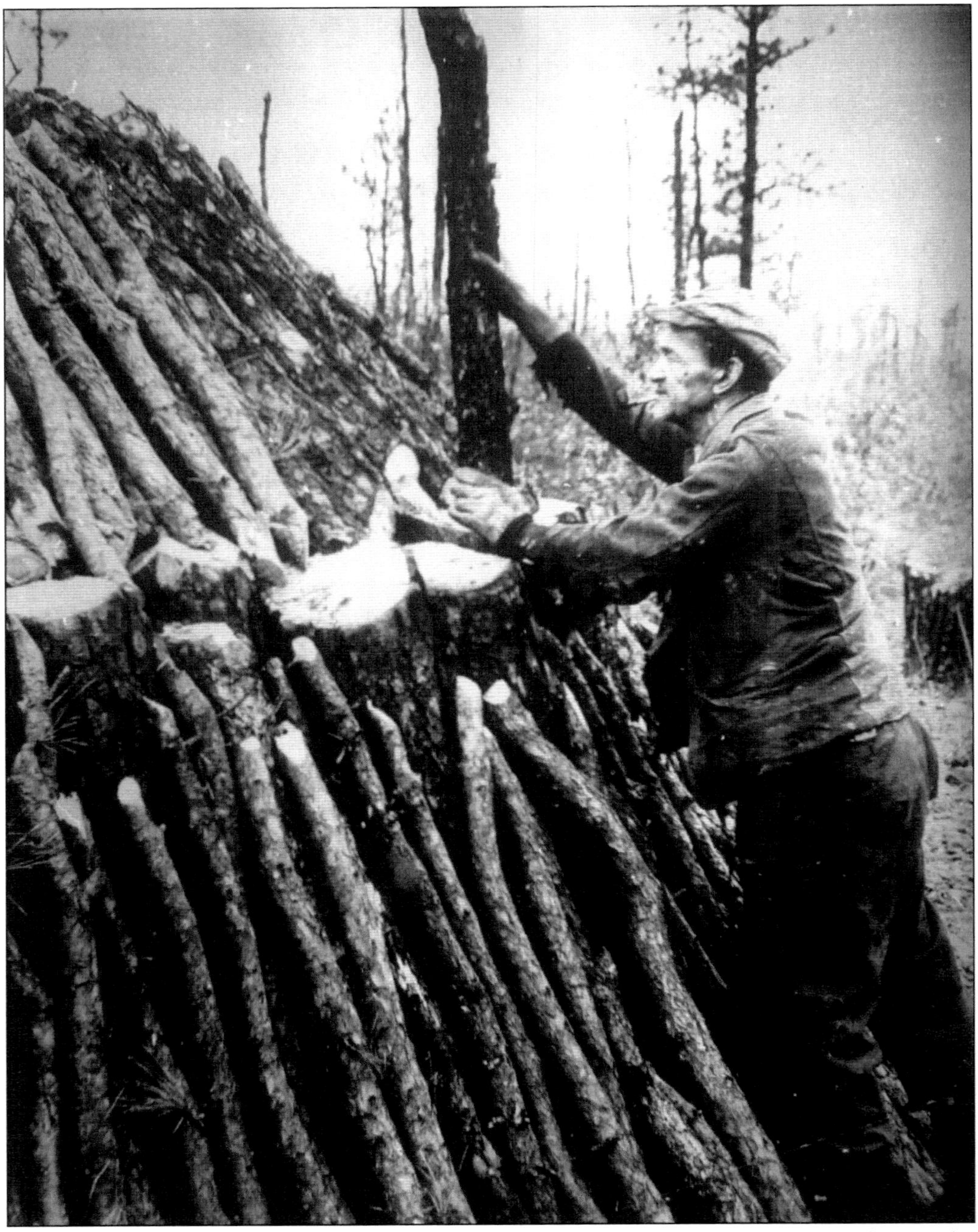

"Indian George" Crummel was supposedly the great-grandson of "Indian Ann" Roberts. The exact line of descent supposedly comes down from Hester Ann Roberts, the daughter of Ann Roberts. Hester Ann supposedly had a child named Annie before she was married. Later this Annie married a Frank Crummel, the collier's father. Not much of this story is verified.

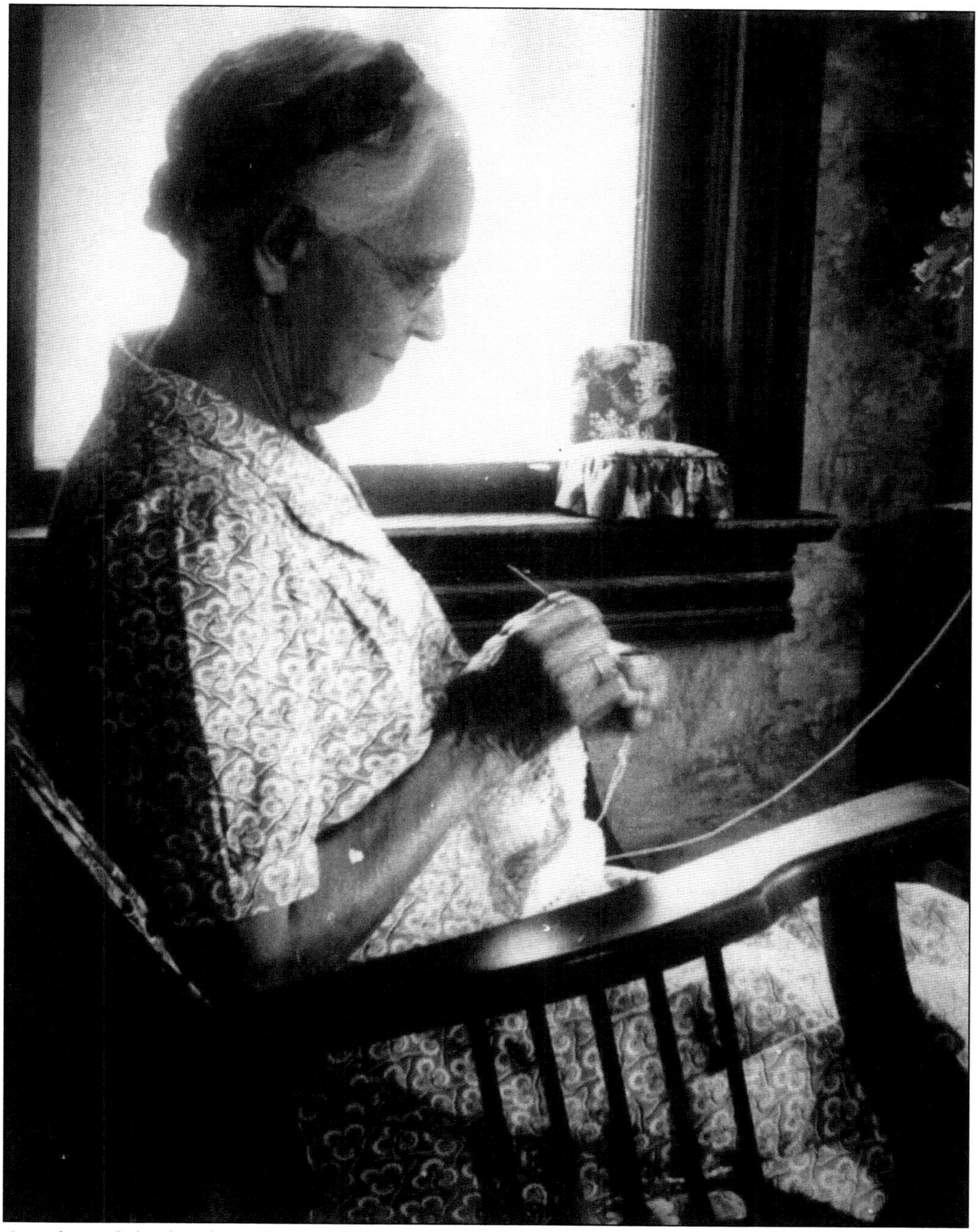

Another of the hardy pioneers of Shamong was named Kate Albor. She loved to crochet and is seen here by the window of her Atsion home, which she shared with Maude Kell, along the shores of Atsion Lake. Albor was formerly a Leek and was a member of one of the oldest families in the Pinelands. She married Charles Albor in 1884. He worked for a time at the paper mill in Pleasant Mills.